Tim Clarkson worked in academic librarianship before setting up a business with his wife. He gained an MPhil in archaeology (1995) and a PhD in medieval history (2003) from the University of Manchester. He is author of *The Men of the North: The Britons of Southern Scotland* (2010).

The Picts

A HISTORY

Tim Clarkson

BIRLINN

This edition published in 2016 by
Birlinn Ltd
West Newington House
10 Newington Road
Edinburgh
EH9 1QS

www.birlinn.co.uk

Reprinted 2017, 2019

First published 2008 by Tempus Publishing

Revised edition first published in Great Britain in 2010 by
John Donald, an imprint of Birlinn Ltd

ISBN: 978 1 78027 403 4

British Library Cataloguing-in-Publication Data
A catalogue record for this book is available on request from the British Library

Typeset and designed by Mark Blackadder

Printed and bound by Clays Ltd, Elcograf, S.p.A.

Contents

Preface

The previous edition of this book appeared in 2010 (reprinted three years later, with corrections). Since then, our knowledge of the Picts has been enhanced by a number of exciting archaeological projects, some of which are still ongoing. These have been reported in the media, both in print and online, bringing the Picts to the attention of a large global audience. The implications are likely to be significant. New archaeological discoveries have the potential to change our perceptions of what kind of people the Picts really were, how they lived and how their society was organised. Interpretation of the evidence can be extended by analogy to neighbouring groups such as the Scots, Britons and Anglo-Saxons. For historians, new archaeological data offers alternative ways to understand how these peoples interacted with one another in the political, social and cultural contexts described in the written sources.

This book is chiefly concerned with Pictish history rather than with Pictish archaeology. An opportunity to give the archaeology more of a presence arose in late 2015, when a scheduled reprint was discussed between the author and publisher. The result is the present revised edition which includes a 'postscript' on a selection of archaeological topics. This mentions some of the recent projects, either as highlighted case studies or set against the backdrop of current archaeological thinking. Space limitations necessarily make the postscript somewhat brief and selective, a mere glimpse of a much larger picture. Readers seeking more than a glimpse should consult Sally Foster's excellent *Picts, Gaels and Scots*, the latest edition of which appeared in 2014.

The postscript is the only major change from the 2010 edition of *The Picts: A History*. A few items have been added to the Further Reading section, to update it with recent scholarship, but the main historical narrative has not been altered.

Tim Clarkson
February 2016

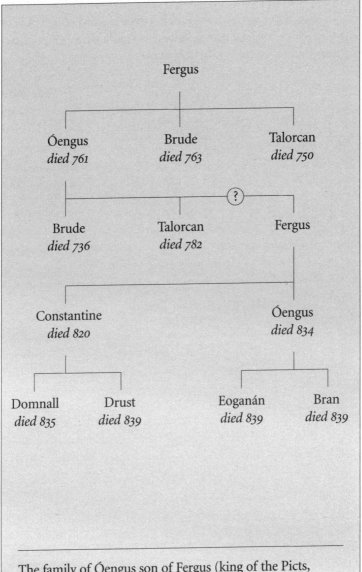

The family of Óengus son of Fergus (king of the Picts, 729–61) showing a presumed link with the family of Constantine son of Fergus (king of the Picts, 789–820).

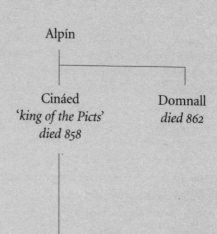

Alpín

Cináed
'king of the Picts'
died 858

Domnall
died 862

Áed Findlaith = [1] Mael Muire
High king of Ireland   *died 913*

Flann Sinna = [2]
High king of Ireland

The family of Cináed mac Ailpín

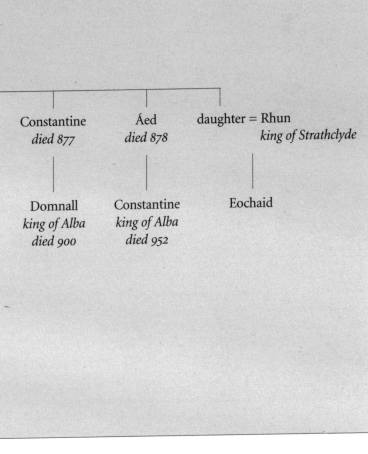

Constantine
died 877

Áed
died 878

daughter = Rhun
king of Strathclyde

Domnall
king of Alba
died 900

Constantine
king of Alba
died 952

Eochaid

The Scottish Highlands: a selection of modern territorial divisions.

CHAPTER 1
A People Apart

'Picts' was the name given to a people who inhabited a large part of what is now Scotland during the first millennium AD. Together with their neighbours – Scots, Britons and English – they played an important role in the early history of the British Isles. They make their first appearance in the historical record at the end of the third century when their raiding activities troubled the authorities of Roman Britain. After less than 600 years, they seem to vanish from the pages of history, leaving behind no written records of their own nor any significant trace of their language. In the wake of their apparent disappearance a fictional tale was created to explain it, and a shroud of myth enveloped the true story of their fall from power. From these legends there emerged a belief that the Picts were a mysterious race whose history was unknown: a strange, almost alien nation who were very different from their neighbours. They became, in other words, a people apart.

The modern visitor to the Highland areas of Scotland usually encounters the Picts through their spectacular artistic legacy. This is most vividly represented by several hundred finely carved stones, many of which are still visible in the landscape. A large number of these stones bear esoteric designs which are repeated and replicated with remarkable consistency across a wide geographical area, from Skye to Aberdeen and from Shetland to Fife. The meaning of these symbols defies interpretation and, despite numerous attempts to decipher them, their original purpose remains an enduring puzzle. It is perhaps ironic that the symbol stones – the most impressive legacy of the Picts – make this ancient people seem even more mysterious.

This book seeks to venture behind the myths and legends to find the real history of the Picts, to 'de-mystify' them in so far as it is possible to do so. It does not take a themed approach, in which aspects of society and culture are discussed as separate topics, but adopts instead a linear structure guided by a simple chronological framework. The span of this chronology is the era of the historical Picts, covering the years 300–850, with some leeway at the beginning and end. This span includes much of the so-called Dark Ages, a term applied rather loosely to the centuries of transition between the fall of the Western Roman Empire and the end of the eleventh century. The phrase 'Dark Age Scotland' certainly has a dramatic impact and conjures an image of mist-shrouded hills brooding in a Celtic twilight, but it also carries negative overtones of ignorance and gloom. As an alternative to 'Dark Age', the more neutral term 'Early Historic' is therefore used throughout this book.

Documentary Sources

This is not meant to be an academic textbook, nor a scholarly investigation, but a narrative history presented as an unfolding sequence of events. The chronological framework guiding the narrative is a list of Pictish kings. This 'king-list' survives in a number of medieval manuscripts which differ slightly from each other in the information they provide. They ultimately derive from an original text that is now lost. This was written at an unknown Pictish monastery and later came into the hands of medieval Scottish monks, whose own versions of it are seen in the surviving manuscripts. In the interests of simplicity the various versions are treated throughout this book as a single source referred to here as 'the king-list'. In reality, the manuscripts fall into two groups, each of which incorporates variant versions of the list together with additional notes relating to the Picts. The basic format of each version is a sequence of some sixty kings giving their reign-lengths and their fathers' names. Based on the chronology of the reigns it becomes apparent that the line of kings begins in the fourth century and ends in the ninth. Recent analysis of the manuscripts has shown the value of the list as a source of data for Scotland's early history, but it has also revealed its shortcomings. Thus, although early versions existed in written form as early as the eighth century, the oldest surviving manuscript is a product of some six centuries later. This means that the text needs to be treated with caution if it is to be employed as a signpost to the Early Historic period. Fortunately, the information it provides for people and events from AD 550 to 850 is frequently corroborated by other sources. This kind of cross-referencing makes the king-list a fairly trustworthy source for the main era of Pictish history between the sixth and ninth centuries.

Among the reliable sources whose testimony corroborates the data in the king-list is the *Ecclesiastical History of The English People*, a book written by the Venerable Bede and completed in 731. Bede spent almost his whole life as a monk at the monastery of Wearmouth-Jarrow in Northumbria and became a scholar of high repute. His *Ecclesiastical History* is an important source of information for the early history of Anglo-Saxon England, but it is also a valuable contemporary source on the Picts. Despite its title, the book deals with secular as well as religious topics and provides a fascinating window on Early Historic society. The nature of kingship was of particular interest to Bede, and it is through his eyes that the modern reader sees how ambitious kings rose to power by defeating their rivals and waging war on their enemies. Bede was not, however, a historian in the modern sense of the term. For him, the course of history was pre-determined by a divine scheme in which the English were a chosen people appointed by God to conquer the native Celtic inhabitants of Britain.

Bede's interest in the Celts was limited to their contact with the English, especially where such contact impinged on religious matters, so the information he provides for political events in Scotland is rather patchy. To learn what was happening in the Pictish regions, historians turn instead to sources of Celtic origin, some of which are far less trustworthy than Bede. The most informative Celtic sources are the Irish annals, a group of texts whose creators noted historical events as brief entries in a year-by-year format. Sometimes these entries were written contemporaneously, as they happened, while others were made retrospectively. The surviving manuscripts are not the original annals but copies made much later than the Early Historic period. However, detailed appraisal of the manuscripts has shown that a substantial number of entries relating to Scotland were part of an original text compiled at the great monastery of Iona in the seventh and eighth centuries. At some point before AD 800, this 'Iona Chronicle' was taken to Ireland, where its information was eventually incorporated into the Irish annals. Many of the annal entries relating to Scotland and the Picts are therefore contemporary with the events they describe and bring to life the figures whose names appear in the king-list.

More controversial than the annals are the *vitae* or 'lives' of early saints whose missionary activities brought them into contact with the Picts. These *vitae* look like biographies, but their purpose was not to give a factual account of their subjects. On the contrary, their authors sought to prove the holiness of a particular saint by describing him or her as a successful performer of miracles. Truth and historical accuracy were secondary considerations or were sometimes dismissed altogether. The *vitae* are therefore difficult to use and need to be treated with caution, although some examples are more trustworthy than others. The most valuable in the context of Pictish history is the *Vita Columbae*, the Life of Saint Columba, written by an abbot of Iona called Adomnán. Iona was founded by Columba in the sixth century and played an important role in bringing Christianity to the Picts. Adomnán was a later successor of Columba as abbot of the monastery in the late seventh and early eighth centuries. He was therefore a contemporary of Bede and almost certainly met him during a visit to the monastery at Jarrow. Because of Iona's status as the mother-church of the Picts, Adomnán had many contacts among their clergy and had dealings with at least two of their kings.

Other sources are more esoteric and include legendary material presented as genuine history. Some of their data on the Picts is reliable, but much of it is based on folklore, myth and other 'traditions' of doubtful origin. An example is the rather odd *Prophecy of Berchan* which probably dates from the twelfth century, although the oldest surviving manuscript was written 600 years later. It contains a number of 'prophecies' which purport to foresee the deeds of 24 Scottish kings but which were in fact made retrospectively. In many instances the prophecies were created several centuries after the lifetimes of these kings. The entire work is essentially a king-list which gives for each monarch his reign-length, his place of death and other information, but not his name. Identifying who is being described in a particular prophecy is not always easy. To make matters even more frustrating, most of the prophecies are so cryptic that their context is barely intelligible, while some incorporate legends and folk-tales. *Berchan* nevertheless contains interesting nuggets of information which can be cautiously added to the general picture presented by the main Pictish king-list, the Irish annals and other sources. It is one example of the many pseudo-historical texts that historians are obliged to consult when searching for information on the Picts. Various sources of similar type are referred to throughout this book at particular points where their testimony becomes relevant.

The Problem of the Picts

A brief glance at the Irish annals shows that the Picts were not regarded as 'a people apart' by their contemporaries. Geographical factors alone ensured that the Pictish lands were caught up in the affairs of northern Britain as a whole. The territory of the Picts was travelled, trampled and invaded by their neighbours – Scots, English, Britons and Vikings – at various times during the Early Historic period. Pictish armies usually returned the favour by launching rampages of their own. When not engaged in warfare, Pictish kings communicated with other kings to shape the political landscape of what eventually became the medieval kingdom of Scotland. To writers such as Bede and Adomnán there was nothing different or special about the Picts beyond the fact that they were a distinct group like the English or the Scots. It is curious, then, that there has arisen in modern times a belief that the Picts were a strange or enigmatic people.

The enigma of the Picts exists because some aspects of their society and culture are indeed controversial. Unlike most of their neighbours, they disappeared from history to become a 'lost' people. Their language – in so far as any trace of it survives – looks like an odd sort of gibberish. Their royal inheritance laws apparently relied on a system of matrilineal succession in which kingship was passed through the female line. Some contemporaries regarded them as a barbarous race, a view seemingly supported by their slowness in converting to Christianity. Most enigmatic of all are the arcane symbols that they carved on standing stones. Other groups may have used a selection of these symbols, but only the Picts employed them as a kind of hieroglyphic alphabet. To a Pictish observer the symbols had special meaning and communicated specific information. Today, in spite of many ingenious attempts to solve the mystery, nobody really knows what the symbols actually mean. This alone would be sufficient to isolate the Picts, to make them seem markedly different from other groups. When added to the other enigmas listed above, it becomes part of a larger puzzle, the so-called 'Problem of the Picts'. Together, the various components of the 'Problem' are responsible for modern perceptions – and misconceptions – of just how mysterious the Picts really were.

Interpreting the Evidence

Perceptions have, however, started to change in recent years, and most of the misconceptions are now in retreat. Interest in the Picts is currently running at its highest level, not only in academic circles but also in the Scottish tourism sector and among the visitor community. More and more Pictish sites are being identified and excavated by archaeologists. Material evidence unearthed by these excavations allows historians to gain new perspectives on the information in the documentary sources. This does not mean that everyone agrees on how the archaeological and documentary evidence should be interpreted. There is much disagreement and debate on many aspects of Pictish history, chiefly because the sources themselves frequently contradict each other's testimony on particular points. The resulting uncertainty breeds a lack of consensus among historians and is another part of the 'Problem'.

The documentary sources and the archaeological data offer a large amount of information on the Picts. Despite the debates about how a particular item of data should be interpreted, there is more than enough data to reconstruct a broad outline of Pictish history. Using this outline to create a more detailed narrative is rather more difficult and less straightforward. It requires the use of sources deemed unreliable or controversial, together with a measure of informed speculation, to bridge the gaps in the framework and so produce a more coherent account. Such an approach is not to everybody's taste and is likely to draw criticism from those who argue that the sources are not suited to the purpose. It is true that the available data does not give a crystal-clear view of the course of events in northern Britain during the Early Historic period, and it is equally true that there are many gaps and uncertainties. Nevertheless, the necessary components of a narrative account are available, and they are retrievable from the sources. By weaving these components together it should be possible to present a coherent, chronological history of the Picts. This is the approach adopted here and is the *raison d'etre* of this book.

Land of the Picts: the Highlands of Scotland.

CHAPTER 2

Caledonia and Rome

*On, then, into action; and as you go, think of those
that went before you and of those that shall come after.*

Words attributed by Tacitus to the Caledonian
chieftain Calgacus, AD 84

Before the Picts made their first appearance in history, their
territory in what is now Scotland was inhabited by an earlier
population. These were the ancestors of the Picts and were the
people encountered by Roman armies during the Empire's attempt
to conquer the northern parts of Britain. Theirs was a typical Iron
Age society of farmers, fishermen and craftsmen grouped into
tribes and ruled by a landowning aristocracy. They spoke a dialect
of Brittonic, the Celtic language used in most parts of mainland
Britain in pre-Roman times. Like other ancient Celtic peoples, the
ancestors of the Picts lived in well-organised communities within a
hierarchical society ruled by a minority upper class. Most of the
population lived in small settlements scattered across the landscape,
owing their primary allegiance to local chiefs who in turn acknowledged the authority of greater chiefs or kings. The economy was
based on livestock – sheep, pigs and cattle – and on crops such as
oats and barley. The majority of houses were built of timber, but
some were of stone. Kings and chiefs built fortified residences on
prominent hilltops, in valleys or in coastal locations. In some areas
prosperous lords constructed large stone towers around which

smaller dwellings were clustered. These towers are known today as 'brochs' and a few still survive in ruinous form. They are the most visible and impressive reminder of the prehistoric forefathers of the Picts.

It was around the time of the broch-builders that the Romans first came to Britain. The island was already familiar to Rome because it lay adjacent to her newly conquered territories in Gaul but its interior was largely unknown. The first Roman forays across what is now the English Channel were made by Julius Caesar in 55 and 54 BC. These brought him into conflict with the south-coast tribes but, on both occasions, he returned to Gaul after making a token show of force. In common with his newly conquered Gaulish enemies, the native Britons who opposed him spoke a Celtic language and were similarly well-organised in tribal groups under the rule of kings. Rome regarded their land as rich in agricultural and mineral resources, but Caesar knew that the warlike inhabitants were unlikely to give up their wealth without a fight. A large-scale military campaign would therefore need to be mounted if Britain was to be brought to heel and drawn within the Empire. Although this was not accomplished in Caesar's lifetime, it was inevitable that Rome would one day return.

Conquest was considered by the emperors Augustus and Caligula but postponed until the middle of the first century AD. In AD 43, during the reign of the emperor Claudius, the project commenced in earnest with a full-scale invasion from Roman Gaul. The initial assault was followed by campaigns against tribes in the southern parts of the island. Some of these surrendered, or made deals with Rome, but others fought bravely to preserve their independence. Within thirty-five years, after crushing all serious resistance and quelling revolts, the invaders successfully brought much of Britain under their sway. Consolidation of the conquered territory proceeded swiftly, driven by a steady process of Romanisation and the reorganising of native political structures. These changes were enforced by a large and permanent military garrison housed in strategically placed forts linked by a network of roads.

Agricola and the Highlands

By the end of the third quarter of the first century the main phase of the conquest was complete. Half the island lay under imperial control and the Britons in these areas became subjects of the Empire. The southern tribal kings were either dead, exiled or working for Rome as urban bureaucrats in newly built towns and cities. The emperor entrusted the task of running the new province to a governor who, because of the volatile character of the natives, was usually an experienced general. In AD 78 the governorship passed to one of Rome's most capable men, Gnaeus Julius Agricola, a career soldier who had already seen service in Britain as commander of the Twentieth Legion. Agricola returned to the province and immediately launched campaigns to subdue rebellious tribes in Wales and the Pennines.

A contemporary account of Agricola's career was written by his son-in-law, Tacitus, whose work has survived. This account bears the simple title *Agricola* and appeared in AD 98, five years after the death of its subject, as a eulogy in praise of his character and achievements. It does not offer a straightforward, factual report of administrative policies or military campaigns, nor is it concerned with presenting an objective view of the peoples and places encountered by Agricola during his time in Britain. Its value for the present chapter lies in what it says about the people of Celtic Britain. Tacitus paid special attention to the northern parts of the island, the area now known as Scotland. It was here that Agricola found his ambitions thwarted by troublesome natives and an inhospitable landscape. In the Highlands across the firths of Forth and Tay, beyond the furthest limit of Rome's early conquests, dwelt tribes of untamed barbarians. Tacitus provides fascinating information about these people, much of it gleaned at first-hand in conversations with his father-in-law, who knew them as well as any Roman could.

The natives of the Highlands are described by Tacitus as having 'reddish hair and large limbs', a typically stereotyped barbarian image rather than an objective view. They were a proud people

11

whose warriors were brave and fierce, but Rome had met such folk elsewhere and did not fear them. As far as Agricola was concerned they stood in the way of a total conquest of Britain and needed to be swept aside. He was not the kind of man to leave such a task to others, nor did he lack the means to accomplish it. First, however, he had to deal with another obstacle: a group of unconquered tribes between the Pennines and the Forth-Clyde isthmus. In AD 80, the third year of his governorship, he marched north into what is now the Scottish Lowlands to bring these tribes within the Empire. They offered little resistance and were subjugated so quickly that the Romans were able to spare time for the construction of new forts in the conquered districts. Before the end of the summer, Agricola's advance brought him to the southern edge of the Highlands. He then crossed the River Forth and led his troops into territory where no Roman army had gone before.

The invaders soon found themselves battling wet, windy weather of the kind familiar to any modern visitor who travels among the lochs and glens. Storms hindered the army's progress after it crossed the Forth into what is now Stirlingshire, but the advance pressed on. Communities of terrified natives could do little but watch helplessly as their lands were plundered by foraging bands of Roman soldiers. The march soon reached the estuary of the Tay, bringing Agricola within sight of the northern mountains, but at this point he decided to advance no further. Instead, he turned around and marched back to the Forth to consolidate his gains in the Lowlands. There he spent the next year building forts and installing garrisons of auxiliaries. The following year, AD 82, saw him campaigning near the Solway Firth in unconquered territory west of Annandale. The tribes of this region were swiftly defeated, their capitulation bringing Roman troops to the shore of the Irish Sea. Agricola briefly considered the viability of an invasion of Ireland but decided against it. A more pressing matter – the subjugation of the far north – still preyed on his mind. With all territory south of the Forth-Clyde isthmus now firmly under Roman control, he knew that the free peoples beyond the Firth of Tay represented a lurking menace. Such a situation was intolerable and had to be resolved by a major campaign of invasion and conquest.

In AD 83 Agricola marched across the River Forth at the head of an army of 25,000 men. Three renowned legions – the Second, the Ninth and the Twentieth – provided the core of his fighting strength, the remainder being cohorts of auxiliaries. These cohorts included some highly experienced infantry units together with several thousand cavalry. As well as these land forces, a fleet of warships under the command of an admiral shadowed the army's progress. The admiral's task was to keep the troops supplied and to make a detailed reconnaissance of the coast. Aboard the ships were units of tough marines who periodically came ashore to scout the best harbours and terrorise the natives. Sometimes the soldiers, sailors and marines camped together to share tales of their achievements and adventures, or to joke about the bad weather and the harsh terrain. Eventually the land forces reached the River Tay and crossed it, entering for the first time a region called Caledonia. Here they were harassed by a group of people whom Tacitus calls *Britanni*, 'Britons', like the other inhabitants of the island. Modern historians generally refer to these folk as Caledonians. They were a tribe or confederation whose core territory included large tracts of the central Highlands as well as most of eastern Scotland between the Firths of Tay and Moray. A memory of their presence survives today in three place-names within their old heartland: Dunkeld ('Fort of the Caledonians'), Rohallion ('Rath of the Caledonians') and Schiehallion ('Fairy Hill of the Caledonians').

Unlike their neighbours in the South, the Caledonians were not content to stand idly by while Roman troops plundered their lands. They retaliated swiftly, launching a series of devastating raids on the forts and camps established by Agricola in the wake of his advance. Using hit-and-run tactics, the native warriors caused such dismay that some Roman officers advised their commander to make a strategic withdrawal. At that moment, however, Agricola learned that the enemy was planning a full-scale attack on his column and decided to thwart it by splitting his army into three divisions. This in turn prompted the Caledonians to amend their original plan by launching a night-attack. Their target was the Ninth Legion as it lay sleeping in a temporary camp, but Agricola anticipated the assault and brought up the rest of his forces behind the enemy's rear. At the same time, the soldiers of the Ninth rose up to defend themselves, not only to expel the raiders but also to show the relief force that they could win the fight on their own. The Caledonians were routed, the survivors vanishing into impenetrable forests and marshlands. Tacitus observed that the Roman victory would have ended the campaign had not the Highland landscape aided the enemy's retreat. This was clearly an echo of his father-in-law's assessment of the battle. Like all Roman generals, Agricola was irritated by an enemy who used hit-and-run tactics. He longed to meet the Caledonians in a pitched battle, but this began to seem like a forlorn hope. Eventually he grew so frustrated by their refusal to stand and fight that he described them as 'just so many spiritless cowards'. This label was unfair and undeserved: the natives were merely waging war in their own way, utilising the landscape of their homeland to its best strategic advantage.

After the failed attack on the Ninth Legion the Caledonians regrouped. They placed their families in safe locations away from danger and began to muster for the kind of encounter that Agricola wanted. Their reasons for abandoning guerilla tactics are unclear. Perhaps their leaders believed that their superior numbers could overwhelm the Roman force in a set-piece battle? Certainly, by the following summer a huge native army was ready to meet the invaders in a final, decisive engagement. Tacitus speaks of tribes forging 'treaties' with each other to unite their warriors under a common purpose, but this is likely to represent a Roman rather than a native way of doing things. In reality, the Caledonians probably rallied around a single paramount leader, the king or chieftain of a powerful tribe, whose authority was strong enough to persuade or coerce other tribal leaders to follow him into battle. Similarly, when Tacitus speaks of native warriors 'flocking to the colours' he is applying the imagery of Rome to a people whose military organisation was markedly different. The Caledonian forces did not have well-drilled regiments of professional soldiers, each with its own standard or 'colours': they were made up from the personal warbands of individual kings and chiefs.

The great clash of arms occurred in late August or early September at Mons Graupius, a name that later inspired the naming of the Grampian Mountains. The slightly different spelling arose from an error on the part of a fifteenth-century Italian writer who, in preparing the first printed edition of the *Agricola*, transcribed *Graupius* as *Grampius*. This mis-spelt name was subsequently applied to the formidable mountain range which since medieval times has been called 'The Mounth', a term of Gaelic origin with the simple meaning 'mountain'. The precise location of the battlefield of AD 84 is a matter of considerable debate, chiefly because Tacitus gives few clues as to where it lay. The hill of Bennachie in Aberdeenshire has been put forward as a likely candidate: its most distinctive peak, the Mither Tap, is certainly deserving of the Latin description *mons*. Another candidate, although hardly a *mons*, is the Perthshire hillock of Duncrub which rises to no great height from the farmlands of Lower Strathearn. Although the name *Dun Crub* might correspond to a Pictish or Gaelic equivalent of Mons Graupius, the site seems too far south to be acceptable to those who envisage Agricola's victory taking place north of the Mounth. The line of Agricolan forts and marching-camps running northward from the Tay suggests that he advanced a long way beyond the fertile valley of the Earn. On the other hand, somewhere in the vicinity of Duncrub lies an unlocated Roman fort whose Latin name was simply *Victoria*, 'Victory'. Perhaps this name was given in commemoration of a great triumph over local natives? Some historians believe that the victory in question was indeed Mons Graupius, despite the insignificance of Duncrub as a landmark. Opponents think it more likely that the Romans named their fort to honour a different battle.

Wherever Mons Graupius lay, it was on its lower slopes that the Caledonians mustered a huge force of warriors, ranging from young men to old veterans, under the command of many kings and chieftains. Tacitus names one of these leaders as Calgacus, whose name is a Latinisation of a Brittonic term meaning 'The

Swordsman'. Tacitus shows this heroic figure giving a stirring speech about courage, freedom and heroism. It is one of the most vivid passages in the entire narrative of the *Agricola*. Standing before the assembled multitude, Calgacus gives words of hope to his people and a solemn vow that Rome will never conquer the Highlands. He predicts that the inexorable advance of the imperial army will be stopped in its tracks by the valiant warriors of the North, whose isolation has hitherto protected them from invasion:

> We, the choicest flower of Britain's manhood, were
> hidden away in her most secret places. Out of sight of
> subject shores, we kept even our eyes free from the
> defilement of tyranny. We, the most distant dwellers
> upon the earth, the last of the free, have been shielded
> until today by our very remoteness and by the obscurity
> in which it has shrouded our name . . . Let us then show,
> at the very first clash of arms, what manner of men
> Caledonia has kept in reserve.

Tacitus describes how this rousing address was greeted with euphoria by the gathering of 30,000 native warriors, who sang and yelled as they eagerly prepared for battle. Above the din, Calgacus closed his speech with these final words: 'On, then, into action; and as you go, think of those that went before you and of those that shall come after'. Historians tend to believe that Calgacus was invented by Tacitus to present an idealised image of a noble savage, but the speech and its setting certainly capture the spirit of a proud barbarian people defying the power of Rome. In similar vein, the account of the ensuing battle – embellished from Agricola's own words – is detailed and full of action. The scene unfolds with the noise of native chariots manoeuvring into position on the flat terrain between the two armies. Both sides then hurl spears at each other before Agricola orders six cohorts of war-hardened German auxiliaries to engage the enemy. Tacitus describes how these tough, disciplined veterans throw the Caledonians into disarray and push them backwards up the hill, 'raining blow after blow, striking them with the bosses of their shields and stabbing them in the face'. Meanwhile, the chariots are easily dispersed by Roman cavalry and career wildly into their own lines. Other Roman horsemen charge the Caledonian rear and break the ranks, causing many warriors to break and flee. Some bravely stand their ground, or rally in nearby woods to launch small counter-attacks, but by then the battle is already lost. With customary efficiency the Romans ensured that they finished the job, and Tacitus tells that 'the pursuit went on till night fell and our soldiers were tired of killing'. He may be exaggerating when he puts the Caledonian losses at 10,000, a third of their force, but the intensity of the slaughter need not be doubted. Roman casualties were less than 400.

Mons Graupius was a resounding victory which could have brought the final conquest of Britain within Agricola's grasp. However, the result did not turn out to be as decisive as he might have hoped or expected. Two-thirds of the barbarian horde survived the onslaught and managed to return to their homes. Moreover, the summer campaigning season was waning and there was no time to establish control over an area as vast as the Highlands. Agricola duly assessed the situation and realised that consolidating his victory would be impossible, especially with autumn approaching and with large numbers of Caledonians still lurking in the hills. The task of rooting them out, while facing the inevitable nuisance of hit-and-run ambushes, presented an unappealing prospect. He and his officers knew that neither the Highland landscape nor its inhabitants were compatible with the Roman way of war. The invading army duly turned about and returned to winter quarters in the south, leaving a small number of garrisoned forts to guard the glens of Perthshire. Hostages were taken from a people called the Boresti, who may have been among the tribes defeated in the great battle, but the Roman advantage was lost. Agricola nominally held sway over all native territory south of the Moray Firth, but political machinations deprived him of an opportunity to consolidate his gains: the emperor Domitian, consumed by jealousy and paranoia after hearing of the victory, ordered Agricola to leave Britain and return to Rome.

After Agricola: The Two Walls

Tacitus tried to portray the victory at Mons Graupius as a spectacular success but could not hide the fact that Caledonia remained unconquered. Calgacus and his warriors, 'the last of the free', were still free. One small consolation for Rome came when the fleet that had shadowed the army's progress completed its operations. After the battle it made a token gesture of dominance by continuing northward along the eastern seaboard and sailing around the top of Scotland, intimidating the natives with a final display of Roman power before sailing home down the western coast. During this voyage the admiral gathered plenty of information about the geography of the northern lands and learned the names of the tribes who dwelt there. This data, together with similar information gathered by Agricola's army, was later reproduced on a Roman map which survives today in a version drawn by Ptolemy, a Greek geographer of the second century. The map is a unique and fascinating document which shows how the British Isles appeared to Roman eyes. As well as naming and locating important topographical features, it identifies the tribes who inhabited Britain and Ireland and indicates the approximate positions of their territories.

The map shows sixteen tribes inhabiting Scotland, twelve of them occupying areas north of the Forth-Clyde isthmus. A number of place-names, denoting Roman forts and native sites, are also shown, but none appear on the map in areas north and west of the Great Glen. This distribution suggests that Agricola's land-campaign never reached beyond Loch Ness or the Moray Firth. The people of Caledonia appear on the map as the Caledonii, but it is curious that the Boresti, from whom the Romans took hostages after Mons Graupius, are absent. The map places the Caledonii across the central Highlands, in territory southwest of a people called Vacomagi, who seem to hold Moray and the Spey valley. Much of what is now Aberdeenshire is shown as lying within the territory of the Taezali, while Fife appears to be the home of a tribe called Venicones.

Within a decade of Agricola's withdrawal, the Romans had become deeply pessimistic about the idea of ever conquering the Highlands. The forts established in Perthshire during the campaigns of AD 80–4 were abandoned, thereby removing the infrastructure for any future invasion. A new legionary fortress at Inchtuthil, on the north bank of the Tay, was dismantled before its construction could be completed. The frontier shrank back to the river's estuary and was marked by a line of wooden watch-towers, but these and their associated forts were abandoned by AD 90. In the Scottish Lowlands the garrisons lingered on for a further ten years, but the second century dawned with an urgent need for manpower on the Danube causing a major withdrawal of troops from Britain. The northern frontier fell back again, shrinking the limits of Empire to the Tyne-Solway isthmus.

The early years of the second century saw the northern barbarians launch a series of attacks on Roman Britain. Whether or not the Caledonians were among these raiders is unknown, but the incursions left a trail of devastation in their wake. The situation became so serious that the emperor Hadrian ordered his soldiers to build a mighty wall of stone along the Tyne-Solway frontier. This great work was begun in 122 or 123 and was still in progress when Hadrian's successor, Antoninus Pius, launched a vigorous campaign in the North. The new emperor's objective was not another attempt to subdue the Highlands but a reconquest of what is now Lowland Scotland and the consolidation of a viable defensive line below the River Forth. Antoninus entrusted the venture to Britain's newly appointed governor, Quintus Lollius Urbicus, who began the campaign sometime around 140. Within a couple of years Roman authority was restored along the Tay estuary and new forts were built to make the gains permanent. The imperial frontier was fixed slightly to the south, being marked by a barrier – the Antonine Wall – across the Forth-Clyde isthmus. The new barrier was not built of stone, but consisted of a turf rampart with a ditch in front. Sixteen forts sited at regular intervals along its forty-mile length accommodated a total garrison of 6,000 men, while several Agricolan forts and some new ones north of the line were maintained as forward outposts. Despite its impressive appearance and large garrison, the turf wall was probably constructed as a display of prestige by Antoninus rather than for practical defensive reasons. For a while it became the new northern border of the Empire and made Hadrian's Wall redundant. It did not, however, survive long as a stable frontier. It was briefly abandoned in the 150s, its soldiers moving south to quell a revolt among the Brigantes of the Pennines, before being permanently evacuated in the following decade. The final withdrawal came soon after the death of Antoninus Pius in 161, which allowed his successors to downsize the northern frontier army. A handful of outpost forts beyond the Forth were still garrisoned, but the imperial boundary shrank back to Hadrian's Wall.

Caledonii and Maeatae

Before the end of the second century the Caledonians were assailing the Scottish Lowlands with increasing ferocity. The Roman writer Cassius Dio described how events took a very serious turn when Hadrian's Wall was overwhelmed sometime between 180 and 184. Although the onslaught on the Wall was brief, it was a symbolic disaster for Rome and a huge achievement for the barbarians. The great stone barrier was quickly recovered, but all the forts to the north of it were temporarily abandoned to the enemy.

The third century dawned on a rather unsettled situation. The Romans now faced two large groups of hostile natives across the war-ravaged isthmus between the Firths of Clyde and Forth. One was their old enemy the Caledonians, who ended the previous century in some kind of uneasy treaty with Rome. The other was the Maeatae, whose territory corresponded roughly with present-day Stirlingshire. A memory of this people survives in two place-names in the region they once inhabited: Dumyat (from *Dun Myat*, 'Fort of the Maeatae') and Myot Hill. According to Cassius Dio, the Maeatae dwelt immediately beyond the Antonine Wall, while the Caledonians inhabited lands further north. This shows that Caledonian territory still included Perthshire, as had been the case in Agricola's time, although the precise extent of these lands in either the first century or the third is unknown. Ptolemy's second-century map shows the name *Caledonii* covering a wide swathe of northern Scotland from the west coast to the east, but this might denote nothing more than Roman perceptions of the fame and status of this people. On the other hand, it is clear that the Caledonians and the Maeatae were large and powerful political entities, each perhaps an amalgamation of peoples under the sway of a single dominant group. Of the twelve tribes shown on Ptolemy's map as second-century occupants of the Highlands, some had already been amalgamated into larger groupings during his lifetime. Using information collected by Agricola's forces, Ptolemy showed four tribes in the area between the Firths of Forth and Moray: the Caledonii, Vacomagi, Taezali and Venicones. By the third century the Caledonii had evidently absorbed the others and subsumed their identities. Given the undoubtedly warlike and 'heroic' character of Iron Age society, it is hard to imagine that the process of absorption or amalgamation was voluntary rather than enforced. Even with the threat of a Roman invasion providing a persuasive argument for smaller tribes to join larger ones, the amalgamation was unlikely to have been peaceful. Between the menace of Rome and the dominance of the Caledonii the leaders of the Vacomagi, Venicones and Taezali may have had little choice but to surrender their sovereignty within the Caledonian 'confederacy'. The alternative was military conquest by one foe or another, the most immediate threat coming not from the legions but from the Caledonians. The Caledonians and the Maeatae are sometimes viewed by historians as voluntary associations formed by separate tribes seeking mutual assurances of protection by amicable agreement. It is more realistic to see these two 'confederacies' as the enlarged hegemonies of powerful kindreds who, in a period of uncertainty, exploited the vulnerability of fearful neighbours to forge large groups that they could control as paramount rulers.

In 197, the emperor Septimius Severus emerged victorious from a destructive civil war in Gaul to deal with the growing barbarian menace on his borders. On the northern frontier in Britain the

Maeatae were still belligerent and were being held back only by large gifts of Roman cash, while the Caledonians were on the verge of breaking a fragile treaty with the Empire. During the early years of the third century Roman diplomacy maintained control of the frontier but, in 205 or 206, the two confederacies launched an invasion. Britain's governor appealed to Severus for more troops or, better still, for the direct involvement of the emperor himself. At that time, Severus was eager to take his sons Caracalla and Geta away from the decadence of Rome to give them some experience of generalship. Bringing them to Britain seemed an ideal solution and so, in 208, he arrived on the island at the head of a large army. Taking personal command of the military situation he marched north, crossing the Forth-Clyde isthmus to attack the Maeatae. Fierce fighting ensued, with the barbarians waging a guerilla war on their home territory until they were beaten into submission. At this point, Severus revived the old Agricolan scheme for a conquest of the North and began to plan the construction of a massive new legionary fortress in Perthshire, at Carpow on the Tay.

In 210, however, the Maeatae rose again, at a time when Severus was stricken by illness. The task of crushing the revolt was given to Caracalla, whose brutal methods provoked the Caledonians under their chieftain Argentocoxos ('Silver Leg') to join the fight against Rome. The decisive event in the drama came in early 211, when the death of Severus elevated Caracalla to the purple. The new emperor consolidated the Antonine frontier, but he soon realised the futility of a permanent scheme to subjugate the North. He eventually made peace with the barbarians and then, like Agricola before him, withdrew his forces south of the Forth-Clyde line while he himself hurried back to Rome. Construction of the new fortress at Carpow had already begun but was promptly abandoned. With Caracalla's withdrawal came the end of any realistic hope of conquering the whole island of Britain. No Roman general would ever again march towards the Tay to threaten the tribes who dwelt in the hills and glens. From that moment on, the destiny of the far North lay in the hands of its native inhabitants.

CHAPTER 3
The Painted People

This chapter looks at how the northern part of Britain fared in the final two centuries of the Roman occupation. It was during these years that the Picts made their first appearance in history. Their sudden emergence in the historical record raises a number of questions about their origins: Where did they come from, why were they called Picts and what made them Pictish? Taken together, these questions form part of the so-called 'Problem of the Picts', the collection of puzzles and mysteries mentioned at the start of this book. The 'Problem' continues to generate competing theories in academic and non-academic circles alike. This chapter does not aim to solve it but will rather try to answer one of its most important questions: Who were the Picts? Finding an answer requires an examination of what traits distinguished the Picts from other peoples. This, in turn, leads into matters of language, culture and social structure. The first of these topics – the Pictish language – will be addressed below, as will the origin of the name *Picts*. A brief survey will identify the areas where this people lived. The chapter begins, however, by following the trail of history through the final phase of Roman rule in Britain.

The trail resumes in the early years of the third century, after the end of the Severan military campaigns. A lack of references to conflict in the contemporary sources suggests that the century was a period of relative calm in Roman Britain, even on the northern frontier. A curious piece of information from these years comes from the southern city of Colchester where, sometime in the 220s or

Roman Scotland and the ancestors of the Picts.

230s, a man called Lossio Veda was commemorated on a tombstone. Lossio was a Caledonian whose sympathies lay with Rome. He undoubtedly spoke Latin and was probably literate, although he retained a devotion to his native religion: he worshipped Mars Medocius, a 'Romanised' Celtic deity who may have been a god of the North. The memorial inscription describes Lossio as *nepos Vepogeni*, which means either 'nephew' or 'grandson' of a man called Vepogenus. Unfortunately nothing more is known about this family. It is therefore difficult to identify their reasons for settling so far south of their homeland. Their migration from the North might be an isolated instance, but it could also reflect a general easing of relations between Rome and Caledonia.

Another interesting snippet comes from Cassius Dio, who refers to a conversation between the empress Julia Domna, wife of Septimius Severus, and the wife of the Caledonian chieftain Argentocoxos. The two women chatted while their husbands negotiated a peace treaty on the northern frontier. Dio relates how Julia spoke disparagingly of the loose morals of Caledonian women. In response, the barbarian lady freely acknowledged her people's relaxed attitude to female promiscuity but compared it to the brazen immorality of Roman women. She remarked that the women of her homeland were right 'to give themselves openly to the best men rather than – as Roman women do – to let themselves be debauched by the vilest'. In reporting (or inventing) this conversation Dio was able to pass judgment on Julia Domna's promiscuous reputation by contrasting her morals with those of untamed barbarians. He was probably far less interested in the question of whether or not 'free love' was ever practised by the ancient people of the Highlands.

Beyond the Wall

Lossio's memorial inscription and Dio's piece of gossip about third-century morality are useful nuggets of information, but they do not prove that Romans and Caledonians were living happily side by side. The situation in the North did, however, seem to be less tense throughout the 200s. Hadrian's Wall began to seem like a secure boundary between the imperial province in the southern parts of Britain and the wild lands beyond. Immediately north of the Wall, in what is now the Anglo-Scottish border region, a handful of outpost forts kept a close watch on the movements of native tribes. Although these forts marked the northern limit of Rome's defences, they had an additional use as bases from which *exploratores* ('scouts') ventured out to gather intelligence. The range of these scouting operations was considerable and extended beyond the Forth to the southern Caledonian lands around the Firth of Tay. The most westerly of the outpost forts lay at Netherby, just north of Carlisle, and bore a name indicative of its primary function: *Castra Exploratorum*, 'The Fort of the Scouts'.

Military intelligence was gathered by various covert means, such as spying, but also via open-air assemblies of the native population. These meetings took place at regular intervals and at designated sites, usually in the presence of Roman officers to whom local civilian leaders were answerable. At each assembly the native Britons aired their grievances and settled their own disputes under the watchful gaze of Roman officers who, in turn, were able to identify troublemakers and potential rebels. The sites where these gatherings occurred were known as *loci*, which in Latin means simply 'places'. Each *locus* served a particular region within lands which, although nominally controlled by Rome, lay north of Hadrian's Wall in territory where forts and other defences had long been abandoned. Summoning the tribes of a particular region to meet at a specific time and place was no easy task, not even for an institution so well-organised as the Roman army. To facilitate the process the *loci* were sited at ancient landmarks where communities had been accustomed to assemble for public or religious ceremonies in pre-Roman times. Thus, the regional meetings for the inhabitants of south-west Scotland were held at *Locus Maponi*, 'The Place of the god Mabon', which was almost certainly the great boulder now known as the Clochmabenstane on the northern shore of the Solway Firth. Further north, around the shore of the

Firth of Forth, the assembly at *Locus Manavi* ('The Place of the Manau district') gathered at a similar sacred rock. The ancient name of this landmark still survives in the town and county name Clackmannan which, in its original Gaelic form *Clach Manann*, means 'The Stone of Manau'. Today the ancient boulder sits on top of a pillar in the town's main square, although its original location lay a few hundred metres away at the oddly named Lookaboutye.

The Britons of the Tweed and Clyde valleys also met with Roman officials at designated *loci*, but the positions of these sites are unknown, as is the whereabouts of what may have been a more northerly assembly place near the Firth of Tay. To modern historians, an incomplete knowledge of the sites is matched by ignorance of how often the assemblies were held and how the proceedings were conducted. It can, however, be assumed that the system of scouting operations and regional meetings was accepted by Roman and native alike throughout the third century. It allowed the Britons living beyond Hadrian's Wall to govern their own affairs under imperial protection, while at the same time enabling Rome to retain a large measure of control as far north as the Tay. On a purely economic level, the system freed the imperial treasury from the huge financial burden of maintaining a permanent presence in Stirlingshire and southern Perthshire, or in the forts along the Antonine Wall. In fact, the frontier zone remained relatively stable until the last years of the century, when an old enemy with a new name emerged from the Highlands.

Picti

In 297, a document known as the *Panegyric of Constantius Caesar* mentioned two barbarian peoples as troublesome foes of Roman Britain. One of these was the *Hiberni*, the inhabitants of Ireland. The other was a group whose name had not been encountered before: *Picti*, 'The Picts'. The identity and ancestry of this new nation was made clear some years later when another Roman text referred to 'the woods and marshes of the Caledonians and other

Picts'. Later still, in the 360s, the soldier and historian Ammianus Marcellinus stated that the Picts were divided into two peoples, the Dicalydones and Verturiones. The latter do not appear on Ptolemy's second-century map, but the former are clearly the Caledonians under a variant of their former name. The first element, *di*, of the name *Dicalydones* implies that the original 'confederacy' of Agricola's time had now split into two sub-divisions.

Ammianus mentioned a series of raids on Roman Britain in 364, and he identified the Picts as prominent culprits alongside Saxons, Scots and an extremely savage race called Attacotti. The Saxons were still based in northern Germany at this time and had not yet made the permanent settlements in Britain that would eventually turn them into Anglo-Saxons. The term 'Scots' was used by Ammianus and his peers as a broad label for any speakers of Gaelic, regardless of whether they lived in Ireland or Britain. It distinguished Gaelic-speakers from those who spoke other Celtic languages, such as the Britons and the Gauls. The term did not therefore denote the inhabitants of 'Scotland', for no such entity existed in Roman times. The Scots of the fourth century were the various Gaelic-speaking groups on either side of the Irish Sea, namely the inhabitants of Ireland and Argyll. The Attacotti were a mysterious people whose identity is unknown, although they perhaps came from Ireland or the Hebrides and were regarded as being distinct from the Picts and the Scots.

Neither Ammianus nor his contemporaries explained the origin of the name *Picti*. The assertion that the Caledonians and Verturiones were the main components of the new nation suggests that both Dunkeld, the 'Fort of the Caledonians', and the later Pictish province of Fortriu (whose name appears to derive from Verturiones), lay within its territory. Historians have traditionally located Fortriu in Strathearn and Menteith, south of the Tay, but recent scholarship proposes Moray as a better alternative. If this new location is correct the Caledonians lay south of the Verturiones, but both peoples were core elements of the Pictish nation. The heartland of the Picts thus extended from Perthshire to the Moray Firth, but the full extent of lands that could be called

'Pictish' was much greater. The previous chapter noted the likelihood that the Caledonians of the second and third centuries were an amalgamation of tribes, each of whom joined – or were forced to join – a larger political entity or confederacy bearing the name of its dominant group. By the end of the third century these 'confederates' had acquired or adopted a new name for themselves, of which the Latin term *Picti* was a Roman variant or equivalent. Overall power within the enlarged nation had fallen into the hands of its two main sub-groups, the Caledonians (or 'Dicalydones') and the Verturiones. The relationships of these two peoples to the Pictish nation as a whole, and to each other, can only be guessed at. Each was clearly a distinct entity, although both exhibited enough shared traits to be called Picts. Of the two, the Caledonians may have been the dominant group, just like their ancestors who had fought Agricola at Mons Graupius 300 years earlier. It is curious, though, to find no fourth-century mention of the Maeatae, whose warriors had formerly posed such a formidable threat to Roman security on the Forth-Clyde isthmus. Were the Maeatae excluded from the Pictish nation? Were they, in fact, a separate group whose cultural affinities set them apart from the Picts? In the third century, Cassius Dio spoke of the Maeatae as being distinct from the Caledonians, so perhaps they were a group of Britons who, for cultural or other reasons, were recognisably non-Pictish. More puzzlingly, no contemporary source reveals the precise origin of the name *Picti*, and it is this enigmatic label that is examined next.

Picti: The Name and the Tattoos

The word *Picti* is a Latin term meaning 'Painted People'. Its Roman origin suggests that it was a nickname given by troops on the imperial frontier to barbarians lurking in the wild lands beyond. The logical inference is that a characteristic of the Picts was body-painting or tattooing, and that this practice distinguished them from their neighbours. The likely origin of the term *Picti* in military slang devised by an enemy suggests that the name in its Latin form was a disparaging one which would not have been adopted by the Picts themselves. They had a name of their own but it is not known what it was: neither they nor their neighbours recorded it for posterity in any of the surviving sources.

Among the Britons, who in the fourth century lay under the sway of Rome, the Picts were called *Priteni*. This term survived the evolution of the Brittonic language into Old Welsh where, in the form *Prydyn*, it came to denote not only the Picts but their homeland as well. *Priteni* and its variant *Pritani* were not originally labels applied to the Picts. Both were very ancient terms that the earliest Greek and Roman travellers had used when referring to all the inhabitants of Britain, and both words may have meant 'The People of the Designs'. Later, the Romans of Julius Caesar's time encountered the term *Pritani* but altered it to *Britanni* and restricted its application to those tribes who eventually came under Roman rule. *Britanni* was in turn adopted by the conquered natives of Roman Britain and, in the form *Brittones* ('Britons') became their own name for themselves. The other term, *Priteni*, soon became obsolete and lost its original meaning but, as the Roman period progressed, the Britons of the imperial province began to use it as a name for the hostile barbarians who dwelt in the wild Highlands beyond the Forth-Clyde isthmus. Later still, Britons and Romans alike started calling these same barbarians *Picti*. Since both the Picts and the Britons were part of a Celtic cultural and linguistic milieu, the Picts may have called themselves by a name similar to the archaic term *Priteni*. It is equally likely that they used a word of their own devising which has since been lost to history. Perhaps this word, when heard by Roman ears, sounded like the Latin slang term *Picti* and was thus adopted not only by Roman soldiers on the northern frontier but also by the chroniclers at Rome. The Picts' own name for themselves probably carried the same meaning as both *Picti* and *Priteni* and signified 'The People of the Designs', or 'The Painted People.'

To Roman eyes these designs were the most striking aspect of the Picts. Had this custom not seemed so unusual or noticeable, the frontier garrisons would have coined a name other than *Picti* from the repertoire of barrack-room slang. The custom of adorning the skin with pictures is apparently what distinguished the Picts from other native groups in the British Isles, and it also gave them a unique and visible identity. To a Roman scout gazing across the River Tay at a group of tribesmen on the opposite bank, any warrior with pictures on his skin was a Pict rather than a Briton or a Scot. But what would this Roman scout actually have seen? The poet Claudian, whose career at the imperial court spanned the years around AD 400, gave a vivid and dramatic answer to this question when he wrote: 'There came the legion, shield of the frontier Britons, check of the grim Scot, whose men had watched the life leave the designs on the dying Pict.' This is clearly a reference to body-painting or tattooing, but Claudian is not the only Roman writer to mention the custom, which had been noted long before by Julius Caesar. In the first century BC, when Caesar's expeditions brought Rome into direct contact with the natives of Britain for the first time, the custom of skin-decoration was apparently widespread across many parts of the island. Caesar wrote that 'all the Britons paint themselves with woad which produces a dark blue colour and for this reason they are much more frightful in appearance during battle', but he makes no specific mention of the northern tribes and does not say if woad was tattooed after being applied to the skin.

In the early third century AD the Greek writer Herodian noted that the barbarians of northern Britain adorned their skin with a range of designs, including representations of animals. Four centuries later, the Christian monk Isidore of Seville believed that the practice of using needles to imprint designs on their bodies had indeed earned the Picts their name. If Isidore's words are taken at face value – and there is no reason why they should not be – they support the idea that the Picts not only adorned their skin with blue designs, but that they also made the decoration permanent by tattooing. This practice had clearly been abandoned by their neighbours, the Britons, whose ancient customs had been severely eroded by 200 years of Roman rule. In Roman and later times tattooing was regarded by non-Picts as barbaric and primitive, the taint of an uncivilised people. The modern image of the tattooed Pict has been regarded in the same way and has added weight to the idea that the Picts were less sophisticated than their neighbours.

Pictish Lands and Language

Turning to matters of geography, there is little precision involved in Roman perceptions of which lands were Pictish and which were inhabited by Britons. To further complicate matters, fourth-century writers probably used the term *Picti* as a vague label for any barbarians dwelling north of the Forth-Clyde isthmus, and not merely for those who dwelt in what historians today think of as the Pictish lands. Nor was the term restricted to the mainland of Britain: the imperial poet Claudian speaks of Picts inhabiting *Thyle*, which is usually identified as the Shetland Islands. However, his poems were works of eulogy rather than of history or geography and were not composed to provide an accurate gazetteer of peoples and places. There may nonetheless be some historical basis to the idea of a 'Greater Pictland' stretching from the Hebrides to the North Sea, and from the Forth-Clyde isthmus to Orkney and Shetland.

For a more precise indicator of where the Picts lived, a useful clue is the distribution of the place-name element *pit*, which derives from a word meaning 'portion of land' in the ancient Pictish language. Names beginning with *pit-* are found all over the Highlands but have an eastern concentration between the Firths of Tay and Moray. This region includes the ancient Caledonian heart-lands and is where writers of the Early Historic period placed many of the key events of Pictish history. It can therefore be identified as the nucleus of Pictish culture, in the sense of its being the region where the most identifiable traits of that culture originated or became concentrated. It is important to acknowledge that outside this heartland, in areas as far afield as Orkney and Skye, local populations considered themselves to be no less 'Pictish' than the inhabitants of Perthshire or Aberdeenshire or Moray where the distinctive *pit-* place-names are most numerous. Indeed, as shall be seen in the following pages, the most recognisable elements of Pictish culture are visible across a wide area of northern Scotland and are not confined to those areas where *pit-* is a common prefix in place-names. The imprecise geography offered by Roman writers is often frustrating, but perhaps they were correct to casually assign the label *Picti* to any band of marauders who emerged from the Highlands and Islands. From Fife to the Isle of Skye, and from Shetland to the Tay, the native inhabitants were almost certainly part of the Pictish nation.

What, then, were the key cultural traits that allow this very large area to be called 'Pictland'? First and foremost, it is known that a common language was spoken throughout the area. This knowledge is not gleaned from ancient documents written in the Pictish tongue: no such texts have survived, if they ever existed. Evidence of the Pictish language comes instead from names of people and places, in so far as these were recorded by contemporary sources or – in the case of place-names – preserved in the landscape of modern Scotland. The earliest records of Pictish place-names come from Roman writers, of whom the geographer Ptolemy is the richest source of information. It has already been noted that Ptolemy's second-century map of the known world included the British Isles, showing not only the names of tribes but also various places that were significant to Rome. These names were not Latin inventions but, in many cases, were simple Latinisations of native originals. Ptolemy's map identified more than forty population groups in Scotland and named the settlements associated with them, together with some prominent topographical features. The latter ranged from large islands such as *Scetis* (Skye) and *Malaius* (Mull) to notable landmarks such as *Epidium Promontorium* (The Mull of Kintyre). Analysis of Ptolemy's data by philologists and other linguistic experts has confirmed that the majority of these names are Celtic in origin. They were given verbally by natives to Roman observers, who wrote them down in Latinised form. The map thus confirms that all the people of Scotland during the Roman period used a Celtic language when giving names to their lands and to their communities. The characteristics of this language, in so far as Ptolemy's map preserves its nomenclature, show that it was part of a group known to linguists as P-Celtic. This group includes Gaulish and Brittonic, respectively the ancient languages of Gaul and Britain, but excludes the Goidelic or 'Q-Celtic' languages, of which the Gaelic of Ireland, Scotland and the Isle of Man are modern representatives. Brittonic is the ancestor of Welsh, Cornish and Breton and was the language spoken by most of the native peoples of Roman Britain. Philologists believe that the language of the Picts was similar to Brittonic, basing this conclusion not only on the P-Celtic elements in the Highland names on Ptolemy's map but also by comparing modern place-names in Scotland and Wales. The prefix *aber-*, for instance, which means 'river mouth' or 'confluence', is very common in Wales but is found also in the Scottish Highlands in names such as Aberdeen, Abernethy and Aberlour. The Welsh word *perth*, meaning a bush or copse, is borne by the Scottish city of that name but is found also in less obvious contexts, such as Muir of Pert.

The prefix *pit-*, already referred to above, was originally *pett* in Pictish and is related to Welsh and Cornish *peth*, 'thing', and to Breton *pez*, 'piece'. In Gaul, where the natives spoke a P-Celtic language related to Brittonic, the equivalent word was something like *petia*, which appears in later Latin documents in the compound *petia terrae*, 'piece of land'. Some 300 place names north of the Firth of Forth begin with *pit-*, which clearly had the same meaning as Gaulish *petia* and similarly denoted a portion of land. There is, as already stated, a marked concentration of *pit-* names in the east of Scotland, from Fife through Perthshire to Aberdeenshire, with instances such as Pitlochry ('Stony Portion') and Pittenweem ('Portion of the Cave'). The occurrence of the prefix in a handful of names along the Great Glen and on the western mainland opposite Skye shows that these areas, too, were places where Picts held 'pieces of land'. However, many of the suffixes attached to *pit-* were not given by P-Celtic speakers: the two examples just quoted – Pitlochry and Pittenweem – contain suffixes that were given after Gaelic supplanted Pictish as the language of the Highlands in the ninth and tenth centuries. Nevertheless, the *pit-* names are so numerous that this uniquely P-Celtic prefix is regarded as important evidence of the essentially Brittonic character of the Pictish language. Interestingly, the rarity of equivalent *peth-* or *pez-* names in Wales, Cornwall and Brittany suggests that units of land were apportioned in a different way in these areas. This implies that the Picts and the Britons did not deal with ownership of land in the same manner, or may point simply to a different application of land-holding vocabulary. Such linguistic differences set the Pictish language apart from the main branch of Brittonic spoken by people living south of the River Forth. Over a long period of time the two branches diverged for a number of reasons. One key factor was Roman influence in the frontier region, where a lengthy military presence may have disrupted native communications to turn northern Stirlingshire and southern Perthshire into a linguistic borderland. This and other factors presumably hastened the separation of Pictish-Brittonic from mainstream Brittonic, with each branch evolving along a different path. The result was a linguistic boundary running alongside a cultural and political frontier in the Forth Valley.

Historians have been puzzled by a number of names on Ptolemy's map which seem to incorporate words of non-Celtic origin. As recently as half a century ago, when Pictish history and culture were less well understood than they are today, a belief arose that these non-Celtic elements indicated the survival of a pre-Celtic culture and language in northern Scotland during the Roman and Early Historic periods. From this came a suggestion that these elements were not only non-Celtic but non-Indo-European, a theory which has greatly contributed to the enigmas and mysteries associated with Pictish society. The idea of a non-Indo-European origin for the Picts arose in the late nineteenth century and held great appeal for those who liked to imagine that the prehistoric people of Scotland were as puzzling as the Basques or Etruscans. The theory persisted for a long time and was still being promoted in the 1930s and 1940s. It retained a foothold even after the publication, in 1955, of Kenneth Jackson's magisterial paper on the Pictish language, which appeared as a chapter in a book entitled *The Problem of the Picts*. Jackson was one of the pre-eminent Celtic scholars of his generation, and his paper remained the definitive work on Pictish linguistic matters for the next four decades. His main conclusion was that the Picts spoke not one language but two: these being a P-Celtic dialect closely related to Brittonic, alongside a non-Indo-European tongue. The former, he suggested, had supplanted the latter during the first millennium BC, when the indigenous pre-Celtic languages of the British Isles were made obsolete after the migration of Celtic culture from Continental Europe. Jackson surmised that, in Pictland, an indigenous pre-Celtic tongue was retained for ritual purposes and was preserved throughout the Roman period and beyond, until Gaelic extinguished both it and the Pictish P-Celtic language in the ninth century AD. Jackson demolished any notion that the Picts should be regarded as non-Celtic or non-Indo-European, and placed them among the Celtic nations of Britain. More recently, new scholarship has substantially eroded his theory of two Pictish languages by identifying many of the presumed non-Indo-European names as being P-Celtic after all. Thus, while a small number of pre-Celtic words may have been retained in place names and personal names, it is now clear that the Picts spoke only one language. This was a Celtic tongue, a variant or close relative of the Brittonic dialects spoken by their neighbours south of the Forth and Tay.

Pictish Origin-Legends

The Picts had their own theory on their origins, but no first-hand Pictish account of it has survived. What has survived is a story of Pictish beginnings contained in a curious origin-legend promoted by their neighbours. This was committed to writing at a time when the Picts had already become absorbed by the medieval kingdom of Scotland, and it is not therefore a Pictish text. It states that the first king of the Picts was Cruithne, whose seven sons divided Pictland between them. The name *Cruithne* is simply a Gaelic equivalent of the Brittonic name *Priteni* which, as previously noted, was a name applied to the Picts by Romanised Britons living south of the imperial frontier. The presence of a Gaelic name raises suspicions about the legend's true provenance, for the Picts were not Gaels and would have been unlikely to give a foreign name to an ancestor-figure. This suggests that both the name and the story were created by non-Pictish folk in a Gaelic-speaking environment in Scotland or Ireland. In the origin-legend, the mythical forefather Cruithne reigned for 100 years, with his sons reigning for a further quarter of a millennium. The names of the sons, and of the seven districts they ruled, are given as Fib, Fidach, Fotlaig, Fortrenn, Cait, Ce and Circinn. Legends such as this are not, of course, a source of authentic history but were constructed for particular purposes and to promote specific interests. Sometimes a late or dubious origin for this type of story is hinted at in a fairly obvious way. In the case of the Pictish origin-legend, the names of the seven sons of Cruithne are derived from territorial divisions which seem to relate in some way to later earldoms of the medieval Scottish kingdom. Fib is the ancient name of Fife, while Fotlaig is a variant of *Athfotla*, an old name for Atholl. Circinn is a name associated by medieval sources with Angus and the Mearns, while Fortrenn is a genitive form (in Gaelic) of the region around Moray commonly called Fortriu. In the previous chapter Fortriu was connected with the Latin tribal term *Verturiones*, both names belonging to the same people and to their territory. Cait is obviously Caithness, but Ce and Fidach are less certainly identifiable. One possible clue is that the Aberdeen-shire hill Bennachie, referred to earlier in the discussion of Mons Graupius, might preserve the name *Ce*. If so, then the Pictish province of Ce could be equated with the medieval earldoms of Mar and Buchan. A twelfth-century version of the Cruithne story clarifies the geography of the seven divisions, linking Ce explicitly to Mar and Buchan while placing Fidach in Easter Ross. It is inter-esting that only the eastern and central Highlands are encompassed by the legend, leaving Argyll and the Isles excluded from this vision of Pictish beginnings. The exclusions suggest that the creators of the legend, whether or not they themselves were Picts or Gaels, regarded the Gaelic West as a non-Pictish zone.

The legend of Cruithne is best viewed as political propaganda originating after the end of the Pictish period to promote a particular ideology during a time of crisis and instability. Peering beneath the story, it can be seen that its creators sought to portray an image of ancient unity among the medieval earldoms of eastern Scotland by linking them to a common ancestor called Cruithne. The likeliest political context for the tale is therefore a period when the seven areas were tenuously unified under an over-arching authority, such as the early Scottish kings of the ninth to twelfth centuries. Their kingdom, as a later chapter will show, was forged from a union of the Gaelic West and the Pictish East. Perhaps these kings hoped to strengthen the cohesion of their newly unified realm by pointing to an earlier period of unity in a remote and mythical past? Alternatively, the legend of Cruithne and his seven sons might go back to the reign of a Pictish overking who wished to give the separate regions of his enlarged kingdom a sense of ancient togetherness and common ancestry.

Some modern historians wonder if the equation of the seven provinces or sub-kingdoms of the Picts with seven major regions of medieval Scotland might be incorrect. The sources which give the identifications are certainly not among the most reliable providers of information, so the equations are unlikely to be geographically precise. However, even allowing for the late and probably non-Pictish origin of the Cruithne story, earlier and more reliable sources show that it preserves an element of truth. The Irish annals, for example, give contemporary information from the era of the Picts, and refer to three of the seven provinces, namely Fortriu, Circinn and Atholl. These three areas, then, were already defined and named during the Pictish period. Perhaps the other four had a similar antiquity? The imprecision of the sources does not allow the matter to be pursued much further. The precise extent of any particular Pictish province is unlikely to be unearthed. Thus it may never be known if the boundaries of Cait were the same as those of the later earldom of Caithness. A particular problem is the location of Fortriu: did it correspond to Strathearn and Menteith, as was formerly believed? Or are modern historians correct in placing it much further north?

The tale of Cruithne is not the only Pictish origin-legend. A rather different story was recorded by the English writer Bede in his *Ecclesiastical History*. Bede was a monk at Jarrow in Northumbria who lived at a time when there was considerable diplomatic communication between the Picts and their English neighbours across the Firth of Forth. Writing in the early eighth century, he states that the Picts sailed from their homelands in Scythia, a region approximating to the wild steppes of Eastern Europe, beyond the reach of Classical civilisation. After being blown about by the wind, the Picts 'in a few warships' eventually landed in Ireland. Their request to stay as settlers was refused by the Irish, who claimed that the country did not have enough room for two nations. The Irish advised the Picts to settle across the sea in Britain and offered unspecified help – presumably of a military nature – if the indigenous population showed any resistance. In a final act of generosity, the Irish gave women to the Picts, who seemed to have none of their own. The gift was bestowed on condition that, whenever succession to a Pictish kingship lay in doubt, the new king should be chosen from the female royal line. Bede added that this custom, which is known to anthropologists as matrilineal succession or matriliny, was still used by the Picts of his own time. His synopsis of the story has a distinctly Irish orientation and presumably originated in Ireland.

Later versions of the tale show Gaelic influence by including the mysterious ancestor Cruithne and linking him to the beginnings of matriliny among the Picts. All versions, including Bede's, probably derived from a legend that was well-established in Ireland before the eighth century. This legend was merely an attempt by the Irish to explain why the Picts differed in certain aspects of their culture from other inhabitants of North Britain: the Gaelic-speaking Scots in Argyll, and the Britons who dwelt south of the Forth-Clyde isthmus. Neither this tale, nor the story of Cruithne, answer the most fundamental questions: Who were the Picts? What did it mean to be 'Pictish'? At this point these queries could be turned on their heads by asking if the Picts really were as different from their neighbours as Bede and other writers suggest. The next chapter will shed some light on these matters by taking a peep inside Pictish society to see how it worked. In the meantime, the focus switches to observe the impact made by the Picts during the final phase of Rome's occupation of Britain. This means that trust must be placed once more, and for the last time, in the hands of Roman writers.

The End of Roman Britain

In 367, according to Ammianus Marcellinus, the various barbarian nations whose warbands had been plundering for many years combined their efforts to launch a huge, well-planned assault. Such co-operation between peoples of widely differing origin – Irish, Saxons, Franks, Picts and Attacotti – was unprecedented and completely unexpected. The joint attack, or 'Barbarian Conspiracy' as Ammianus called it, was made simultaneously on all fronts. Its leaders were assisted by men called *arcani* or *areani*, members of a shadowy Roman organisation operating as spies or secret agents beyond the northern frontier. These were no doubt associated with, or were the same as, the *exploratores* who had scouted beyond Hadrian's Wall in the previous century. In 367, they collaborated with the barbarians by providing key geographical and military information in return for a share of the loot. The co-ordinated attack overwhelmed the imperial forces, throwing them into utter disarray. Some high-ranking officers perished in the mayhem. In the South, the Count of the Saxon Shore was killed in an attack on his coastal defences, while the general in charge of the northern garrison, whose headquarters lay at York, was ambushed and captured. Roman Britain now lay at the mercy of barbarian warbands who, along with deserters from the imperial army, rampaged through towns and villages with impunity. The defenceless inhabitants, having relied on Roman protection for 300 years, were brutally plundered and terrorised. Only when the emperor Valentinian I sent four elite regiments under the renowned Count Theodosius was some semblance of order restored, but it was a further two years before things returned to normal.

The situation did not remain stable for long. By the end of the fourth century, Britain again came under barbarian attack. This was the time when the poet Claudian mentioned Roman soldiers fighting tattooed Picts on the northern frontier. Claudian referred to a victorious imperial campaign, but its results were short-lived. Before the end of the first decade of the fifth century, the military situation in Britain had become dire and perilous. Successive withdrawals of Roman troops to support ambitious generals on their personal adventures in Gaul had reduced the garrison to dangerously low numbers and, to make matters worse, the barbarian attacks continued. In desperation, the civilian leaders of the major cities of Britain took matters into their own hands: they formed their own armies to defend themselves against the raiders. Finally, in the year 410, and after requesting direct military intervention from Rome, they were told by the emperor Honorius that no further assistance would be forthcoming. This dismissive response effectively signalled the end of Roman rule in Britain.

It is easy to imagine the Picts jumping for joy at the news and relishing the prospect of looting their southern neighbours without fear of meeting a Roman legion along the way. This, indeed, is an image consistent with the picture painted by Gildas, a British monk of the mid-500s. Gildas wrote a long essay in which he warned that the lax morals of his own time would provoke God to unleash the kind of chaos seen in the previous century. From him comes a dramatic picture of moral corruption and political instability taking hold after the Roman withdrawal in 410. Much of what he wrote was essentially accurate. South of Hadrian's Wall, in territory formerly administered by the Empire, the administrative bureaucracy swiftly disintegrated. From its ruins arose a patchwork of native political groups which, by the beginning of the sixth century, had evolved into small kingdoms under the authority of kings. Gildas was extremely scornful of these rulers and their successors, the kings of his own lifetime, and expended much ink on bemoaning their abuses of power. His greatest scorn was reserved for Maglocunus, a sixth-century monarch of Gwynedd in North Wales, who epitomised everything that was corrupt and degenerate about Britain's post-Roman leadership. Gildas gives few clues about the fifth-century origins of royal authority, but native kingships evidently sprouted soon after 410 when, in the absence of imperial rule, local leaders divided what had once been Roman Britain among themselves. Whether or not these post-Roman rulers sprang from the same urban elites who had appealed to Honorius is unknown. They may have owed their positions to ancestral links with the old tribal aristocracies of pre-Roman times, or to military contacts in the final occupation phase of the Roman garrison. Some individuals seized power through wealth, land ownership, personal ambition or political opportunism. Whatever the true origins of their authority, within a few generations their descendants were calling themselves kings and were starting to wage war against their neighbours.

Gildas believed that the conditions which allowed these men to seize power were created as soon as the Britons were told by Rome to solve their own political problems without the Empire's help. He stated that the period after 410 saw a wave of new barbarian attacks, including destructive raids from the North and West. 'As the Romans went back home,' he wrote, 'there eagerly emerged from the coracles that had carried them across the sea-valleys the foul hordes of Scots and Picts, like dark throngs of worms who wriggle out of narrow fissures in the rock when the sun is high and the weather grows warm.' To Gildas, the Scots of this period were the Gaelic-speakers of Ireland and Argyll. He recognised certain cultural distinctions between them and the Picts but, in his eyes, both groups were equally loathsome and savage: 'They were to some extent different in their customs but they were in perfect accord in their greed for bloodshed, and they were more ready to cover their villainous faces with hair than their private parts and neighbouring regions with clothes.' To combat these attacks the native British leaders, who were apparently still capable of joining together as a national 'council', invited groups of Saxons to settle in southern and eastern Britain as mercenaries. Saxon warbands duly sailed over from Germany to provide a bulwark against the Scots and Picts, and received substantial payments from the Britons. For a while the

Saxons performed a useful job but, after establishing settlements and bringing in reinforcements from their homelands, they rose in revolt against their employers. Much bloodshed ensued until the Britons achieved a major victory, at an unidentified place called Mount Badon, which led to an uneasy truce. This brought the narrative of Gildas to the end of the fifth century and the beginning of the sixth, when he himself was born. He was aware that in spite of the victory at Badon the Saxons still remained on the island. With them were members of two other Germanic nations: the Angles and Jutes. All three peoples had established settlements in the eastern parts of Britain during the fifth century, in a wide tract of territory stretching northward from Kent to Yorkshire. Today these settlers are usually called Anglo-Saxons, but they themselves used the term *englisc*, 'The English'. Their descendants in the seventh, eighth and ninth centuries were to have a major impact on the fortunes of the Picts.

The Northern Britons after 410

The fifth century was a time of great political change for the Picts and their neighbours. The end of Roman Britain meant the withdrawal of the northern frontier garrison that had stood as an obstacle to barbarian attack for almost 400 years. Most of this army was withdrawn in phases before the emperor Honorius told the Britons to stand on their own feet. By c.400 there is unlikely to have been more than a shattered remnant of troops in the forts along Hadrian's Wall, and these were a far cry from the formidable garrison that had once held the line. After 410 no more pay came from the imperial coffers, and the disillusioned soldiers vanished into the local communities from whom, by this time, they were probably indistinguishable. Whatever remained of Rome's once-mighty northern frontier army simply faded away, casting aside its uniforms and insignia to merge with the native population. The old network of forts and signal-towers that had once defended the frontier people from Pictish assault quickly disintegrated. A few forts were re-used as strongholds by the new local leaders who appeared at this time, but the majority were abandoned to dereliction. Gildas referred to a brief re-manning of Hadrian's Wall by the Britons themselves, but this is unlikely to have happened and is either a confused folk-tradition or an invention by Gildas himself. It would seem, then, that nothing now lay between the Picts and the lands south of the old imperial frontier. The great Wall between Tyne and Solway was deserted, the outpost forts beyond it lay derelict, and the *exploratores* were little more than a memory. However, the departure of Rome allowed new powers to arise, and the Picts of the fifth century found the Forth-Clyde isthmus once again held against them.

Gildas mentions the recruitment of Saxon mercenaries to defend Lowland Britain against the Picts and Scots, but these soldiers were confined to eastern districts and were settled no further north than Yorkshire. As far as Gildas was concerned, they were not recruited to help his countrymen in the lands beyond Hadrian's Wall. His account of affairs in what is now the Anglo-Scottish borderland conjured gruesome scenes of bearded, half-naked Picts using hooked spears to drag feckless Britons from the parapet of the Wall itself. This report, although colourful and dramatic, has no basis in fact. It painted a suitably terrifying image of savage barbarians for the secular and religious elites of the southern parts of Britain, to whom Gildas addressed his words. The real situation in the North during the fifth century was actually quite different. Far from lying open to Pictish attack, the lands south of the Tyne and Solway were protected by a buffer-zone extending northward as far as the Forth and Clyde. In earlier times this zone had lain under direct Roman rule while the Antonine Wall held firm. Later, when the imperial frontier fell back to Hadrian's Wall, the Britons who dwelt in the lands between the two walls maintained close links with the Empire and were regarded as subjects or allies of Rome. The main tribes of this area were the Novantae of Galloway in the south-west, the Selgovae in the centre, the Votadini in the east and the Damnonii in the north-west. These tribes were among those who had formerly assembled under

Roman supervision at designated *loci* and whose territories had been patrolled by *exploratores* from the outpost forts.

The lands of the Votadini and Damnonii bordered on the Highlands and therefore faced the Picts, whose incursions they resisted during the final phase of Roman rule. After the imperial withdrawal in 410, a resurgence of independence among the Britons increased the defensive role of these two tribes to make them a powerful bulwark against Pictish attack. At times they were defeated or plundered but, at the end of the fifth century, they still held the Forth-Clyde line intact. By then, both tribes had evolved into kingdoms, their respective heartlands being Lothian and the Clyde Valley. The Votadini, whose rulers dwelt in a fortress on Edinburgh's impregnable Castle Rock, emerged into the sixth century as the realm of Gododdin. To the west, the Damnonii created a kingdom centred on their ancient citadel at Dumbarton, which they called *Alt Clut*, 'Clyde Rock'. The inhabitants of both kingdoms were Brittonic-speaking populations who regarded themselves as distinct from the Picts. Their cultural affinities lay rather with their fellow Britons in the lands south of Hadrian's Wall. By 500, the southern Britons were also emerging from the upheavals of the post-Roman period with kings and kingdoms of their own. For the Picts, then, the departure of Rome did not leave their neighbours helpless and vulnerable and ripe for ravaging. On the contrary, the chaos of the early fifth century swept away the last remnant of an ailing imperial garrison and allowed the kings of the Britons to replace it with their own warbands. Thus, by playing a major role in the collapse of Roman rule, the Picts unwittingly paved the way for powerful new rivals to enter the political arena.

CHAPTER 4

Into the Sixth Century

The middle years of the first millennium AD saw North Britain emerging from the Roman era to enter a period commonly known as the Dark Ages. This name is somewhat misleading: it conjures a bleak image of gloom and anarchy in which hairy savages hack at each other with axes while society as a whole reverts to cultural ignorance and a primitive way of life. It is an image that is not only negative but also inaccurate, which is why many historians have abandoned the term 'Dark Ages' altogether. A more useful terminology draws on the period's importance as the time when the barbarian peoples of Europe first began to create their own documents and write their own histories. In the British Isles this period can be loosely defined as the centuries between the withdrawal of Rome and the coming of the Normans, whose arrival in 1066 heralded the dawn of a new epoch: the High Middle Ages. During these centuries the peoples of Britain and Ireland evolved from barbarian kingdoms to become well-organised proto-states ruled by sophisticated and literate kings. Under the patronage of these kings an influential Christian clergy compiled the annals and chronicles that have survived to become the main sources of information for the Picts and their neighbours. These texts are acknowledged as the earliest historical writings produced by the native inhabitants of Britain, and it is chiefly for this reason that 'Dark Ages' is not employed in the following chapters to describe the years between 500 and 1000. A more informative term, the Early Historic period, is used instead.

Pictish Society

In the previous chapter it was observed that the Picts did not find the rich lands of the South a soft target after the end of Roman rule in 410. The inhabitants of what had once been Roman Britain rose to the challenge, took up arms and defended their homes or, in wealthier districts, hired bands of Germanic mercenaries to do the job. Meanwhile, in the North, two large and powerful groups of Britons – the kingdoms of Alt Clut and Gododdin – guarded the Forth-Clyde line. The Picts' response to this stiffening of resolve was a strengthening of their own identity. Why this happened is unknown but they seem to have promoted an image of themselves as a distinct, loosely unified nation rather than as a patchwork of separate groups. In the documentary sources – the chronicles and annals – the territory inhabited by this nation is often called *Pictavia*, which means simply 'Pictland'. This term will be used here and in the following chapters to denote the realm of the Picts in the Early Historic period. When historians refer to 'The Picts' in a political sense, what they are really speaking about are the upper strata of society: the kings, the high-ranking clergy who served them and the aristocratic warbands whose military muscle gave potent force to the idea of kingship. But what is meant by 'kingship' in the context of sixth-century Pictavia? To answer this question, we must take a look not only at the high-status kindreds from whom the kings were drawn, but also at Pictish society as a whole.

First, it should be acknowledged that the Picts were not very different from other barbarian peoples who dwelt beyond the frontiers of what had once been the Roman Empire. Despite their location in the far northern parts of Britain, they were neither isolated from their neighbours nor impervious to external influences. By the beginning of the sixth century the Pictish nation was no longer the patchwork of 'tribes' seen on Ptolemy's map, but a group of small provinces or sub-kingdoms whose identities more or less related in some way to the seven regions named in the legend of Cruithne. Continuity with the remote past was maintained by a recognition that the nation was divided into two parts, a division noted long before by the Romans when they had identified the Dicalydones and Verturiones as two groups who together consti- tuted the Picts. Irish and English writers of the seventh and eighth centuries identified the divide between the two Pictish areas as the Grampian Mountains, otherwise known as the Mounth, a boundary whose roots lay deep in prehistory. The divide was geographical rather than human, and the Picts maintained a well- defined cultural unity in spite of it.

By far the most vivid example of a distinct Pictish culture was the use of a range of symbols not encountered elsewhere. These were undoubtedly of very ancient origin, having been created in prehistory as a kind of alphabet. It is not until the Early Historic period, however, that the symbols become uniquely visible in the landscape. In prehistoric times they probably appeared as decora- tions on small objects such as jewellery or even as tattoos, but their use changed after the end of the Roman era. By AD 500 they were starting to appear as carvings inscribed with great skill on standing stones. The consistency of the 'alphabet' of symbols across a vast swath of territory is astonishing, with an identical repertoire of designs appearing on stones and other objects in places as far apart as Orkney, Skye, Shetland and Perthshire. All these areas, then, were Pictish, or were places where high-status Picts held sufficient authority to commission the carving of distinctive and meaningful designs on stone monuments.

The meaning of the symbols is unknown, but the lure of solving the mystery generates endless debate among scholars and laymen alike. The puzzle is part of the so-called 'Problem of the Picts' and, for many people, the symbols are its most fascinating aspect. They are dealt with in great detail by numerous studies of the subject, but the topic lies mostly outside the scope of this book. Various theories have been proposed, each with its own merits as an explanation of the meaning behind the symbols. Some theories see the designs as emblems of important Pictish families linked by marriage alliances. Others wonder if the symbols relate to nature or agriculture. All of the theories are argued convincingly by their adherents, but no particular one stands out as the best or the most likely solution. A typical theory is nevertheless presented here, as an example of one viewpoint in the debate rather than as a hypothesis to be preferred above all others. This theory, which has been previously aired elsewhere, interprets the symbols as representations of personal names. At its heart lies the fact that the symbols carved on stones in the landscape began to appear in the late fifth or early sixth centuries. The timing of their appearance is likely to be no accident and points to the carved stones being memorials of a type that were created in other parts of Britain at around the same time. Memorial stones from Wales, Cornwall and other western areas are usually Christian grave-markers commemorating (in Latin) a named individual, 'X son of Y'. The Pictish stones perhaps served a similar purpose, with the symbols corresponding to the names of the deceased and a parent. This could explain why most symbols appear in pairs. A similar 'alphabet' of emblems to identify specific individuals or their families was used effectively in medieval heraldry, and this could provide a model for the practical use of Pictish symbols. Thus, to a sixth-century farmer in southern Perthshire or northern Skye, a symbol stone could have conveyed the same kind of message that a knight's painted shield conveyed to a thirteenth-century yeoman in England or France. By analogy, then, the Pictish symbols were perhaps a code or alphabet by which a person's name could be easily identified in a society where writing was largely unknown. All of this, of course, amounts to little more than one hypothesis among the many that have been proposed. It offers one possible context or 'meaning' for the Pictish symbols but is not necessarily the most plausible one available.

Culturally, then, the Picts were a defined group who possessed an artistic tradition that was unique in the British Isles. On a social level they differed little from other barbarian peoples in Northern Europe. Their society was structured in a similar way to the societies of their neighbours and bore scant resemblance to the fondly imagined image of backward 'tribes' or 'clans' living as idyllic rural co-operatives under the rule of benevolent chiefs. Barbarian society in Early Historic Europe had long since discarded any lingering egalitarian traits and was heavily stratified in terms of wealth and

Figure 1. Pictish symbol stone found at Craigton, Sutherland, now located in the grounds of Dunrobin Castle. Reproduced from J.R. Allen and J. Anderson, *The Early Christian Monuments of Scotland* (1903).

status, with the bulk of the population living as peasants on agricultural land ruled by lords who in turn constituted a sophisticated aristocracy. This is the image that should be kept in mind in any study of Pictish society. Tacitus and other Classical writers presented a stereotyped view of primitive Caledonian chiefs standing proudly in ragged furs, but such notions originated in Roman propaganda and were unrealistic. They were certainly not applicable to the leaders of the historical Picts.

By the beginning of the sixth century the Pictish aristocracy was a prosperous upper class with expensive tastes and a luxurious lifestyle. Its members were a selective elite holding absolute control over the peasants, who comprised the majority population. Peasants were unlikely to be free farmers working their own fields and were probably bound to the land of their lord, enjoying few privileges and with minimal rights under law. They almost certainly took no active part in warfare. In most parts of the British Isles, the Early Historic period was a time when the lower classes were excluded from military life. There was no mass mobilisation of agricultural labourers armed with clumsy weapons; no local militia like the Anglo-Saxon *fyrd* of the tenth century. Like hunting and feasting, war was the exclusive pursuit of the landowning aristocracy, and it provided the main route of social advancement for ambitious young noblemen. Service in the armed retinue or warband of a powerful lord, such as a king, brought the prospect of wealth and fame. Young aristocrats became soldiers to win riches and renown, fighting for their king in the hope of being rewarded with a grant of land after a few years of loyal service. A military career offered the prospect of material benefits in the form of loot distributed among the warband after a successful raid or a great victory. Movable loot, such as livestock and human beings, formed the main spoils of war and was a major part of the currency of gift and exchange in this period. Cattle and slaves, together with ornate craft-goods and jewellery, were the essential trappings through which a high-born warrior displayed his wealth and status to his rivals and dependants.

The most powerful Pictish nobles lived with their kinsfolk and retainers in dwellings protected by a combination of natural topography and artificial defences. In northern and western Britain the hilltop stronghold, consisting of a timber hall rising above lesser buildings within a circuit of walls, was a favoured abode for great lords and their followers. Such sites were often the residences of kings, most of whom ruled small districts of a type that modern terminology calls 'petty kingdoms'. The origins of these kings and their dynasties are generally unknown and were probably varied. Some kings undoubtedly sprang from earlier, possibly ancient, local aristocracies who may have considered themselves 'royal' for many generations. Others emerged as leaders of prominent families in a particular locality, or as accomplished warlords who fought their way to power and sealed their achievement by calling themselves monarchs. By the middle of the sixth century the institution of kingship in the British Isles was itself becoming stratified, with groups of lesser kings within a region acknowledging the authority of a dominant overking and becoming his clients. This clientship could be given freely, through an act of homage, in return for high-status gifts and pledges of protection. Sometimes it was imposed by force through raid or conquest, or by the threat of destruction. In time of war, an overking's clients or 'sub-kings' were expected to lead their warbands under his banner when he rode on campaign. In peacetime, the overking conducted regular journeys through the domains of his clients to avail himself of their hospitality. This kind of 'circuit' was conducted on a smaller scale by the sub-kings themselves through the lands of the local aristocracies who acknowledged their authority. Agricultural produce gathered from the peasantry was consumed during these circuits at lavish feasts where important rituals, such as the renewal of oaths of allegiance, were performed in the presence of assembled dignitaries.

Like his peers elsewhere in Britain a Pictish king was supported by no bureaucracy and had no civil service to administer his realm. Trusted henchmen or family elders advised him when required, but he was essentially a lone figure who ruled according to his own personality. Any hint of weakness, especially in the face of an enemy outside the borders, might result in his replacement by a more vigorous rival. The greatest and most powerful kings of this period were bold, ruthless leaders who conquered their external foes by reducing vast territories to subjection. Their success in war brought a constant flow of booty back to their homelands and made their henchmen rich. War, of course, carried lethal risks in an era when kings fought alongside their soldiers in close combat, and it is no surprise that the chronicles and annals report frequent royal casualties. One historian of modern times suggested that the normal expectation of a seventh-century king was to die in battle. This observation was made in relation to Northumbria, the only Anglo-Saxon kingdom to share a frontier with the Picts, but it applied equally to any region of the British Isles during the Early Historic period.

This, then, was the social world of the Picts: a typical North European barbarian society comprising a lower class of more-or-less unfree peasants whose labour supported an aristocratic warrior elite headed by kings. The nature of kingship itself was dynamic rather than static: it evolved and changed as the larger kingdoms of Britain and Ireland moved gradually along the road to proto-statehood. In the sixth century this process was still in its early stages, and some kingdoms had only recently been formed in the wake of the Roman withdrawal. From the fifth century onwards in Continental Europe, and from the sixth century in southern Britain, the evolution of kingship accelerated under the influence of Christianity. Conversion to the international religion of the Romans became a major factor in the development of new and sophisticated ways for barbarian kings to rule their domains. The Picts, however, were slow to embrace the Faith and clung to paganism for a longer time than did any of their neighbours. The various attempts by successive Christian missions to make headway against the old religions of Pictavia will be dealt with in this and subsequent chapters. For the moment, the trail of history resumes at the point where Pictish kings begin to emerge as real figures whose names and deeds appear in the sources.

The Earliest Kings

After giving the legend of Cruithne and his seven sons, the Pictish king-list names roughly sixty monarchs and gives their reign-lengths. Historians usually regard these men as overkings whose authority was acknowledged not only in their own heartlands but also in the lands of subordinate kings. This paramount kingship may have encompassed, at certain periods, a very large hegemony incorporating many Pictish territories. At other times, especially when the sovereignty was divided between two or more rivals, its territorial extent may have been much smaller. Some Pictish overkings might have ruled, in reality, little more than an individual sub-kingdom such as Atholl or Fortriu.

The list begins with an obscure and probably mythical figure called Gud and ends with a historical king called Drust in the mid-ninth century. Drust's reign coincided with the rise to power of Cináed mac Ailpín, a controversial figure who ruled the Picts and Scots simultaneously. More will be said of Cináed in Chapter 11 but, for the moment, the focus is on the start of the king-list to see where legends end and real history begins. Gud, who stands at the head of the list, is unknown in any other source. He was invented by the list's creators when they extended the sequence of names backwards to give Pictish overkingship a more ancient origin. Each king in the list is given a reign-length in years, although the numbers sometimes vary between different manuscripts. Also, some kings appear in one or more manuscripts but not in others. The discrepancies mean that the format and chronology of the lost original list, from which all the surviving versions derive, is difficult to reconstruct. Only when the name of a king can be linked securely to a known historical event does the information in the list become reliable and authentic. The Irish annals, for instance, associate many Pictish kings with real and dateable events, thus placing firm chronological markers in the list. Since no such markers are provided for Gud and other early figures, they must be consigned to legend and pseudo-history.

The annals noted the death of Brude, Maelchon's son, paramount king of the Picts, in 584. His exploits are looked at more closely in the next chapter. For now, it will be sufficient to note that he appears in the king-list with a reign-length of thirty years, which would place his accession in the mid-550s. Using Brude as a fixed point and working backwards, his predecessors can tentatively be placed in a chronological framework. If the first twenty or so obscure kings are ignored as fictional, the list eventually arrives at Wradech whose name, in its Gaelic form *Feradach*, is borne by several historical figures in the Irish annals. The early Pictish king who bore this name might himself be more than a character of myth and pseudo-history, for he is perhaps the ruler of Pictavia mentioned in an Irish tale about the Munster king Conall Corc, who was known to be active in the early fifth century. The events in Conall's tale are likely to be fictional but, since he really existed, the reference to a contemporary Pictish king called Feradach may be significant. If this Feradach is the same as the Wradech of the king-list, the latter was probably a real person.

Nothing more can be said of Wradech. Two more kings follow him in the list, but of these no other source speaks. All that can be surmised about them is that, if they ever lived, their reigns occurred in the first half of the fifth century. One is Gartnait and the other is Talorc, two names which become very common in later portions of the list. After Talorc comes Drust, son of Erp, on whom a note adds: 'In the nineteenth year of his reign the holy bishop Patrick arrived in the island of Ireland.' The figure of nineteen need not be accepted as precise, but Saint Patrick certainly arrived in Ireland sometime between 430 and 470. He might have conducted his Irish mission at a time when a king called Drust did indeed rule the Picts. To Drust the king-list attributes 100 battles and a curiously long reign of 100 years. With him the list draws towards the end of the fifth century and to the period when Christianity first came to northern Britain.

Legends of the Early Saints

Two texts written by Saint Patrick – a 'Confession' and a letter to the warband of a king – have survived. Both refer briefly to his life and work and together offer an important insight into the mind of an Early Christian missionary working among the barbarians. By birth Patrick was a Briton of wealthy parentage, from a prosperous landowning family. He spent his childhood in a refined Christian environment in some western district of Britain between the estuaries of Severn and Clyde. During his youth he was captured by pagan Irish raiders, from whom he eventually escaped. After entering the priesthood back home in Britain, he returned to Ireland as a missionary, his aim being to baptise the country's heathen inhabitants. He evidently had no desire to labour in the remote northern parts of Britain, where old religions still competed with Christianity. He was, however, acquainted with the Picts and held them in low regard, not least because of their paganism. During his mission to Ireland he learned, to his horror and dismay, that numerous young people among his flock of newly converted Christians were being abducted by pirates and sold to Pictish slave-traders. The pirates were Britons from Alt Clut, the mighty Rock of Clyde at Dumbarton. Their ruler was a king called Coroticus, a man who outwardly presented himself as a Christian. The soldiers of Coroticus received from Patrick a stiff letter of protest and an angry rebuke for their lucrative but immoral dealings with heathen Picts. In fact, the Dumbarton raiders were so reprehensible to Patrick that he could barely bring himself to regard them as his own countrymen. Like him, they were Britons, but he felt ashamed of their deeds and refused to address his letter to 'my fellow-citizens' or to 'fellow-citizens of the holy Romans'. To him they were rather 'fellow-citizens of demons, because of their evil actions. Like the enemy they live in death, as allies of Scots and Picts and apostates.' His greatest scorn was reserved for King Coroticus himself, at whose command the marauders had come slave-raiding to Ireland. In his letter, Patrick wrote of this monarch: 'Far from God's love is the man who delivers Christians into the hands of Scots and Picts.' It is not known if Coroticus responded to the letter, but Patrick was not the kind of man to let such serious issues rest. What further action he took is uncertain.

Medieval Scottish tradition refers to Patrick's disciple, Saint Kessog, undertaking missionary work in North Britain, but this might not have extended to the Picts. At Luss on the western shore of Loch Lomond, in the territory of the Britons, Kessog is said to have founded a church, a tradition supported by the discovery of Early Christian gravestones in the churchyard. In Pictavia itself he is associated with the church at Auchterarder and with the medieval Saint Kessog's Fair at Callander, but there is no proof that he actually journeyed so far eastward. It is probably prudent to regard his activities as confined to Luss and its environs, all of which lay under the authority of the Britons – perhaps those of Alt Clut. It would appear that neither he nor any of Patrick's alleged disciples took up the challenge of converting the Picts but, as will soon be seen, other missionaries might have been less reluctant.

The Pictish king-list shows Drust, son of Erp, being succeeded by another Talorc. The latter is then followed by Nechtan Morbet, also a son of Erp. The compiler of the king-list clearly regarded Nechtan as Drust's brother, but there was evidently little love between the siblings. In one version of the text Drust banished Nechtan from Pictavia, for reasons that are not given. From the compiler's point of view the banishment served a useful literary purpose in bringing Nechtan to the monastery of Kildare in Ireland. Here the exiled prince is said to have met Saint Bride or Brigid, one of the most renowned figures in Celtic Christianity, who foretold that he would one day rule the Pictish kingdom in peace. Brigid's lifetime straddled the late fifth and early sixth centuries, and her chronology is fairly secure. If her alleged contact with Nechtan has any basis in fact then he, too, was a figure of the same period. He eventually went home to claim the kingship and, according to notes added to the king-list, the early years of his reign saw the arrival in Pictavia of a Christian mission from Kildare. The missionaries were led by an abbess called Darlugdach, one of Brigid's disciples, who received from Nechtan a grant of land on which to establish a church. From this base she and her followers began to evangelise the heathen Picts. Her church was built at Abernethy where, in subsequent centuries, an important monastery flourished under the patronage of Pictish kings. Today the most prominent landmark in the town is the eleventh-century round tower, an impressive sandstone structure which looms above the present-day kirk of St Bride. By contrast, Darlugdach's church would have been a typical outpost of early Celtic Christianity: a simple wooden building enclosed by a fence or earthwork.

If the story of the Kildare mission has any basis in historical fact, it would give Abernethy a special status as the birthplace of Pictish Christianity. Unfortunately, in the absence of better data than is currently available, historians can do no more than admit the story as a possibility. It seems to have originated in old traditions preserved by Abernethy's clergy throughout the medieval period, but how far these reflect reality is unclear. To cloud the issue still further, different traditions give varying accounts of the foundation of the earliest church. In some, for instance, Abernethy's first patron was not Nechtan Morbet but a later Nechtan who reigned at the end of the sixth century. Despite the uncertainty there is strong evidence of high-status or royal activity at Abernethy in the fifth or sixth centuries, namely a fragment of a stone monument incised with Pictish symbols. This now stands at the base of the round tower and could be a sixth-century commemoration of King Nechtan's gift of land to Darlugdach.

Abernethy's kirk carries a dedication to 'Saint Bride' and is one of many Scottish churches whose traditions claim a direct link with Brigid of Kildare. The place-name Kilbride, which derives from the Gaelic *Cill Briohde* ('Brigid's Church'), is fairly common, but not every occurrence of this and of other 'Brigid' names represents a mission by early disciples of the saint. Some instances have a much later origin and can be attributed to the ninth or tenth centuries, when Irish Vikings began to make permanent settlements in Scotland. Brigid was especially venerated by Christians of Hiberno-Norse ancestry, and many of the old churches bearing her name owe their 'Bride' dedications to this later era. From the ninth century onwards the Picts increasingly adopted the Gaelic language and culture of their neighbours, the Scots of Argyll, and may have felt inclined to take an interest in Brigid and other Irish saints. It is therefore difficult to identify places where actual sixth-century missionaries from Kildare might have operated in Pictavia. The ruined medieval church at Blair Atholl, for instance, is known as St Bryde's Kirk and occupies an inland site deep in the Pictish heartlands, but the dedication to Brigid is not recorded before 1275. Similarly, Kilbride in Strathearn lies within a southern Pictish province or sub-kingdom, but its location near a key route of penetration from the Gaelic West raises doubts about an early association. Another factor to keep in mind is that there were more than a dozen Celtic saints called Brigid in addition to the famous abbess of Kildare.

Nechtan Morbet seems to make another appearance in ecclesiastical tradition of dubious origin. On this occasion the source is the *Vita* or 'Life' of Saint Boethius, also known as Buite, an Irishman who hailed from a royal kindred of Munster. Although this text looks at first sight like a genuine life story it is not a biography in the modern sense. As noted in Chapter 1, the *vitae* of early saints are works of hagiography rather than of history and should therefore be treated with appropriate caution. They form part of a genre of ecclesiastical writing designed to promote the cults of saints and the economic or political interests of their cult-centres. The presentation of real history played a subordinate role in these texts and was largely irrelevant to their primary purpose, which was to advertise the sanctity of holy men and women by whatever methods suited the writer. A favourite technique involved creating scenarios in which tragedy or disaster was averted by a miracle performed by the saint, whose reputation was consequently enhanced. The Life of Boethius is typical of the genre, being a product written several centuries after the subject's lifetime and surviving today in manuscripts of an even later date. Boethius is a little-known figure who, according to the Irish annals, died in 521. In his *Vita* he is said to have miraculously restored to life a Pictish ruler called Nectanus, who might be the Nechtan Morbet of the king-list. The miracle occurred at a fortress which Nectanus later gave to Boethius in token of gratitude and where the saint established a church. This place is assumed to be Kirkbuddo, a Roman fort southeast of Forfar, whose name derives from an earlier *Caerbuddo*, which might indeed mean 'Fort of Boethius'. This fort is near the ancient stronghold of Dunnichen Hill, originally *Dun Nechtáin*, 'Nechtan's Fort', although the identity of the Nechtan in the place-name is not known. It could be the sixth-century king or a later namesake. As with the tale of Darlugdach the historical facts are entangled with ecclesiastical fiction. Like the Abernethy foundation-legend the *Vita* of Boethius might preserve some kernel of truth about the religious policies of Nechtan Morbet, but its testimony cannot be taken at face value. It is a work of hagiography, drawn from traditions of uncertain provenance and compiled by writers who did not claim to be historians.

Another early saint with alleged Pictish connections was Fillan, a monk from Ireland who lived around the late fifth and early sixth centuries. Medieval Irish tradition makes him a member of the Munster aristocracy whose centre of power lay at the great fortress of Cashel. In Pictavia he is associated with the hillfort of Dundurn near the village of St Fillans in Strathearn. Excavations at Dundurn have yielded evidence of high-status occupation during the Early Historic period, the inhabitants being a prominent family of Picts, perhaps even a royal kindred. A curiously shaped rock known as Saint Fillan's Chair is still visible on the summit of the hill but its name originated in local folklore relating to the saint's cult in later times. Irish texts place Fillan's activities east of Druim Alban – the 'Spine of Britain' or Highland massif – and associate him with Rath Erenn, a name with a Gaelic first element meaning 'fort' and a second element which might refer to the River Earn. If the name *Rath Erenn* refers to Dundurn, it would be consistent with local traditions about Fillan's activities in the valley. In Gaelic the name of the village of St Fillans is *Dun Fhaoláin*, 'Fillan's Fort', which was undoubtedly applied to Dundurn at one time. The hillfort overlooks a ruined church known as St Fillan's Chapel, which itself occupies a site of great antiquity. The chapel's origins are unknown, but it is possible that it played a role in whatever work Fillan is presumed to have undertaken among the Picts of Strathearn.

The various references to missionary campaigns by Darlugdach, Boethius and Fillan suggest that these saints were the first to bring Christianity to the Picts. Although this idea is not necessarily wide of the mark, it is based on sources and traditions of uncertain relia-bility. On the other hand, a kernel of truth is embedded in most hagiography to lie hidden until layers of later myth are peeled away. There is thus no need to relegate Darlugdach, Boethius and Fillan to the realm of ecclesiastical legend until expert analysis of the relevant sources says otherwise. Envisaging early Irish missions to Pictavia does, however, contradict what Bede believed. He wrote that the southern Picts were evangelised by a Briton called Ninian, while their northern compatriots did not receive the Faith until Saint Columba came from Iona in 565. Bede stated that Columba was preceded by Ninian, who laboured in Pictavia 'a long time before'. Given Bede's reputation for reliability his words on the beginnings of Pictish Christianity cannot be lightly set aside. His ignoring of the early Irish missionaries named above weakens the case for their historicity, although his silence is not definitive. He might simply have been unaware of events in Pictavia before the time of Ninian and Columba, or he may have chosen to ignore other saints. In due course, the role he ascribed to Columba will be examined here in more detail. For the moment the focus now turns to Ninian who, as Columba's predecessor, was regarded by Bede as the first successful missionary to the Picts.

Ninian and the Picts

Bede believed that the Pictish nation was divided into two parts by the Grampian Mountains. This imposing range, the Mounth, forms a natural division between Perthshire and the north-east Highlands. How far this barrier served as a political or cultural boundary across Pictavia is difficult to assess, but Bede clearly regarded it as a dividing line. For him, it split the Picts into those converted by Ninian and those converted by Columba.

Ninian is a controversial figure who continues to provoke debate among historians. Bede identified him as a Briton who was buried with other saints at *Candida Casa*, 'The White House'. This place is now Whithorn in Galloway and it was here, in the eighth century, that a Northumbrian monastery thrived at the site of Ninian's shrine or tomb. In the same century a monk at Whithorn composed a Latin poem, 'The Miracles of Bishop Ninian', which identified the saint's Pictish converts as members of a people called *Naturae*. This group is unknown, and their name is in any case likely to be an English corruption of a Pictish word whose original form cannot now be retrieved. Later still, when Galloway became part of the medieval kingdom of Scotland, the shrine at Whithorn attracted a cult of pilgrimage which eventually prompted the production of a *Vita* or 'Life' of the saint. This appeared in c.1160 and was written by Ailred, abbot of the monastery at Rievaulx in Yorkshire, who assigned Ninian's Pictish mission to the fifth century. Support for Ailred's and Bede's statements about Ninian comes from archaeological evidence of early Christianity at Whithorn and in southern parts of Pictavia. In both areas, however, the evidence belongs to the sixth century rather than to the fifth. Excavations at Whithorn revealed a religious settlement founded in c.500, while similar work in Fife and Angus unearthed Christian cemeteries from the sixth century but no earlier. The dating of the evidence raises doubts about Ninian's alleged mission to the Picts in the fifth century and is consistent with Saint Patrick's view that they were still a pagan people in the late 400s.

Not long after the publication of Ailred's *Vita*, another of Scotland's early saints, Kentigern of Glasgow, was commemorated in similar fashion by an Anglo-Norman monk called Jocelin of Furness. Jocelin wrote that the Picts, after being converted to Christianity by Ninian, subsequently relapsed into paganism and had to be re-evangelised by Kentigern in the early seventh century. Since neither Ailred nor Jocelin were primarily interested in presenting historical fact for its own sake, their accounts are generally treated with suspicion. Like all hagiographers, their main objective was to enhance the importance of a saintly figure upon whose continuing fame rested the popularity of a cult associated with his or her achievements. The *vitae* of Ninian and Kentigern duly incorporated the usual collection of miracle-stories and monkish folklore and therefore served their genre well. Ailred's text gave the Whithorn cult a boost by reassuring the pilgrims who visited Ninian's shrine that the saint entombed there possessed

God-given supernatural powers. The pilgrims happily purchased souvenirs and went home. They were unlikely to have shared modern scepticism about whether or not Ninian converted the Picts in the fifth century, nor would they have felt inclined to wonder – as historians wonder today – where the traditions reported by Bede, Ailred and Jocelin originated. Analysis of the *vitae* of Ninian and Kentigern suggests that, in each case, the writer's sources included folklore which may or may not derive from real events. However, when reliable information about the Picts is looked for in these traditions the search tends to yield large amounts of fiction and few facts.

In Ninian's case, the matter is confused by an erroneous belief in the Middle Ages that the inhabitants of Galloway during the fifth and sixth centuries were Picts. This fictitious notion conveniently linked the hub of his medieval cult with Bede's story of the Pictish conversion, for it placed heathen Picts in the vicinity of the saint's tomb and shrine at Whithorn. In reality, the people of Galloway during Ninian's lifetime were Britons whose ancestors appeared on Ptolemy's Roman map under the name *Novantae*. After the Romans left, these people regarded the Picts with hostility as pirates and brigands who plundered their coastlands. In the twelfth century, however, when Ailred and Jocelin wrote about Ninian and Kentigern, English people often equated the ancient Picts with the inhabitants of Galloway. This notion of 'Galloway Picts' is of uncertain origin and derives partly from a lack of knowledge, especially in medieval England, about the early inhabitants of Scotland. It has little relevance to the fifth and sixth centuries but will be looked at in more detail in the final chapter of this book.

This still leaves Bede's information about Ninian's mission to Pictavia. As a contemporary and compatriot of Whithorn's English monks, Bede knew that the monastery lay among Britons, the descendants of the Novantae, so he had no delusions about Galloway being inhabited by Picts. Where, then, did he acquire his story about Ninian's Pictish mission? One source was Pecthelm, an Englishman and a contemporary of Bede, who served as bishop of Whithorn in the 720s. Other sources were Pictish priests who at that time were communicating closely with Bede's own monastery at Jarrow. It is from these Picts that Bede received his best information about Ninian's mission to their homeland. One crucial piece of data was missing: a precise chronology for the mission. Bede usually liked to give specific dates in his *Ecclesiastical History* but, as this was not provided for him by either Pecthelm or the Pictish clergy, all he could say was that Ninian worked among the southern Picts 'a long time' before Saint Columba arrived among their northern cousins in 565. If Ailred's vision of a fifth-century Ninian is rejected in favour of the archaeological evidence, Bede's 'a long time' before Columba can be interpreted as meaning the decades before 565. Ninian thus emerges into history as a Briton who converted some part of the Pictish nation in the early 500s before retiring to his monastery at Whithorn in Galloway. His mission to Pictavia would have followed the typical pattern of the time. Being an influential cleric, and thus a person of noble birth, he would have first approached a Pictish king to formally introduce himself. Having secured permission to preach Christianity under royal protection, he and his monks would have begun the process of conversion. A grant of land – given by the king – would have allowed the missionaries to build a small wooden church to serve as their base. Eventually, Ninian returned to his principal monastery at Whithorn in Galloway, bequeathing the Pictish venture to his followers. At some point thereafter, and for reasons unknown, the conversion ground to a halt. The missionaries gave up and left before their presence became established, leaving no trace except the cemeteries in Fife and Angus where their Pictish flock was buried in Christian graves. Because of Bede's testimony, Ninian can be regarded as the leader of this first successful programme of Christian conversion in Pictavia. Earlier missions by other individuals apparently made little headway. This should mean that the alleged Pictish activities of Darlugdach, Boethius, Fillan and other obscure saints failed to achieve their objectives. Archaeological excavation may yet uncover early sixth-century cemeteries associated with these three figures but, until then, their stories hover in a kind of limbo between history and legend.

Drust and Drusticc

After Nechtan Morbet, his successor in the Pictish king-list is a second Drust, whose chronology suggests a reign ending in the early sixth century. Nothing is known of him, nor of his successor. The next two kings also bear the name Drust and are said to have held the kingship jointly, which presumably means they ruled separate regions of Pictavia at the same time. Their location in the list as figures of the early sixth century coincides with the approximate dates of a certain King Drust who appears in an Irish tale concerning Saint Finnian of Moville. The setting for this tale is again the monastery of Whithorn in Galloway. Although established in British territory, Whithorn is here depicted as operating under the authority of an Irish abbot called Mugint and with Irish monks such as Finnian among the brethren. The story revolves around Drusticc, daughter of Drust, 'king of the northern Britons'. This princess was sent to Whithorn by her father to become a pupil of Mugint, but she fell in love with one of the younger monks. Finnian became involved as a go-between but incurred Mugint's wrath and was lucky to emerge alive. The tale originated in monastic folklore of unknown origin and probably includes only a few grains of genuine history, despite the fact that both Finnian and Mugint were real figures of the sixth century. Other Irish sources tell how Finnian studied at Whithorn in his youth, and this might be true, but the rest of the story looks like an amalgam of names and places from various obscure traditions. Drusticc appears in another Irish text as 'Dustric, daughter of Trust', where she is said to have been the mother of a Galloway saint called Lonan. Whether she really existed is hard to say but, since the name Drust is Pictish rather than British, her father was perhaps meant to be one of the Drusts whom the king-list describes as ruling Pictavia in the early sixth century.

The next six kings in the list are given very short reigns, and nothing is known of them. The seventh was Galam *Cennaleph* ('Head-Wound' or 'Freckled Head'). He ruled the Picts for three years before sharing the final year of his reign with Brude,

Figure 2. Symbol-bearing cross-slab from St Vigeans, Angus, where it resides today in the museum. Reproduced from J.R. Allen and J. Anderson, *The Early Christian Monuments of Scotland* (1903).

Maelchon's son. Brude is the first Pictish king to enter the pages of authentic history and more is known about him than about any of his obscure predecessors. The start of his reign in 554 marks the point when Pictish history finally emerges from the era of legend and uncertainty.

CHAPTER 5

Maelchon's Son

The middle of the sixth century marks the 'historical horizon' of the Picts, the point at which their history becomes clearer. For earlier periods the documentary sources give plenty of legends but few verifiable facts. From c.550 the information becomes more reliable, chiefly because some of the more important sources began to be written around this time. In the monasteries of Britain and Ireland, scribes now began to note historical events in their records, thus creating the texts from which the Irish annals were later compiled. Likewise, later observers such as Bede – who was born in the seventh century – lived and wrote when memories of the previous century were still fresh. Thus, while the overall picture never becomes completely clear, the second half of the sixth century seems less of a mystery than the preceding era.

In 563 Saint Columba left his monastery in Ireland and sailed to Britain. He came, according to Bede, to preach Christianity to 'the kingdoms of the northern Picts'. Bede believed that the southern Picts had already been evangelised by Saint Ninian and, as the previous chapter showed, Ninian's mission might explain the presence of Early Christian cemeteries in Fife and Angus. At the time of Columba's arrival, the Picts had been ruled for eight or nine years by Brude, son of Maelchon, whom Bede calls 'a most powerful king'. The Pictish king-list and the Irish annals give Brude a reign of three decades, the annalists noting his death in 584. All three sources – king-list, annals and Bede – agree on the bare facts about Brude, namely that he reigned for thirty years and that his father's name

Kingdoms, peoples and provinces in the 6th century.

was Maelchon. The latter would have lived in the early sixth century but does not appear in the list as a Pictish king.

Maelgwn and the North

The name Maelchon is of great interest, partly due to its rarity but also because its most famous bearer was Maglocunus, king of the Britons of Gwynedd in North Wales. *Maglocunus* is a Latinisation of *Maelchon*, and both forms represent an original Celtic name meaning 'princely whelp'. This king was a contemporary of Gildas and bore the brunt of his tirade against the corrupt despots who ruled Britain in the sixth century. Gildas believed Maglocunus to be the epitome of a ruthless tyrant and castigated him for his evil deeds. To Gildas, Maglocunus was the mightiest king of all, the *insularis draco* or 'Dragon of the Island', but also a person of shameless immorality. This was particularly reprehensible to Gildas because Maglocunus was a Christian and had even spent some years as a monk. Fate or divine retribution eventually caught up with him in 547, when he perished in a great plague which swept through the British Isles. In Gwynedd tradition he was remembered as Maelgwn, a later Welsh form of *Maglocunus*, and this is the name by which he is more commonly known. In some medieval Welsh texts he appears as *Mailcun* and it is this early form of the name that makes him of interest to students of Pictish history. The interest stems from some versions of the Pictish king-list in which the father of Brude, son of Maelchon, is called *Mailcon* or *Maelcon*. No other figure in the list bears this name, or any variant of it, nor is it borne by a Pict in any other source. The name *Mailcun* or *Maelchon* is in fact unique in Britain and is applied in only two contexts: as the infamous tyrant of Gwynedd and as the father of a Pictish king. Since both contexts refer to the first half of the sixth century, many historians regard Maelgwn and Maelchon as the same man and envisage Brude as Maelgwn's son by a Pictish princess.

The circumstances which might have led to royal inter-marriage between Wales and Pictavia are not easy to identify. There is no record of a connection between Maelgwn and northern Britain, but this does not make his alleged Pictish marriage any less likely. It is possible that he spent time in the North during his youth, perhaps as an exile seeking sanctuary, and thus came into contact with Picts. The only record of dealings between Gwynedd and the North appears in a controversial work called *Historia Brittonum* ('The History of the Britons') which was carefully constructed by a Welsh monk in c.830 from a plethora of older material. According to the *Historia*, a man called Cunedda led an army of Britons from Manau Gododdin – part of the district of Manau around the lower reaches of the River Forth – to North Wales at the beginning of the fifth century. Gododdin was the kingdom of the Britons of Lothian, the descendants of the Votadini of Roman times, whose northern border lay adjacent to Manau. The *Historia Brittonum* states that Cunedda cleared Gwynedd of Irish raiders who had settled there. Afterwards, he and his eight sons founded several small kingdoms from whose dynasties a number of later Welsh kings claimed descent. The entire tale is usually regarded by modern historians as a piece of fiction created in eighth-century Wales to provide a suitably exotic foundation-legend for the royal family of Gwynedd. This type of political propaganda was useful because it gave an aura of legitimacy and antiquity to the notion of Gwynedd being senior to other Welsh kingdoms, but it has little relevance to the fifth century or to northern Britain. This has not prevented some historians from trying to glean authentic post-Roman history from Cunedda's story and using its suggestion of early links between Gwynedd and the North as a context for Maelgwn's later paternity of Brude. In reality, Cunedda and his sons are unlikely to have left their northern home to fight Irish settlers in distant Wales. Cunedda's existence as a historical figure outside the realm of legend is not even proved beyond doubt. In any case, finding a connection between Wales, Gododdin and Pictavia to justify Maelgwn's marriage to a Pict is not necessary. Inter-dynastic marriage was a regular feature of Early Historic diplomacy, and it should come as no surprise to find at least one instance of a Welsh king producing a crown prince for the Picts. The significance of political marriage in Pictavia will be addressed in the next chapter but, for now, the spotlight falls on a different topic.

The Scots of Dalriada

Two key events are known from Brude's reign: Columba's visit to Pictavia, and the first record of war between Picts and Scots. These two incidents are connected by the fact that Columba had his ecclesiastical headquarters in the land of the Scots and relied on the support of their kings. In addition, both incidents were early episodes in a long process which eventually gave birth to the medieval kingdom of Scotland. In Brude's time, of course, there was not yet a political entity called 'Scotland' but there were, in the far western parts of northern Britain, a people who called themselves Scots. Their importance in Pictish history cannot be overstated and, for this reason alone, their emergence as enemies of Brude needs to be explained. This requires an examination of their society, their culture and their origins.

Who were the Scots? This is a big question and the answer to it is still unclear. Until recently, conventional wisdom asserted that the Scots in north-western Britain originated as Irish colonists. In Roman times the label *Scotti* was evidently applied by Latin writers to speakers of Gaelic and was duly interpreted by modern historians as denoting the inhabitants of Ireland. The idea of Gaelic-speakers – 'Scots' – dwelling in mainland Britain before the fifth or sixth centuries was usually regarded as unrealistic. This was because the conventional view firmly believed that Scottish Gaelic developed from a dialect of Irish Gaelic imported to Argyll after the end of the Roman period. The native tongue of the Irish is indeed the forerunner of the language spoken in the Scottish Highlands throughout the medieval and early modern periods. Gaelic still survives in the Gaidhealtachd areas of Scotland, particularly in the Western Isles, where it can be heard in everyday speech. But did it really arrive in Britain no earlier than the late fifth century? This is certainly the view presented by medieval Scottish tradition and accepted without question by generations of later historians. It forms the basis of the origin-legend of the Scots and was long regarded as irrefutable and unassailable.

According to the origin-legend, a dynasty of Irish kings transferred its seat of power from Antrim to Argyll sometime around AD 500. This dynasty then established a new kingdom in Cowal, Kintyre and Islay. The kingdom's name was Dalriada, which is usually encountered in the sources in its Gaelic form *Dál Riata*, this being also the name given by the legend to the dynasty's ancestral home in Ireland. In this tale of eastward migration from Antrim, historians have traditionally found a logical explanation of how the Scots emerged as the dominant power in Argyll and, in later centuries, as the masters of northern Britain. It is a vision found in most modern histories of Scotland and has long formed the bedrock of the country's origins, chiefly because it incorporates long-held and deeply embedded perceptions of national identity.

The idea that the Scots of mainland Britain came originally from Ireland was moulded and refined by their own later rulers, but its core elements already had widespread currency as early as the eighth century. Bede included a version of the origin-legend in his *Ecclesiastical History* of 731, in which he referred to an Irish tribe, led by a leader called Reuda, acquiring lands in Pictish territory 'either by friendly treaty or by the sword'. These settlers took their leader's name and called themselves *Dalreudini*, a name peculiar to Bede but clearly a variant form of Dalriada. Later sources of Irish and Scottish origin tell similar versions of the story but attribute the founding of the settlement to Fergus mac Erc, whom they identify as Dalriada's first king. A medieval genealogy of Fergus makes him tenth in succession from a king called Coirpre Riata and thirteenth after Eochaid Riata, the founder of Dál Riata in Antrim. The latter kingdom is traditionally assumed to be the Irish 'homeland' of the mac Erc dynasty. Under the year 501, the Irish annalists retrospectively noted that Fergus 'with the people of Dalriada occupied a part of Britain and died there'. Subsequent annals recorded the deaths of a son of Fergus called Domangart in 506, and of Domangart's son

Comgall in 538. By the middle of the sixth century, when Saint Columba came from Ireland to preach Christianity among the Picts, the 'overkingship' of Dalriada with its constituent kingships were well-established. The ambitious elites of Argyll were already beginning to look eastward. Since the kings who led these elites spoke Gaelic, the language of Ireland, and bore Irish names, it was easy for Bede and his contemporaries to believe that the mac Erc dynasty was indeed an offshoot from Antrim. It likewise seemed reasonable to regard the entire Gaelic-speaking population of Argyll as immigrants.

But is this tale of Irish colonists really a true record of Scottish origins? Was Scottish Dalriada nothing more than the transplanted colony of an Irish namesake? Recently, a radical re-interpretation of the sources has gained considerable academic support. This alternative view identifies a discrepancy between the origin-legend and the archaeological evidence, which provides little support for the idea of a migration from Ireland to Britain. If the legend is true, archaeologists should expect to find evidence of a sixth-century Irish presence in Argyll. Colonisation should be recognisable in the landscape, especially in the surviving remains of human habitation. However, the types of settlement that are so characteristic of Ireland during this period, including the circular enclosures known as raths, are not found in Argyll. Indeed, there is nothing in the archaeological record to suggest that the area underwent any significant change of population during the first millennium AD. Nor is there any evidence for a seizure of power in Argyll by a small but vigorous elite group from Ireland. If this had happened, excavation should unearth high-status artifacts of Irish design in the area's Early Historic archaeology. In Ireland, for example, aristocrats of the period displayed their wealth by fastening their cloaks with ornate brooches of a particular type, which differed from types worn in Britain. In Argyll, however, it is the British design – not the Irish – that comes to light. Instead of finding clear traces of an immigrant Irish culture supplanting an indigenous one, archaeologists find no indication that such a process ever occurred. Nor do linguists see any sign of a language change, which is what normally happens when one cultural group conquers and colonises another. If an elite from Antrim imposed Gaelic on a non-Gaelic population, traces of the latter's former language should survive in place-names. In the landscape of Argyll there are no traces of any language other than Gaelic. It seems, in fact, that the natives – whoever they were – were neither pushed out in the sixth century nor taken over. The combined evidence of archaeology and place-names suggests rather that these people – although they spoke Gaelic – were not of Irish origin. On the contrary, they seem to have been an indigenous population of Gaelic-speaking 'Scots' who had always been there.

Who were these non-Irish Scots and what was their relationship to the Picts? To answer this question we must glance back to Roman times, to the second century, and to Ptolemy's map of the British Isles. The map shows Argyll as being occupied by a people called Epidii; the conventional view of Scottish origins usually regarded them as Picts or Britons – speakers of a P-Celtic language rather than a Q-Celtic one like Gaelic. Historians have generally assumed that the descendants of the Epidii were ousted by an influx of Gaelic-speaking colonists from Antrim three or four centuries later. This assumption is now giving way to a belief that the Epidii already spoke Gaelic in Roman times and simply re-emerged in the Early Historic period as the Scots of Dalriada.

Although this alternative view is radical and controversial, it is almost certainly correct. The idea of a Gaelic-speaking population inhabiting Argyll since prehistoric times is consistent with the physical geography of north-west Britain. The core territories of Dalriada are separated from the eastward lands, the territory of the Picts, by Druim Alban – a mountainous barrier whose harsh terrain hindered communication and settlement as much in the first millennium as it does today. Few routes have dared to traverse this obstacle, which includes the main massif of the central Highlands and many of the highest peaks in Scotland. To the people of Argyll, the prospect of forging viable economic and social relationships with communities dwelling on the other side of the 'Spine of Britain' must have seemed daunting. By contrast, the coast of Antrim is less than fifteen miles from the Mull of Kintyre, is clearly visible across the narrow strait between and can be reached easily by boat. The Gaelic-speaking inhabitants of north-east Ireland were the nearest and most accessible neighbours of the people of Argyll long before the Romans came to Britain. It requires no great leap of imagination to envisage Argyll's native folk regarding themselves as part of a Gaelic cultural milieu embracing maritime communities on both sides of the Irish Sea. Trade and social interaction gave these communities similar economic interests and a shared dependence on the seaways which, far from being a barrier, provided a major artery of communication. With language providing the key to forging mutually beneficial relationships, it is not difficult to see how Gaelic became the common speech of Argyll.

Where, then, does this leave the traditional origin-legend? The shortest answer is that if the inhabitants of Argyll were already speaking Gaelic before the fifth century there is no need to envisage an influx of settlers from Ireland. A longer answer requires taking a look at possible reasons for the creation of the legend which, as well as being widely circulated in medieval Scotland, was certainly known to Bede as early as the 730s. The legend has recently come under scrutiny and its various versions have been subjected to critical analysis. Historians now believe that the story of Fergus mac Erc and his migration originated in the ninth or tenth centuries rather than in the fifth or sixth. It was created to provide an Irish origin for the kings of Scotland by turning their forefathers into immigrants from Dál Riata in Antrim. This provided an appropriate ancestry for Scottish kings of the tenth to thirteenth centuries whose policies were strongly influenced by Irish ideas about kingship, but it was not the only motive for the story's creation. Bede's eighth-century version of the legend – the earliest version known today – was probably created by the Scots of his own time to justify territorial claims on Irish Dál Riata. The legend sees their kingdom in Argyll as an offshoot of a motherland in Antrim but, with traditional views now standing on shaky ground, the reverse seems far more likely. If so, then Dál Riata in Ireland was a 'colony' of its namesake in Britain rather than vice versa.

An acceptance that the Scots of Argyll had always lived in Britain has profound implications for how historians view their relationship with the Picts. It means that both peoples were indigenous and had deep ancestral roots in their respective lands. Neither group was a new or immigrant population, but their cultures travelled along different paths. The harsh geography of the Highlands lay between them to keep them apart, ensuring that they shared few cultural traits and did not even speak the same language. The Picts spoke a language akin to that of the Britons beyond their southern border, and the two dialects were to some extent mutually intelligible. This was not the case with their Gaelic-speaking neighbours in the West. The people of Argyll were as foreign to the Picts as if they had indeed just arrived in a fleet of boats from Ireland. Their material culture – the form of their settlements and the design of their jewellery – gave them an affinity with people in other coastal areas of Britain, but their speech made them appear 'Irish'. Throughout the Roman period they had some kind of relationship with the Picts and probably engaged in small-scale trading activities across Druim Alban. It would seem that neither group had much to fear from the other until Dalriada's kings began to look east in the sixth century.

Before AD 500, the Scots were merely one of several Gaelic-speaking communities along the northern shores of the Irish Sea. They happened to be located in Britain rather than in Ireland but, like the Irish, with whom they shared a common language, they were a people whose main economic activities were maritime trade and seaborne raiding. By the middle of the sixth century they were grouped into a number of distinct kingdoms, each with its own royal dynasty or ruling kindred. These kindreds were known in Gaelic as *cenéla*, which loosely means 'tribes' or 'peoples'. Of these the most powerful were Cenél nGabráin of Kintyre, Cenél Comgaill of Cowal and Cenél Loairn of Lorn. For much of the Early Historic period these three competed vigorously for the overkingship of Dalriada, leaving other kindreds – such as Cenél nOengusa of Islay – in a marginalised role on the periphery. At the same time as the emergence of the *cenéla*, a shift of policy occurred, perhaps because of economic pressures caused by a lack of good agricultural land in Argyll. Dalriada's kings began to adopt an increasingly aggressive stance. They became more ambitious in their political dealings and more belligerent towards their neighbours. It was not long before this aggression led to open war with the Picts.

In the Irish annals, under the year 559, is the following entry: 'Flight of the Scots before Brude, Maelchon's son, king of Picts, and the death of Gabran, son of Domangart.' The annalists associated this event with 'an expedition by Maelchon's son, King Brude'. Domangart and Gabran were respectively a son and grandson of Fergus mac Erc who – in spite of his presence in the origin-legend – may have been a genuine historical figure. Little is known of the heirs of Fergus, but Gabran was regarded by the annalists as being of sufficient importance for his death to warrant a mention. The annal for 559 is especially significant because it represents the earliest report of a clash of arms between Pict and Scot. Its location is not given, but the outcome is clear: Brude won and the Scots withdrew. Since no further clashes between the two peoples are recorded for a further fifteen years, it is possible that the battle of 559 marked a decisive Pictish victory which forced Dalriada to acknowledge Brude as overlord.

Columba and the Picts

It was during Brude's reign that Saint Columba crossed Druim Alban to bring Christianity to the northern Picts. Columba was an Irishman of noble birth whose parentage linked him closely with the powerful Uí Néill kings of northern Ireland. Had he not chosen a religious career he would have become a warrior, perhaps even a king. He was born in 521 and began training for the priesthood at an early age, although he made use of his family's high-level contacts and played an influential role in political as well as religious affairs. He was charismatic and clever, a dynamic figure whose piety and humility concealed a forceful personality and a fierce ambition. In 563 he left his homeland, for reasons unknown, and sailed to Britain with a small group of followers. Whilst there is a suspicion that he was forced to leave Ireland, his main objective – according to Bede – was 'to preach the Word of God to the northern Picts'. Most of what is known about Columba comes from a 'Life' written by Adomnán, seventh abbot of Iona, sometime around the year 700. Adomnán was a hagiographer of great skill and his *Vita Columbae* is therefore not a historical biography but a literary homage to the holiness and spiritual powers of Iona's founder. Nevertheless, it is through the *Vita* that modern historians gain a glimpse of sixth-century Pictavia under the rule of Brude, Maelchon's son.

As soon as Columba arrived in Britain he established a monastery as a base for missionary activities. This was located not in the land of the Picts but on the western fringe of Argyll, on the island of Iona off the coast of Mull. According to the Irish annals Iona was a gift from Conall, son of Comgall, the overking of Dalriada. Bede tells a different story, attributing the gift to Brude, but this is probably a later version created by the Picts of his own time in an attempt to portray Iona as part of their territory. By envisaging the holy island as removed from Dalriada's influence, the eighth-century Pictish clergy could promote their ancestors' conversion to Christianity as a process in which the Scots played no significant role. However, Iona is so far removed from the Pictish heartlands in the east, and so close to the core territory of Dalriada, that the story of Conall's gift need not be doubted. A base in the land of the Scots was in any case a logical choice for Columba who, like them, was a Gaelic-speaker. Iona lay not too far from Ireland, where he still maintained a network of contacts and interests. He shared with the Scots a common language, which facilitated the swift integration of his Irish monks. The Picts, on the other hand, were a people whose heartland lay across the mountains in territory that was barely accessible to the Scots and largely unknown to the Irish. To Columba and his companions, as to the natives of Argyll, Pictavia probably seemed like an alien place with which they had little in common. By establishing his headquarters on Iona, Columba was not so much seeking a springboard for missionary work among the Picts as aligning himself with the powerful elites of Dalriada. The elite with whom he eventually formed the closest bond was the royal dynasty of Cenél nGabráin, whose realm encompassed the long peninsula of Kintyre. Indeed, within a few years the monastery on Iona became the premier royal church of this dynasty and the place to which the kings of Kintyre looked for spiritual guidance. The development of this relationship is less likely to have been an accidental by-product of Columba's arrival in Argyll than the fulfilment of one of his principal aims. It could be argued that a similar political objective prompted him to make his first foray into Pictavia.

Bede dates Columba's mission to the Picts in 565, two years after the saint's arrival in Britain. The conversion was not, however, a single event at which the entire Pictish nation was baptised *en masse*, but rather a long process of journeying and preaching. Success rested on securing and maintaining the goodwill of Brude who, at that time, was the pagan ruler of a pagan people. Convincing the king to abandon the old gods and sacred rituals of his ancestors was unlikely to be an easy task, nor indeed a rapid one. Adomnán's passing mention of Columba's 'first tiring expedition to King Brude' suggests that more than one visit was made to the royal court. Elsewhere in the *Vita*, Adomnán gives a fictional account of how the first visit began rather badly. In what was hardly the most auspicious or optimistic start, the Pictish king refused to open the gates of his fortress after Columba and some monks approached along a steep path. Undeterred, the saint stood before the gates and made the sign of the Cross, at which point the bolts drew back and the gates opened. In hagiographical terms this was a fairly small miracle, but Adomnán included it because it served his purpose, which was to show Brude being so impressed by Columba's powers that he welcomed the travellers from Iona with courtesy and respect.

For Adomnán, the incident at the fortress gates was not about the Picts or their king. It was invented to provide an illustration of Columba's miracle-working talent and thus gives no real insight into the saint's first encounter with Brude. In reality a group of

Irishmen would not have turned up unannounced at the residence of a foreign king in the chance hope of gaining access. It is far more likely that Columba arrived at the fortress in response to a formal invitation from the Pictish monarch. Both men were members of an aristocratic social stratum encompassing the secular and religious elites of every kingdom in the British Isles. Their first meeting would have been marked by public expressions of mutual respect, together with formal gestures of courtesy and generosity. This is how high-status relationships were conducted in the Early Historic period, and such rituals were not lightly set aside.

What was Brude likely to gain by allowing a delegation from Iona to enter the heart of his realm? The answer probably lies in an awareness that the old gods of Pictavia now had little to offer. In every corner of the British Isles, paganism was retreating in the face of a sophisticated international religion whose leaders were rapidly gaining influence at the centres of political power. By contrast, the cults of the old gods operated in local contexts which must have seemed small and petty by comparison. To a wise and ambitious king such as Brude, the eventual triumph of Christianity may have seemed inevitable. To a hagiographer like Adomnán, the conflict between the old religion and the new required a more dramatic image. It was presented in the *Vita* as a face-to-face confrontation between Columba and the high priests of Pictish paganism. These 'wizards' or druids were trounced by a few spectacular miracles which proved the superiority of the Christian God. The chief druid was Broichan, Brude's own foster-father, who continued to resent Columba even after the saint miraculously saved him from death. Broichan's antipathy was not shared by Brude, for the monks were granted permission to preach throughout the kingdom, and some Picts received Christian baptism from Columba. The actual number of converts is unknown, but Adomnán gives no indication that Brude himself was among them. The king may have remained a pagan to the end of his days, perhaps as a matter of personal choice, or to maintain the goodwill of those among the Pictish elite who felt little enthusiasm for change.

Brude and His Realm

Bede describes Brude as *rex potentissimus*, 'a most powerful king'. This means that he was an overking who held lesser kings as clients and from whom he received hostages, tribute-payments and military manpower. His elevated status will have been achieved through aggressive warfare, threats and intimidation, driven by strength of will and ruthless ambition. Overkingship in this period was not hereditary: it did not pass by default to the royal heir but had to be earned through success on the battlefield. Victory in war resulted in easy plunder, the defeat of enemies and the confiscation of their wealth via the receipt of tribute. Some foes were internal ones, and every king had to contend with them – dynastic rivals and competitors – whenever they rose up inside his kingdom. Other enemies hailed from lands beyond the border and included rebellious under-kings as well as challengers from further afield. A ruler who waged successful military campaigns, and who placed enemy territory under tribute, was likely to become the overlord of a wide domain. This was how Brude, Maelchon's son, increased his power to achieve the status of *rex potentissimus*.

In warfare and in all other royal ventures, a king of the Early Historic period commanded by personality and reputation. Some consultation with trusted advisers among the secular and religious elites occurred from time to time, but there was no governmental structure in the modern sense. Adomnán speaks of a Pictish *senatus* or 'council' accompanying Brude during Columba's visit, but these men were senior warriors rather than bureaucrats or administrators. A king in this period ruled alone, using his individual qualities to turn himself into a successful warlord who thus earned respect from friend and foe alike. Brude certainly possessed these qualities and used them to consolidate his hold on the outer fringes of Pictavia, but his enlarged realm was basically a one-man show which could not be bequeathed to an heir. When he died in the early 580s his overlordship of distant provinces and faraway territories died with him.

A measure of Brude's power is that he held other kings under his sway. An indication of the wide extent of his authority emerges from the *Vita Columbae* in a story about Cormac, a monk of Iona. Columba told Brude that Cormac and some other Ionan monks wanted to sail away in search of a remote place where they could establish a monastic retreat. Among those present at the royal court was the *regulus* or 'under-king' of Orkney, into whose territorial waters Cormac was likely to venture. This ruler was in a tributary relationship to the Pictish overking, but his continuing loyalty was ensured because members of his family were living at Brude's court as hostages. Neither Adomnán nor the Irish annals mention Brude warring in Orkney but, at some point during his reign, he subjected the islands to his rule. His authority was therefore not confined to mainland Britain but extended beyond the Pentland Firth to encompass the outer fringe of Pictish territory. There is no doubt that the Orcadians – the inhabitants of Orkney – regarded themselves as Picts. At the Brough of Birsay, a high-status site on the largest island in the group, a carved stone adorned with four Pictish symbols and three spear-bearing warriors once stood in an old graveyard. The stone dates from the seventh or eighth centuries and is therefore later than Brude's time, but it adds to other archaeological evidence indicating that the Brough of Birsay was an important residence of Orcadian kings. The three warriors on the stone might even represent descendants of the *regulus* who acknowledged Brude's authority in the sixth century.

Columba visited Brude at a royal fortress near the mouth of the River Ness. The site is not named in the *Vita*, but it was clearly some kind of elevated stronghold or hillfort, accessed via a steep path. Many historians identify it as the old fort of Craig Phadraig, which lies close to Inverness on a ridge overlooking the Beauly Firth. Excavations have shown that this was built in the fourth century BC and abandoned in the early centuries AD. Sometime later, in the fifth or sixth century, it was re-occupied as a residence for people of high status. This phase of occupation was the last and was marked by signs of neglect. Despite the discovery of a metalworking mould and other indications of an elite presence, the gradual dereliction and eventual abandonment of the site in the 500s has cast doubt on the theory that this was where Brude met Columba. However, one curious factor in its favour is that the approach to the summit involves a strenuous ascent, which brings to mind Adomnán's mention of the steep path trodden by the monks. Aside from this anecdotal support the case for Craig Phadraig does not look very convincing, but it is not the only candidate. Two other possible locations for Brude's fortress have been suggested. One of these is the Castle Hill at Inverness, which stands in a dominant position above an important ford, while another is the hillfort of Torvean. Archaeologists might one day pinpoint the the site of the royal residence more closely but, until such time, its location remains unknown.

The image of Brude holding court beside the River Ness has led to a belief that the core of his domain lay in northern Pictavia. This seems to be supported by Bede's reference to Columba converting the northern Picts rather than their southern cousins. However, neither Bede nor Adomnán explicitly states that Brude did not also rule south of the Mounth. In Chapter 4 it was observed that one of the characteristics of Early Historic kingship was an itinerant royal court, which enabled a monarch and his entourage to conduct regular 'circuits' of the kingdom, visiting prominent local lords who offered gifts and hospitality. At various prestigious sites scattered around his realm the king presided over rituals and ceremonies where bonds of fealty and clientship were cemented through mutual gift-giving and the renewal of oaths. Brude's fortress on the River Ness may have been an occasional royal residence of this sort, but there were probably other places of equal status elsewhere in his domains. Some may have lain further south, in Perthshire, but were not necessarily of lesser importance than the northerly stronghold visited by Columba. There is in fact no reason to assume from the testimony of Adomnán that Brude did not hail from southern Pictavia. This was an ideal power-base for ambitious rulers, being an area of prime agricultural land and thus a source of wealth. On the other hand, since the sources associate later Pictish kings with the province of Fortriu, an area now identified with Moray, it may be assumed that this was Brude's home territory. It is worthwhile to note that the name *Brude*, borne by a number of kings of Fortriu, may have been especially associated with this area. Maybe Brude himself hailed from Fortriu and was a northern Pict by birth? If so, then his stronghold near the River Ness was probably an ancestral residence, the citadel of his forefathers, as well as being a suitable venue for dealing with sub-kings from Orkney, Caithness and other northerly districts.

How far Brude's realm extended westward is uncertain. During his reign there was military conflict with Dalriada and pressure by the Scots on Pictish communities in frontier areas. In the far west these areas may have included the Isle of Skye, which was certainly inhabited by Picts at this time. Three stones bearing Pictish symbols have been found on the island, but a significant piece of additional information comes from Adomnán's story of Columba meeting an old pagan called Artbranan. The latter, described as the leader of the 'Cohort of Geona', arrived on Skye in a small boat when the saint was visiting the island. He asked Columba for baptism and, after this was performed, promptly died and was buried on the spot. During the baptism the two men communicated through an inter-preter, whose presence indicates that Artbranan spoke a language other than Gaelic. This suggests that he was a Pict from Skye or from some other place not far away. He was the leader of a distinct group, perhaps a warband, and therefore a person of high or aristo-cratic status. Ultimately, he may have been answerable to Brude or to some other Pictish ruler whose authority included the coastlands around Skye. An alternative possibility is that Artbranan already acknowledged the kings of Cenél nGabráin as his new overlords and felt compelled to show this allegiance by seeking baptism from their spiritual patriarch.

The story of Artbranan contains a few details, but little is really known about the people of Brude's kingdom. One family of Picts appears briefly in the *Vita Columbae* as pagans encountered by the saint near Loch Ness. Columba interrupted a journey on foot to make a detour to this family's residence, which lay within a prosperous agricultural estate at Glen Urquhart. There he baptised an old man called Emchath who lay on the brink of death.

Emchath's son, Virolec, also received baptism, as did other folk of the estate. Emchath and Virolec belonged to a family of high status who ruled a 'household' of retainers, tenant-farmers and other dependants. The family's main residence may have been the Early Historic fort located by archaeologists beneath the ruins of Urquhart Castle at the mouth of the glen.

The Columban Mission

Adomnán's brief allusions to Pictavia do not give any indication of the success of Columba's missionary activities. Monasteries were established among the Picts and Scots, but Adomnán names only two, both of which lay on Hebridean islands in Dalriadan territory. There are no clues as to where the Pictish ones were located. In later times the monastery at Deer in Buchan claimed Columba as its founding-father and supported the claim with a suitable legend. In the absence of corroboration from other sources the claim raises scepticism, but there is nothing inherently improbable about it. Deer was certainly an important church in later Pictish times and, sometime around AD 900, its monks produced an illuminated manuscript of the Gospels. This volume, known today as the Book of Deer, was used in the early twelfth century as a notebook for jottings about land owned by the monastery. Preceding the notes is a foundation-story which not only mentions Columba but adds that he was assisted by a Pict called Saint Drostan. Recent analysis of the tale suggests that the earliest traditions at Deer attributed the foundation to Drostan alone. Unfortunately, little is known of this saint and historians cannot confirm that he existed outside monastic folklore, although the notes in the Book of Deer probably preserve local traditions of much older origin. The foundation-story describes Drostan as a disciple of Columba on his journeys in Pictavia. Together they came to Aberdour on the coast of Buchan, where a local lord granted land for the building of a monastery. An additional grant made provision for a second monastery at Deer, twelve miles to the south. Other traditions identified Drostan as a

Scot of royal blood who received education in Ireland, although his name suggests Pictish ancestry. His tomb is said to be at Aberdour, but he apparently spent his final years as a hermit at Glenesk in Angus.

The Deer foundation-story may be based on real events of the sixth century embellished by layers of ecclesiastical folklore. A Pictish monastery once stood there, and it could have been founded by Columba or his disciples during the reign of Brude. The mysterious Drostan, a Christian Pict, may have accompanied Columba to assist in missionary work or to act as an interpreter. Most of Iona's clergy were Irishmen, but some newly baptised Picts probably joined Columba's entourage to train as priests. Drostan might have been one of these. The same can be said of Saint Talorcan who, like Drostan, bore a distinctively Pictish name. Folklore associates Talorcan with the church at Fordyce in Moray. Both he and Drostan may have been Pictish converts who helped Columba and his disciples in the late sixth century.

Of Columba himself there are inevitably many commemorations throughout Scotland, where his name is encountered in numerous contexts. These sometimes use his Gaelic nickname *Columb Cille*, 'Dove of the Church'. Finding authentic traces of his mission to Pictavia is a rather different matter. Both Bede and Adomnán believed that the Pictish monasteries of their own time – around the turn of the eighth century – were daughter-houses of Iona and therefore part of the *familia* or family of Columban churches. Some of these may have been personally founded by Columba, while others owed their origins to his successors in the abbacy of Iona. An Irish poem called *Amrae Coluimb Chille* ('The Praise of Columb Cille') was composed within a few years of his death in 597 and credits him with converting 'the tribes of the Tay'. The contemporary provenance of this source adds value to its testimony and implies that his missions enjoyed a measure of success along the Tay valley, in the Pictish heartlands of Atholl and northern Perthshire. In these areas a scatter of minor place-names and early church dedications incorporating his name might reasonably be expected. It is strange, therefore, that the valley of the

Tay yields no such pattern, the only certain example of a Columba commemoration being the much later dedication of Dunkeld Cathedral. One reason for this could be that his activities might not have made a huge impact in Pictavia but instead laid a solid groundwork for later missions sent forth from Iona in the seventh century. An alternative explanation is that Columba laboured primarily north of the Mounth, in the same region where King Brude maintained a royal residence on the River Ness, and there founded a small number of monasteries of which Deer was probably one. As in the case of Saint Brigid, an appraisal of Columba's impact in the sixth century is complicated by the active promotion of his cult by later Gaelic influences and by the ecclesiastical policies of medieval Scottish kings for whom he became an iconic figure. Within 100 years of his death, the cult of Columba was already well-established in both Britain and Ireland under the direction of his successors at Iona. In subsequent chapters the influence on Pictavia of these later abbots will be looked at more closely but, for the moment, the focus returns to political events of the late sixth century.

Brude, Áedán and the Neighbours of the Picts

In 574, King Conall of Dalriada died and was succeeded by his cousin Áedán mac Gabráin, a member of the Kintyre dynasty. Columba ordained Áedán as king of Cenél nGabráin in a ceremony on Iona. The accession of the new monarch gave his family a warlord of considerable skill who had the ability to raise their fortunes. His father was the same Gabran who had perished in 559 in the first recorded battle between Scots and Picts, but Áedán's ambitions were far greater. He soon embarked on raids against his neighbours and it was only a matter of time before he challenged Brude, son of Maelchon, the powerful Pictish overking. The challenge came in 580 with an attack on Orkney, which at that time lay under the rule of kings who acknowledged Brude's authority. Áedán's assault was an attempt to disrupt Brude's relationship with the Orcadians by demonstrating that their overking was unable to protect them. Nor was this the only eastward incursion undertaken by Cenél nGabráin forces at that time. Adomnán refers to a victory over a people called Miathi, the fearsome Maeatae of Roman times, in which Áedán lost two sons. The territory of the Miathi lay in Stirlingshire near the borders of Strathearn, making them neighbours of Brude. Their leaders were probably tribute-paying clients subjugated to Brude's overlordship, just like the *regulus* of Orkney whom Columba saw at the royal residence beside the River Ness. Áedán's campaign in Stirlingshire may have been a southern counterweight to his raid on Orkney, its purpose being to threaten the Miathi and to destabilise their relationship with their Pictish patron.

Brude died in 584, probably in battle rather than peacefully. His successor was a king called Gartnait, who repulsed a Cenél nGabráin attack deep inside the heartland of Pictavia. The battle happened in 598, in the province of Circinn, and was a major defeat for Áedán. Its precise location is unknown, but it lay east of the River Tay in what is now Angus and marked an important victory for the Picts. It was their final encounter with the Scots during Áedán's reign and resulted in the death of another of his sons.

Within a couple of years Gartnait was dead. His passing, noted in the annals around the year 600, coincided with an event of ominous significance for Pictavia. This was the battle of *Degsastan*, in which Áedán mac Gabráin was massively defeated by the northern English while campaigning in their territory. The victor was Aethelfrith, king of Bernicia, whose chief stronghold lay at Bamburgh on the North Sea coast in what became the great realm of Northumbria. Bede celebrated the victory as a turning-point in the political history of Britain, noting triumphantly: 'From that time no king of the Scots has dared make war on the English nation to this day.' From a Pictish perspective, the thwarting of Áedán's southward ambitions signalled the emergence of the English as one of the great northern powers.

At that time, the English or Anglo-Saxons had been settled in Britain for several generations. Northumbria was the most northerly of their territories and consisted of two kingdoms, Deira and Bernicia, each with its own royal dynasty. Much of what is now Yorkshire lay within Deira, founded by Germanic mercenaries who wrested control from native Britons in the fifth century. Bernicia was established later, perhaps in the mid-sixth century, after the seizure of a British coastal fortress at Bamburgh or, less dramatically, after an English faction came to power in a native kingdom whose rulers used Bamburgh as their principal residence. Vigorous warfare by Bernicia's kings brought more territory under their control and allowed them to threaten or coerce their Deiran neighbours. In the person of Aethelfrith, these two English kingdoms were united for the first time under one ruler but continued to retain separate identities for the next 100 years. Not until the time of Bede did the notion of a single, unified Northumbria become the dominant ideology.

In the early seventh century the English shared no common frontier with the Picts. The two peoples were separated by Gododdin, the large British kingdom whose territory included Lothian and the great citadel of Din Eidyn on a site now occupied by Edinburgh Castle. Gododdin's southern border came under intense pressure from Bernicia and was the scene of an English victory in the closing years of the sixth century. An account of this battle was subsequently dramatised by a British poet who composed a series of heroic verses to honour the Gododdin casualties. Historians usually identify Catraeth, the site of the battle in the poem, as Catterick in Yorkshire, but a location along Gododdin's southern frontier in Lothian or Berwickshire seems more plausible. The poem survives today and is one of the most controversial sources for Early Historic Scotland, partly because it has resided for more than a thousand years in Wales, far from its place of composition. In the hands of medieval Welsh poets and scribes, the original version received many additions and alterations. It also received the title by which it is more commonly known today: The Gododdin. Although its creation may belong to the time of the battle of Catraeth, traces of the early version are difficult to identify in the surviving text, which consists of a series of stanzas in Welsh. This has not deterred some historians from treating the poem as the authentic diary of a sixth-century war correspondent, which it certainly is not.

One verse in the *Gododdin* refers to a man called Bubon who may have been a Pict fighting alongside the Britons at Catraeth. He is described by the poet as hailing from 'beyond the Sea of Iddew'. The Welsh term *Iddew* is usually equated with *Giudi*, a name applied to Stirling in Early Historic times, and the 'Sea of Iddew' might therefore be the Firth of Forth. If this is the correct identification, it implies that Bubon was a Pictish ally of the Britons, perhaps a freebooting nobleman seeking wealth and renown. Neither the poem nor any other source sheds light on political relations between Pictavia and Gododdin at the time of the battle. At all times there would have been outbreaks of warfare between the two in what is now eastern Stirlingshire – the old frontier region of Manau – alternating with periods of uneasy peace. By AD 600, however, the Britons of Lothian were rapidly losing ground to Bernicia. Their defeat at Catraeth was merely one episode in a process that was soon to culminate in the final collapse of Gododdin. The kingdom's eventual demise would bring the Picts face-to-face with a far more aggressive people.

CHAPTER 6

Neighbours and Kinsmen

The early seventh century saw the Picts turning away from the old gods and embracing the religion of Rome. The process of Christian conversion began at the higher levels of society before gradually permeating down to the peasantry, who gave up their heathen beliefs rather more slowly. To the Pictish upper classes the new religion seemed attractive and beneficial. With its literate personnel and international links, the Church offered an exotic and sophisticated alternative to the paganism of their ancestors. Becoming Christian enabled these aristocratic Picts to avoid being marginalised in a world where the new religious elite played an increasingly influential role in power and politics.

From c.600 the main documentary sources are generally reliable. The Pictish king-list is still the basic chronological guide, but detailed information now comes from contemporary observers such as Bede, Adomnán and the Irish annalists. Some legends and uncertainties appear here and there but, on the whole, the key events of the seventh century were accurately reported by contemporary writers. The century also saw the Picts joining their Celtic and Anglo-Saxon neighbours to change forever the political map of northern Britain.

Dynasties

The sixth century ended with a man called Nechtan, grandson of

Uerb, becoming paramount ruler or overking of the Picts. Like his predecessors he would normally be regarded by historians as a member of one of the royal families of Pictavia, a prince who attained the kingship through right of succession. It is curious, then, to find a complex web of academic conjecture surrounding him. At its heart stands the question of whether he was a Pict rather than a Briton from Alt Clut. A surviving royal genealogy of the latter kingdom includes a king called Neithon – a Brittonic form of Nechtan – who reigned in the early seventh century. Some historians think Neithon of Alt Clut may have been Nechtan, grandson of Uerb. In Chapter 4 it was noted that the people of the Clyde, the Damnonii of Roman times, were ruled in the Early Historic period by a powerful dynasty of native kings whose chief residence lay on the rocky height where Dumbarton Castle stands today. The modern name derives from an older one coined by Gaelic-speakers who knew the ancient stronghold as *Dun Breatann*, 'The Fort of the Britons'.

One possible connection between the Pictish Nechtan and his Clyde namesake Neithon rests on a poem relating to a later king of the Picts, Brude son of Beli, who defeated the Northumbrian English in 685 while fighting 'for the inheritance of his grandfather'. The context of this battle is dealt with in the next chapter but, for the moment, it will be sufficient to observe that Brude's paternal grandfather was the Clyde king Neithon. Brude's father Beli was Neithon's son and succeeded him in the kingship of Alt Clut. The obvious implication is that Beli had a marriage – or some other kind of liaison – with a Pictish princess and that the child of this union eventually became the Pictish king Brude. In the Clyde genealogy mentioned above, the father of Beli appears as 'Neithon, son of Guipno' but some historians prefer to see him as 'Nechtan, son of Cano', whose death was recorded in the Irish annals at 621 and who was probably a Pict. This would make the name *Guipno* either an error in the Alt Clut genealogy or a corruption of *Cano*, but only if Cano's son and Guipno's son were indeed the same man.

Those historians who equate Neithon of Alt Clut with Nechtan, grandson of Uerb, draw support from the likelihood that the two figures were contemporaries. Because Neithon's grandson became the powerful Pictish king Brude, it has been suggested that Neithon – in his Pictish guise as Nechtan – ruled the Picts as well as the Britons. The basis for this theory sees the royal family of Alt Clut maintaining dynastic control in Pictavia for at least two generations after c.600. Central to the theory is a belief that the 'inheritance' for which Brude, son of Beli, fought in 685 was the Pictish segment of an extensive hegemony ruled by his paternal grandfather Neithon. The scenario is certainly interesting and thought-provoking. It represents a plausible attempt to simplify the appearance around the same time of three men called Nechtan or Neithon by blending them together as a single individual. It does, however, require tampering with the Alt Clut genealogy in order to dispose of Guipno as a scribal error for Cano. It also envisages a dynasty of Britons seizing control in Pictavia – or even a Pictish dynasty doing something similar on the Clyde – without any pressing need for such conjecture. No surviving source implies that a single paramount king simultaneously ruled the Picts and Britons in the early seventh century. A simpler alternative is to regard the coincidence of two kings with the same name ruling at roughly the same time as a quirk of history and nothing more. This would make Nechtan, king of the Picts, and Neithon, king of Alt Clut, contemporaries and neighbours but not the same man. A related topic is discussed in the next chapter in the context of Brude, the son of Beli and grandson of Neithon, who fought a battle over 'the inheritance of his grandfather'.

The reign of Nechtan, king of the Picts, witnessed several important political events. According to the Pictish king-list, he ruled for twenty years, from c.600 to c.620. This coincided with a time of dynastic strife between Bernicia and Deira, the two kingdoms of the northern English, each of which was ruled by its own king. The unified realm of Northumbria – bearing a name meaning 'lands north of the Humber' – was at that time a temporary entity rather than a permanent feature of the political landscape. The Bernician king Aethelfrith, whose army had decisively defeated the Scots at Degsastan in 603, expelled the royal kindred of Deira to establish himself as the first king to rule all the Northumbrians. His Deiran rival Edwin fled into exile among the Britons before finding an English protector in the person of Redwald, king of the East Angles. In 617, at a great battle in the midlands, Redwald destroyed Aethelfrith to pave the way for Edwin's restoration. The victory was so decisive that Edwin not only regained Deira but also seized the embryonic overkingship of Northumbria. It was now the turn of the Bernician royal family to flee into exile. Unlike Edwin, the sons of Aethelfrith sought refuge in the Celtic North. The younger sons, including the future kings Oswald and Oswiu, fled to Dalriada, seeking sanctuary among the Scots. The eldest son, Eanfrith, went to Pictavia, where he married a Pictish princess and fathered a son.

Meanwhile, Edwin of Deira imposed his rule on Bernicia and, like Aethelfrith, ruled the two northern English kingdoms as a single realm. Aethelfrith had died a pagan, but Edwin perceived the political benefits of Christianity and became a convert. He joined his wife – a princess from Kent – in following the ways of the Continental or 'Roman' Church, which had recently established itself as the religious mentor of the southern English. So, just as the Celtic North acknowledged the spiritual authority of the abbot of Iona, so the South looked to the archbishop of Canterbury for guidance. In the seventh century, the 'Celtic' Church was based in the northern and western parts of Britain and also in Ireland. It was not a single institution but three groupings loosely defined by geography. Columba's Iona and its *familia* of dependent monasteries in Argyll and Pictavia formed one group, while Ireland formed another. The Britons of Wales, Cornwall and the North were part of a third group which also included any other native Christian communities not absorbed by the English. It should be noted at this point that Celtic Christianity was not distinct from mainstream Roman Catholicism. The monasteries of the Celtic lands never considered themselves sundered from Papal authority, but were merely slow to adopt new ecclesiastical developments because of their geographical isolation. This meant that they continued to use practices which made them seem archaic or

Figure 3. Pictish cross-slab from Ulbster, Caithness, now in Thurso Museum. Reproduced from J.R. Allen and J. Anderson, *The Early Christian Monuments of Scotland* (1903).

backward to the so-called 'Roman' clergy of Continental Europe. One outmoded practice was the style of clerical tonsure, but the most contentious issue was the Celtic method for annually calculating the precise date of Easter Sunday. Later in this chapter it will be seen how these issues came to a crisis in the 660s, with far-reaching consequences for the Picts.

Matrilineal Succession

The Pictish king who fostered Eanfrith, Aethelfrith's eldest son, during his exile was either Nechtan, grandson of Uerb, or his successor Ciniod, son of Lutren. Fosterage of a foreign prince meant more than merely giving shelter and protection. It was a political gesture of profound significance, uniting foster-father and foster-son in a bond of imagined kinship sealed by oath and ritual. Such a relationship carried firm promises of mutual benefits when the period of fosterage was over. The Pictish king who gave hospitality to Eanfrith therefore expected something in return, presumably a promise of non-aggression if the young English prince managed to regain the Bernician kingship. Such a promise would have placed on Eanfrith an obligation to acknowledge his debt by regarding his Pictish foster-father as an overlord to whom tribute would eventually be paid from the Bernician royal coffers. Among the formal rituals sealing this bond was a marriage between Eanfrith and a Pictish woman and, more significantly, his fathering of a son who could be groomed as a future king of Pictavia. Arrangements of this kind between dynasties did not necessarily demand a formal or permanent marriage but were nevertheless an important part of diplomacy between kingdoms.

The sources show numerous instances of inter-dynastic union, not all of which were necessarily marital, occurring all over the British Isles in this period. In most cases the matchmaking of princes and princesses from different dynasties sealed political relationships between powerful kings in a period when the art of diplomacy, in the modern sense of written treaties and alliances, was virtually unknown. The Picts seem to have employed inter-dynastic union in a way that their neighbours did not, using it to provide biological fathers for the future high kings or overkings of Pictavia. Many historians take this idea further by seeing Pictish overkingship passing not through the male line of the royal families, but through a line of princesses whose husbands or designated partners were excluded from the succession in favour of the sons whom they sired. Such a system of royal inheritance is known as matriliny, to distinguish it from the more common patrilineal system in which kingship routinely passes from father to son. In a matrilineal system, a king is rarely succeeded by his son and more commonly bequeaths the kingship to his own womb-brother ('son of the king's mother') or to his sororal nephew ('son of the king's sister'). Matrilineal succession was not a widespread practice in the

British Isles, nor indeed across Europe as a whole, in any period of recorded history. It did however occur in other parts of the world, even in comparatively recent times, and was prevalent among several African societies of the pre-Colonial era. The Ashanti of Ghana, for example, were a matrilineal society whose customs have been studied extensively by modern anthropologists. If matrilineal inheritance really did prevail among the Picts, even if it was restricted to royal succession and was not practised by the general population, it would make them unique in a European context. This topic is one of the most controversial aspects of their society and warrants a detailed examination. It requires a digression from the unfolding sequence of historical events to consider the so-called 'matrilineal hypothesis' of the Picts.

The earliest information on Pictish royal succession comes from Bede, in his introductory remarks about the peoples of Britain. Of the Picts, he says that they originated in Scythia and from there sailed westward to the British Isles. Arriving first in Ireland, they were turned away by the Irish, who directed them to settle across the sea in Britain. Bede describes how the Irish, on seeing that the Picts had no wives, gave them a number of women but only on the condition that 'in all cases of doubt, they should elect their kings from the female royal line rather than the male; and it is well known that the custom has been observed among the Picts to this day'. What Bede is here describing, albeit in the form of a legend, is a custom of matrilineal succession which was apparently still current in Pictavia during his own lifetime in the early eighth century. The Pictish king-list is in fact consistent with such a custom: no king is succeeded by his father until the dynastic upheavals of the ninth century, when the kingship began to enter a period of profound change.

All the kings in the list were identified as sons of fathers, with only one possible instance of a mother's name replacing that of the father. At this point it is important to recognise that matriliny carries no implication of matriarchy. There is no evidence for Pictish women holding greater political power than their counterparts among the Irish, Britons, Scots or English. Nor should matriliny necessarily accord them a special importance in contemporary annals, chronicles or other literature. Early Historic society was thoroughly patriarchal and rarely mentioned women in its records. Furthermore, even high-status females are sometimes insignificant in the histories and genealogies of matrilineal societies, regardless of their important roles as mothers or sisters of kings. This is a normal characteristic and has been observed by anthropologists in studies of Africa and other parts of the developing world. The name of a dynastically important female, even if she is the revered ancestress of the tribe, is frequently forgotten in the oral tradition of a matrilineal people. It is therefore unsurprising that the Irish annals name only two or three women whom we can tentatively identify as Picts.

A quarter of the rulers in the Pictish king-list were succeeded by a brother, this being a normal feature of matrilineal systems, because a man's brother is his mother's son and therefore a scion of the female dynastic line. Brothers are identifiable in the list when two or more kings are given a common patronymic (a son's name followed by the father's name), a prime example being three sons of a man called Gwid, all of whom ruled consecutively in the early seventh century. Other close kin, such as cousins who shared a common grandmother, possibly appear in the king-list, but this type of familial relationship is not easy to identify. If the matrilineal system was indeed the guiding principle in Pictish royal succession, many kings would have been succeeded by their sister's sons but, as with cousins, such relationships are invisible because the names of women are excluded from the list.

Most kings in the list bore typically Pictish names drawn from a curiously limited pool. Thus, there are numerous Brudes, Drusts, Talorcs, Nechtans and Gartnaits, but these names were clearly not restricted to one family. They appear to have been used by a number of designated kindreds whose representatives were eligible for the overall kingship of Pictavia. Another popular name, Talorcan, seems to be a diminutive with the meaning 'Young Talorc' and should be regarded as interchangeable with the name Talorc. The very small pool of names, while showing remarkable consistency over several centuries, contrasts sharply with the many and varied names of the kings' fathers. This suggests that baby boys earmarked as potential overkings of Pictavia were given a suitable 'kingly' name from the small selection available. Their mothers belonged to what must have been a powerful group of royal families whose male offspring competed for power in some kind of formal king-making system. How this system worked in practice is unknown, but it allowed not only full-blooded Picts but also the sons of non-Pictish fathers to acquire kingship. These half-Picts, having been born of foreign fathers and Pictish mothers and having been given 'kingly' names, were eligible under the rules of matriliny to be anointed as kings of Pictavia.

Some historians have suggested that men whose blood was only half-Pictish were accepted as royal claimants through a policy of exogamous marriage – marriage outside the kindred – by which husbands for Pictish princesses were found not only outside the province or sub-kingdom but frequently also in foreign lands. Exogamy was probably the norm within Pictavia, and marriage alliances between Pictish royal families – or between minor provincial dynasties – were no doubt common, but only two figures in the king-list can be securely identified as sons of foreign fathers. The fathers in question were Eanfrith, son of Aethelfrith of Bernicia, and Beli, king of the Clyde Britons. During his period of exile among the Picts, Eanfrith fathered a son called Talorcan who ruled Pictavia in the middle of the seventh century. There is no similar record of Beli being exiled from his homeland, but this is due primarily to a general lack of information on the kingdom of Alt Clut. Beli's son Brude ruled the Picts in the latter part of the century and is one of the most renowned figures in the history of Early Historic Scotland, as the next chapter will show. Two possibly non-Pictish fathers in the king-list were Domnall Brecc of Dalriada, who died in 643, and Maelgwn of Gwynedd. Maelgwn has already been mentioned, for he is usually identified as the Maelchon of the king-list whose pagan son Brude met Saint Columba in 565. Domnall Brecc was the grandson of Columba's royal patron Áedán mac Gabráin and is tentatively equated with Donuel, whom the list names as the father of a Pictish king called Gartnait. *Donuel* looks like a Pictish variant of Gaelic *Domnall* which, in turn, appears among the Britons as *Dyfnwal* and corresponds to the modern name Donald. Gartnait's reign spanned the years between Talorcan, son of Eanfrith, and Brude, son of Beli and fits the expected chronology for a son of Domnall Brecc, but this is as far as the data can be pressed. The Donuel of the king-list could feasibly have been a Scot, a Pict, a Briton or an Irishman: his name in the various forms given above was common in many parts of the British Isles at this time.

Royal princes who sprang from non-Pictish fathers were almost certainly raised among the Picts. The youngsters were probably kept close to their mother's kin, to be nurtured as candidates for the overkingship of Pictavia. Nothing in the historical sources indicates that these princes sought political advancement in their fathers' foreign kingdoms, nor is there any indication of a parallel movement of non-Pictish princesses being acquired as wives for Pictish men. It may have been a pre-condition of an inter-dynastic 'marriage' that a non-Pictish father took no part in the child's development and that he surrendered responsibility for such matters to the woman's family. These princes, then, regarded themselves as Picts and most likely spent their formative years in an entirely Pictish setting. It is worthy of note that the non-Pictish fathers, who were undoubtedly men of royal status in their own lands, were apparently willing to participate in such an arrangement. More remarkable still, in a wider sense, is that the neighbours of the Picts found this unusual succession system acceptable and were happy to contribute to it (in a biological sense). It seems likely that the foreign fathers-in-law – as kings themselves – gained from the arrangement in some meaningful way. If the 'marriage' was a permanent union formalised by customary ritual, rather than merely being a temporary liaison for purely reproductive purposes, a foreign king might expect economic or political benefits in exchange for his son becoming breeding-stock for future Pictish royalty. On the other hand, some coercion by the Pictish side may have been employed, especially if the foreign king and his son were already tributary to the Picts and thus – to a certain extent – subservient to their whims in matters of inter-dynastic policy.

What, then, were the advantages of a matrilineal system? Why was it apparently practised by the Picts but not by the other peoples of Britain? The answer lies in the nature of overkingship when more than one royal family is eligible to claim it. An overking of Pictavia was the acknowledged ruler of a group of provinces or sub-kingdoms, each of which had its own royal kindreds. The princes of these kindreds were eligible for the overkingship, but only one among them could be selected as the best candidate. Inter-marriage between royal families, together with marriages involving Pictish princesses and non-Pictish men, created a varied pool of candidates. The process of selecting an overking would therefore benefit by using a matrilineal system, for the heir would be selected by quality rather than merely by birth. Thus, a weak son of a strong king could not succeed his father. Instead, the brothers and nephews of the king – his mother's sons and his sister's sons – would become eligible to succeed him, the best among them being selected. The absence of father-to-son inheritance prevented overall power being monopolised by one dominant bloodline, for inter-marriage would ensure a rotation of power. Each family needed to maintain its stake in the succession process by constantly arranging strategic marriages between its own princesses and the princes of other families. However, outside the network of royal kindreds the normal inheritance system may have been patrilineal. In other words, inheritance of property and status in Pictavia as a whole was probably through a system of father-to-son succession and only the overking, the paramount ruler of the Picts, was succeeded by his brother or by his sister's son.

Some historians oppose the idea that Pictish royal succession was matrilineal. They usually focus on Bede's assertion that succession through the female line occurred 'in all cases of doubt', a phrase which could be taken to mean that matriliny was the exception rather than the norm. Opponents of the matrilineal hypothesis argue that these 'cases of doubt' were unusual circumstances in which a prince's eligibility for the overkingship had to be proved by reference to the female line. If this was the case, the normal succession system was not matrilineal but patrilineal. Such an argument is difficult to sustain, chiefly because the king-list – the primary source of information on Pictish royal succession – conforms to what anthropologists expect to find in a matrilineal society. The strong case for matriliny therefore remains intact and continues to provide the simplest explanation of the data.

Ciniod, Edwin and the Sons of Aethelfrith

The trail of Pictish history now resumes in the early seventh century, around the year 620. Ciniod, the successor of Nechtan, ruled as overking of Pictavia from then until the early 630s. His reign witnessed a number of important events which were to have major repercussions for his people. The first of these was the continuing exile of Eanfrith, eldest son of Aethelfrith of Bernicia. At some point, perhaps quite early in Ciniod's reign, Eanfrith married a Pictish princess who bore the future king Talorcan. This child's formative years, and his grooming for kingship, were spent in Pictavia during Ciniod's reign. Both Eanfrith and his son received Christian baptism from priests of the Pictish Church, whose personnel lay under the authority of Iona, and both were under the protection of the Pictish overking.

Eanfrith remained in exile for many years, staying away from his homeland while Edwin ruled both Deira and Bernicia as a unified realm. Aethelfrith's other sons spent their exile among the Scots of Dalriada where they, too, were baptised by priests of the Columban Church. Their baptisms took place on Iona and therefore placed them under the spiritual influence of its abbot. There is no record of hostility between Picts and Scots at this time nor, indeed, is either nation recorded as warring against Edwin. Some degree of amicable relations may have existed between the respective overkings of East and West, these being Ciniod of the Picts and Eochaid Buide of Cenél nGabráin. Both kings were members of the Columban Church and both looked ultimately to Iona for religious guidance and, more importantly, for ecclesiastical assistance in political affairs. They thus shared a bond which may have been strong enough to defuse tensions along their shared frontier in the Highlands. This is merely a theory, but it offers a plausible context to explain why Ciniod and Eochaid simultaneously fostered the exiled sons of an English king.

Several entries in the annals show the Scots becoming entangled in Irish wars during Eochaid's reign. These conflicts lie outside the scope of this book, but they helped to divert the predatory intentions and military resources of Dalriada away from Pictavia. The Picts, meanwhile, seem to have enjoyed a relatively peaceful and stable period during the 620s. Their neighbours in the West were preoccupied with Ireland while, in the South, Edwin warred primarily in Wales and the English midlands. It is curious that he chose not to pursue Aethelfrith's sons, his surviving Bernician rivals, into their lands of exile. Perhaps he considered them a more remote threat than the Welsh, Mercian and West Saxon enemies with whom he fought vigorously? Or, maybe, the combined power of Eochaid and Ciniod was too formidable, especially if some kind of military accord existed between them?

Two changes affecting the pattern of power in the North occurred at the end of Ciniod's reign, the first being the accession in 631 of the aforementioned Domnall Brecc ('Freckled Donald') to the kingship of Cenél nGabráin. At that time, the claim of Domnall's family upon the Dalriadan overkingship was being contested by Cenél Comgaill, a rival kindred based in Cowal who shared a common ancestry with the house of Gabran. Domnall's father Eochaid Buide had probably been ousted from the overkingship by a Cowal king called Connad Cerr. After 631 Domnall himself may have faced similar rivalry from Connad's son Ferchar. The second key event at the close of Ciniod's reign came in 633, probably the year of his death. In that year, at a battle on the border of Mercia and Deira, Edwin was defeated and killed. The victor was Cadwallon, king of the Britons of North Wales. Edwin's demise paved the way for Aethelfrith's sons to return from exile and regain their inheritance. As the eldest son and the rightful monarch of

Bernicia, Eanfrith promptly left Pictavia to claim his birthright. He duly became king, but his reign was brief and brought catastrophe upon his people. Renouncing the Christianity received in exile, he returned to the pagan religion of his forefathers, an act of apostasy bitterly condemned by Bede in the following century. Eanfrith's rejection of the baptism conferred on him by the Columban Church had implications beyond his personal choice of religion. It was a political act to symbolise his rejection of the Pictish patrons upon whose hospitality he had relied for so long. His motives for doing this are unclear, but he presumably nurtured some grievance against the Picts and wanted to end his relationship with them. This effectively sundered him from his son, Talorcan, who remained in Pictavia with his mother and her people.

At the same time, a cousin of Edwin who claimed the kingship of Deira was slain in battle with Cadwallon. In the wake of his victory the Welsh king unleashed a terrible fury on the northern English, ravaging Bernicia and Deira for a whole year and slaughtering the population in droves. The hapless and desperate Eanfrith attempted to negotiate a peace, but his embassy to Cadwallon ended in tragedy when he and his companions were assassinated. Northumbria now teetered on the brink of disaster: the kings of her two constituent kingdoms lay dead and her people cowered in the face of a huge army of rampaging Britons. The Picts probably wondered which way the tide of fate would turn, but they were not in a position to intervene. Any advantages they may have hoped to gain south of the Forth were already gone: Eanfrith's apostasy had severed his bond with Pictavia while Bernicia, his own kingdom, now lay leaderless at the mercy of fierce foes. The Picts themselves may have wondered if they, too, would soon face the ravaging sword of Cadwallon.

All this changed in the following year, 634, when Aethelfrith's younger sons returned from exile to reclaim their heritage. They were led by Oswald, next in line after Eanfrith, who proclaimed himself king of Bernicia. The princes' return was undertaken with the permission of Domnall Brecc, king of Cenél nGabráin, who may have sent a military force to assist them in dislodging

Cadwallon. The Welsh king was brought to battle near Hexham in the shadow of Hadrian's Wall. There his warbands were decisively defeated and he himself fled the battlefield. The final drama was played out on the banks of a nearby stream, where Cadwallon made a last fateful stand before being cut down by English swords. Bernicia was thus restored to Aethelfrith's family in the person of Oswald, a Christian king whose religious affiliations lay not with the archbishops of Canterbury but with the abbots of the Celtic North.

It was not long before Oswald summoned monks from Iona to convert his heathen people. The island of Lindisfarne off the Northumbrian coast was given to the missionaries as a base. Behind the spiritual moves lay a political agenda involving the Bernician dynasty and its Cenél nGabráin allies. Neither Oswald's departure from Kintyre to fight Cadwallon nor his request for Columban monks would have been possible without the blessing of Domnall Brecc. Indeed, with Oswald firmly installed in Bernicia, the descendants of Gabran now had a useful friend on the south-east flank of their territory. The Picts, too, may have felt relieved that Bernicia was now ruled by a king who shared their adherence to Celtic Christianity and whose elder sibling – despite his treacherous actions – had fathered their own royal prince Talorcan. There is no evidence that Oswald subsequently reversed his friendly stance towards the Scots and Picts. Bede asserts that he eventually held all the northern peoples under his dominion, but this is hard to believe and is probably no more than a slice of retrospective wishful thinking. Elsewhere in the *Ecclesiastical History*, Bede contradicts this exaggerated vision of Oswald's hegemony by stating that his authority was no greater than that of Edwin, whose power is unlikely to have reached into Pictavia or Argyll. The extent of English dominance in the North is in fact unknown before the reign of Oswiu, the successor and younger brother of Oswald. Bede himself states that Oswiu was the first English king to attain a truly extensive overlordship. Neither the *Ecclesiastical History* nor the Irish annals record military campaigns by Oswald against the Scots or Picts. Given the previous goodwill shown by both peoples to

Aethelfrith's sons during their long exile, this is hardly surprising.

However, one campaign by Oswald had profound implications for the Picts. This was the English conquest of the Britons of Lothian whose kingdom, Gododdin, was ruled from Edinburgh Castle Rock. The key event in the campaign was noted in the Irish annals under the year 640 as *obsessio Etin*, 'the siege of Etin'. The annalists give no further details, but the reference is almost certainly to a Bernician attack on Edinburgh which, at that time, was called by the Britons *Din Eidyn*, 'The Fort of Eidyn', a name for which *Etin* is an expected genitive form in Old Irish usage. The history of Gododdin is unclear, but it certainly fell under the sway of Bernicia before the middle of the seventh century and thereafter ceased to exist as a political entity. The siege of Eidyn in 640 marked a crucial moment in Northumbria's expansion and can be credited with some confidence to Oswald. Few folk in Pictavia and Dalriada would have mourned the demise of the Gododdin kings who, like their fellow-Britons on the Clyde, had a long tradition of hostility to Picts and Scots. In Late Roman times the Votadini – the forefathers of Gododdin – had functioned as a buffer state between Roman Britain and Pictavia in the frontier districts near the Antonine Wall. Old memories of ancient border strife were unlikely to have faded in northern folklore, and many Picts no doubt rejoiced at the news of Gododdin's collapse. Others may have felt less reassured by the arrival of English warbands on the shorelands of the Firth of Forth.

During Oswald's relatively short reign the Picts were ruled by three successive overkings, each of them a son of a certain Gwid (a name sometimes written as Wid, Guid or Foith). These kings were Gartnait, Brude and Talorc, but little is known about them except the dates of their deaths. Brude, who died in 641 or 642, was ruling Pictavia in 640 when Domnall Brecc led a Dalriadan army against unknown foes at a place known to the Irish annalists as *Glend Mairison* (or *Mureson*). This battle occurred in the same year as the siege of *Etin* and may have taken place at Glen Moriston to the west of Loch Ness, not far from the border between Picts and Scots. The identification of *Mairison* or *Mureson* with Moriston is not certain, but the 'glen' prefix suggests a location in the Highlands and the battle marked the end of a long period of peaceful relations between Scots and Picts. Domnall was a very belligerent warlord and it should come as no surprise to find him behaving aggressively towards his eastern neighbours. Despite fighting many battles in Ireland and Argyll, his military record was singularly unimpressive and was not improved at *Glend Mairison*, where he suffered another defeat. If his adversaries were Picts, the victor was possibly Brude, son of Gwid.

Oswiu and Talorcan

Oswald's main enemy lay in the south, in Mercia, where an expanding English kingdom lay under the rule of a mighty warlord called Penda. It was Penda who had helped Cadwallon against Edwin, and it was he who now challenged Oswald for the overlordship of southern and midland Britain. In August 642, at either Oswestry in Shropshire or some other site in the English midlands, Oswald was defeated in a great battle with the Mercian king and his numerous allies, most of whom were Britons from Wales. Oswald was slain and, in an act of terrible savagery, his corpse was ritually dismembered and displayed on stakes. His overkingship of Northumbria died with him, and the kingdom again split into its two constituent parts. Oswald's younger brother, Oswiu, became king of Bernicia but was in no position to extend his rule. At the same time, the dynasty of Deira reasserted itself in the person of Oswine, the son of a cousin of Edwin. Both kings had little choice but to fall under the sway of Penda who, after his victory over Oswald, became the most powerful ruler in Britain. In December of the following year, in the valley of the River Carron near Falkirk, Domnall Brecc died in battle against the Britons of Alt Clut. The Britons were led by their king, Owain son of Beli, whose defeat of the Scots made him the strongest ruler in the North and a potential rival to Penda. The political relationship between Owain and Penda is not known, nor is there any record of them challenging each other in battle, but the Mercian king still had unfinished business with his Northumbrian neighbours.

The *Historia Brittonum* adds that the riches yielded up by Oswiu were distributed by Penda among the kings of the Britons, who were either Welshmen or northerners or a mixture of both. Iudeu is usually identified as the ancient fortress at Stirling known to Bede as *Urbs Giudi*. Many historians see Giudi and Iudeu as variants of the same name, a Brittonic place-name supplanted in later centuries by *Strivelin*, a name of uncertain origin from which the modern form *Stirling* evolved. In the Early Historic period this stronghold commanded an imposing position befitting the abode of a ruler of high or royal status. The immediate area under the citadel's control was the region of Manau, the likely homeland of the Maeatae. One plausible context for the tradition preserved in the *Historia Brittonum* sees the Maeatae – who can be identified as Britons – as allies of Penda in his campaigns against Northumbria. Their fortress of Giudi was perhaps utilised by the Mercian king as a suitable venue for his dealings with Oswiu. Another possible context envisages Oswiu wielding authority in Stirlingshire, having wrested it by force from the Clyde Britons whose victory on the Carron in 643 had made them overlords of the area. Did Oswiu flee northward to Giudi and there pay homage to Penda? A more radical theory casts doubt on the identification of Iudeu as Stirling-Giudi and looks instead to a geographical context much further south, perhaps at a site in Deira or Mercia. Wherever it occurred, we can be sure that Oswiu's tribute-payment marked a low point in his career. Bede gives a different version of the sequence of events, telling us that the payment was scornfully rejected by Penda, but here we may cautiously accept the *Historia Brittonum* as a more accurate record.

Although the Picts evidently played no part in all of this, they cannot have been unaffected by the presence of a powerful Mercian king bringing a huge army close to their southern border. Despite their earlier fostering of Eanfrith, they had no obligation to give military aid to his brother Oswiu and may simply have acknowl-edged Penda as the supreme overlord of Britain. As far as is known, Oswiu had little contact with Pictavia and was in no position to seek

Pictish aid in his war of survival. His nephew, Talorcan, was in every significant sense a Pict and may have felt little or no affinity with his English uncle. In any case, he had not yet attained the kingship, which was held at that time by Talorc, son of Gwid, whom Talorcan succeeded in 653. Since the name Talorcan seems to mean 'Little Talorc', there is a strong possibility that these two kings were closely related by blood. Perhaps Talorcan's mother and Talorc were brother and sister, with the sister's son succeeding his uncle to the kingship? This scenario fits well with the theory of matrilineal succession, in which royal power was regularly inherited by the son of the king's sister. The absence of any record of hostile relations between Pictavia and Mercia at this time further suggests that Talorc son of Gwid wisely chose a policy of non-interference in Penda's northern affairs. Had he chosen to join the Britons as Penda's military ally, the twin kingdoms of Northumbria would almost certainly have been crushed and their royal dynasties exiled or extinguished.

Talorcan's accession in 653 placed a half-English king over the Picts, but this was not necessarily advantageous for Oswiu. Some historians regard Talorcan as a puppet imposed on Pictavia by his Bernician uncle, but this seems inconsistent with the evidence. Oswiu was an ambitious king who hoped to regain the paramount status formerly enjoyed by Oswald and Aethelfrith but, in 653, his capacity for intervention in the North or anywhere else was hindered by the continuing menace of Penda. Oswiu mustered an army for a power struggle with Oswine, the king of neighbouring Deira, but his primary concern was the dark shadow cast by the Mercian ruler. It is therefore difficult to imagine him diverting military forces away from his southern frontier to foist a puppet-king on the Picts. If Talorcan had ruled as a Bernician stooge, his uncle would surely have defused the hostility between Picts and Scots which culminated in a battle at Strathyre in 654. During his childhood exile Oswiu had been baptised on Iona, and his family had maintained peaceful relations with Cenél nGabráin for many years thereafter. If he had really held any political influence over Talorcan, the conflict at Strathyre, which saw the death of a Cenél nGabráin prince, should never have happened. The fact that the battle did occur points to a cool or neutral relationship between nephew and uncle. The two men may even have been openly hostile to one another.

The political situation shifted again in 655, when Oswiu finally defeated Penda at a great battle near Leeds. The Mercian king perished, leaving his Bernician conqueror in an unassailable position as master of Deira and overking of all Northumbria. In the immediate aftermath of the battle, Oswiu also held Mercia under his sway, at least until Penda's sons were strong enough to regain power. Bede states that Oswiu 'subjected the greater part of the Pictish race to the dominion of the English' but does not say when or how this was accomplished. In 657 Talorcan died, but it is not known if this happened before or after Oswiu's subjection of the Picts. It is clear from Bede's words that some parts of Pictavia did not fall under the English king's sway, but the 'greater part' should mean Perthshire and other southern regions. This would place a large portion of the Pictish heartlands in Oswiu's dominion, but here Bede's rhetoric may be stretching the truth. He had a tendency to make grand statements about the extent of Northumbrian royal authority at the expense of historical accuracy. Thus, by depicting Oswiu as a mighty conqueror, Bede was reminding his audience of the earthly rewards that come to good Christian kings. His report of Oswiu's subjection of large tracts of Pictish territory might therefore be an exaggeration. In reality, the English overlordship probably did not reach as far as the River Tay, although some portion of Pictavia did fall under Oswiu's direct control. The territorial gains, made presumably after a war against Talorcan or one of his successors, were sufficiently secure to allow the establishment of a Bernician bishopric at Abercorn on the southern shore of the Firth of Forth. Abercorn was an English foundation with ecclesiastical authority over the Picts and it was not founded until 681, eleven years after Oswiu's death, but its location suggests that the conquests were limited to Fife and did not encompass large parts of Perthshire. If this was the case, then the River Earn perhaps marked the northern limit of Oswiu's territorial gains, but his martial reputation ensured that other parts of Pictavia acknowledged him as overlord. In practical terms this probably meant that Talorcan and his successors were obliged to send regular tribute-payments southward.

Among the casualties of English expansion north of Lothian were the Maeatae, the Britons of Manau. Their lands had bordered Pictish territory since Roman times, but the Early Historic period brought them into conflict with the Scots of Dalriada and, after the collapse of Gododdin, with the Northumbrian English. Sandwiched between three powerful nations and nestling in a volatile frontier region, the native rulers of Manau were unlikely to survive. Their great citadel of Giudi, which may have been used by Penda as the venue for his humiliation of Oswiu, would not have been left unconquered when Oswiu's warbands came north after 655. Like their Gododdin neighbours, the Britons of Stirlingshire were effectively wiped off the seventh-century political map.

It was during this period of Northumbrian overlordship that an expedition to Pictavia was made by Cuthbert, a monk at Melrose in the Tweed Valley, who subsequently became bishop of Lindisfarne and Northumbria's patron saint. With a couple of companions he set off on a winter voyage by sea, intending to sail north to a part of Pictavia inhabited by a people called Niduari. During the journey a fierce storm forced the travellers ashore in a desolate coastal region where, while the weather continued to deteriorate, they began to run out of provisions. By way of a miracle and in answer to their prayers, they found dolphin meat and thus survived until the storm relented after three desperate days. The sources for this incident are a *vita* of Cuthbert written by an anonymous monk of Lindisfarne together with a later *vita* derived from it and written by Bede. Neither author stated the purpose of Cuthbert's visit to the Niduari Picts, nor did they say who this people were or where they lived. Given the likelihood that Oswiu's military campaigns conquered parts of Fife, the Niduari probably lived in the same region.

Talorcan's successor as paramount ruler in Pictavia was Gartnait, son of Donuel, who reigned from 657 to 663. This king's father may have been Domnall Brecc of Cenél nGabráin, as some historians have suggested. On the other hand, as previously noted, the name was fairly common among the Britons in the form *Dyfnwal* and so could have been borne by a royal prince of Alt Clut. Alternatively, and more simply, the name of Gartnait's father could have been a Pictish variant of *Domnall* or *Dyfnwal* and therefore not of 'foreign' origin at all. Gartnait was eventually succeeded by his brother, Drust, whose seven-year reign coincided with the zenith of Oswiu's ascendancy as overlord of Britain. Drust's army fought the battle of *Lutho-feirnn* in 664, in Fortriu. The battle-site defies identification, but it presumably lay north of Perthshire and beyond the range of Oswiu's overlordship. The Irish annalists thought it worthy of note, even if they chose not to describe its cause or outcome. Its likeliest context was an internal scuffle between Drust and a dynastic rival, one of whom may have fought with Oswiu's moral, if not material, support.

The Synod of Whitby

The year of the battle of *Lutho-feirnn* saw an event of huge religious significance whose repercussions were felt across every part of northern Britain. This was an assembly or synod, a gathering of prominent churchmen, convened by Oswiu at the Northumbrian monastery of Whitby. The synod's purpose was to debate differences between the 'Celtic' and 'Roman' clergy, which were now becoming acute. The Celtic tradition was by no means independent of Roman orthodoxy and its leading figures acknowledged the authority of the Pope. However, the clergy of the Celtic lands – namely Ireland and the northern and western parts of Britain – were marginalised by geography and therefore less receptive to ecclesiastical developments on the Continent. This made them seem conservative and insular, and unwilling to adopt new practices. Celtic monks, for instance, were tonsured not according to the 'Roman' method (a crown of hair encircling the shaved top of the scalp) but by shaving the front of the scalp from ear to ear. By far the most important difference, however, was the method used for calculating the date of Easter. Adherence by the Celtic clergy to an archaic form of calculation meant that Easter Sunday on Iona did not always coincide with Easter Sunday in Rome.

Matters came to a head in the seventh century, partly because both traditions were practised among the northern English. Bernicia, for example, had been evangelised by priests of the Celtic tradition invited from Iona by King Oswald. Lindisfarne and other important Bernician monasteries, such as Whitby, were essentially satellites of Iona and bastions of Celtic Christianity. They formed part of the *familia* of the Columban Church, whose influence stretched across much of northern Britain. By contrast, the southern English kingdoms had received Christian baptism via

Figure 4. Christian symbolism and mythical beasts on the Boar Stone of Gask. Reproduced from J.R. Allen and J. Anderson, *The Early Christian Monuments of Scotland* (1903).

missionaries sent directly from Rome in 597 under the leadership of Saint Augustine. After gaining a foothold in Kent, the mission had consolidated its presence when Augustine became the first archbishop of Canterbury. It was Canterbury's 'Roman' tradition that Edwin of Deira enthusiastically embraced after his marriage to a Kentish princess and into which his children were baptised. In this he differed from Oswiu of Bernicia, whose childhood baptism on Iona had made him a devotee of the Celtic Church. However, when Oswiu married Edwin's daughter in 643, the situation at the Northumbrian royal court became rather awkward around Eastertime. The king and queen often found themselves celebrating Christ's Resurrection on different Sundays, a situation so absurd that Oswiu eventually took steps to prevent it.

At the time of the synod the churches of Pictavia lay securely within the orbit of Iona and were answerable to its abbot. This was Columba's legacy in the East and stemmed directly from the seeds of Christian conversion planted by his journeys during the reign of Brude, Maelchon's son, in the late sixth century. The extent of Iona's influence among the Picts in the seventh century can be seen in the pattern of place-names and church dedications commemorating its principal figures, such as the men who followed Columba in the abbacy. These abbots were usually Irishmen of noble stock, like their founder, and often hailed from powerful families closely related to Columba's own kin. The exception was Fergna or Fergan, evidently a Briton, who held the abbacy of Iona from 605 to 623. In Pictavia his memory is preserved in the names of wells near Pitlochry and Tomintoul, where the Gaelic *Tobair Fheargáin* ('Fergan's Well') commemorates him at two ancient holy places where water deities were worshipped in pagan times. The well near Tomintoul lies on a hill called Cnoc Fergan and is near an old church at Kirkmichael. Close proximity of holy well and ancient church suggests the focus of an early cult devoted to this little-known saint. It is not known if Abbot Fergna ever ventured east of Druim Alban but, if he did not, the place-names could have been bestowed by Columban missionaries working among the Picts during the period of his abbacy. Fergna's sister was the mother of an

Ionan priest called Comman or Comanus, to whom the Perthshire church of Rossie was dedicated. A cross-slab dating from the eighth century unearthed in the graveyard points to Rossie having been a centre of Pictish Christianity. When the church was re-consecrated in 1243 by the Bishop of St Andrews, a new dedication was made in the names of Saint Laurence and Saint Comanus 'the confessor'. The cross-slab provides firm evidence of ecclesiastical activity at Rossie at a time when Iona still held sway over the Pictish churches, and it is tempting to envisage the place as an early cult centre where Comman, the nephew of Abbot Fergna, was venerated.

Iona's seventh abbot was Cumméne the White who wrote a *vita* of Columba that preceded Adomnán's but which has not survived. He is commemorated in several areas of Pictavia where names such as Kilchumin (from Gaelic *Cill Chuimein*, 'Cumméne's Church') near Fort Augustus and *Suidhe Chuimein* ('Cumméne's Seat') in Moray might mark districts in which his followers laboured. It was during Cumméne's abbacy that the Synod of Whitby convened to debate the future status of Iona in Northumbrian ecclesiastical affairs. The great gathering of churchmen included representatives from both traditions, Roman and Celtic, together with King Oswiu himself. The ensuing debate was a matter of enormous significance to everyone involved. Upon its outcome hung the question of whether Northumbria would stay loyal to Iona or transfer its ecclesiastical allegiance to the archbishop of Canterbury. The proceedings were chaired by Abbess Hild of Whitby, herself a prominent figure of the Columban Church in Northumbria. Colman, the Irish bishop of Lindisfarne, put forward the Celtic case but was vehemently opposed by Wilfrid, the English bishop of Ripon. In the person of Wilfrid, the cause of Roman orthodoxy had a lucid and forceful advocate against whom the Celtic side struggled to present their views. Bede, giving a report of the debate more than half a century later, depicted it as a slanging-match between Colman and Wilfrid, but this perhaps reflects his own deep antipathy towards the Celtic tradition. The synod finally ended with Oswiu placing his support firmly behind Rome, a decision which effectively ended Iona's association with Aethelfrith's dynasty. Soon after, Colman and many of the Lindisfarne brethren left Northumbria and returned disconsolately to Iona.

Little of this seems at first sight to be relevant to the Picts, but the long-term effects were profound. The most immediate change was an alteration of the ecclesiastical map of Britain, which now showed Iona's influence restricted to Dalriada and Pictavia without any foothold south of the Forth-Clyde line. The Clyde Britons still adhered to Celtic Christianity, but their bishops had never been under Iona's sway and had more in common with their compatriots in Wales and Cornwall, where native kings still resisted English encroachment. The outcome of the synod of 664 effectively sundered Oswiu's people from the Celtic Church which had brought them into the Christian fold. More significantly, it gave Roman orthodoxy a valuable northern base from where its bishops could plan their next move against Iona.

Skye

Sometime during the reign of the Pictish overking Drust, son of Donuel, the remaining Picts of the Western Isles became locked in a bitter struggle with Dalriadan foes. The precise circumstances are unclear but, according to a couple of entries in the Irish annals, hostilities broke out on Skye in the late 660s. In one entry, placed under the year 668, the annalists noted 'the voyage of the sons of Gartnait to Ireland, with the people of Skye'. The second entry relates to 670 and states simply that 'the people of Gartnait came from Ireland'. Neither entry says who Gartnait was or why his sons spent two years in Ireland, nor does any other source describe what was happening on Skye at this time. An earlier entry in the annals refers to a war in 649 between the descendants of Áedán mac Gabráin and a certain Gartnait, son of Accidan. If this Gartnait is the same man whose sons and 'people' journeyed to and from Ireland two decades later, he should be envisaged as a king or chieftain of Skye who contested lordship of the island with Áedán's descendants, and whose heirs later sought refuge among Irish allies.

ymbol stone at Abernethy.

Symbol stone at Abdie Old Kirk, Lindores, Fife.

Left. Symbol stone at Strathpeffer. This is known as the Eagle Stone because of the lower symbol which represents a bird.

Below. Dundurn in Strathearn, a major fortress of the Picts.

Above. Urquhart Castle, beside Loch Ness, on the site of a northern Pictish centre of power.

Right. Abernethy: the eleventh-century round tower on the site of an earlier Pictish monastery.

Left. Meigle: the present church stands on the site of the Pictish monastery of *Migdele.*

Below. Portmahomack, Easter Ross: St Colman's Church, where a monastery stood in Pictish times.

Restenneth Priory in Angus. This may be the site of an eighth-century Pictish church.

Neighbours of the Picts: Dumbarton, stronghold of the Strathclyde Britons.

Neighbours of the Picts: Stirling Castle Rock, site of Giudi, chief citadel of the Britons of Manau.

Abercorn on the southern shore of the Firth of Forth. Site of a Northumbrian bishopric with jurisdiction over conquered Pictish territory.

The famous battle scene on the reverse of the Aberlemno cross-slab. This is usually seen as a memorial to the Pictish victory over Northumbria in 685.

The Picts at war: warriors armed with swords, spears and shields.

The Picts at war: an armoured horseman confronts a foot-soldier.

The Picts at war: a horseman flees from battle.

The Picts in peacetime: cattle, a symbol of wealth and status.

Reverse of a Pictish cross-slab at Dunfallandy, Perthshire.

Dunblane Cathedral: a cross-slab from the late Pictish period.

Conserving the Pictish past: a replica of the Dunnichen stone. The original is in Dundee Museum.

Conserving the Pictish past: a replica of the cross-slab at Fowlis Wester, Perthshire. The original is in the nearby church.

Logierait, Perthshire: a broken Pictish cross-slab in the graveyard of the old church.

The Priest's Stone, near Pitlochry, Perthshire: the shape of a cross can still be seen on this weathered stone.

All photographs were taken by Barbara Keeling.

Gartnait is usually identified as the father of Cano, an obscure figure who features as the hero of an old Irish story called the *Tale of Cano Son of Gartnan*. This survives in a single manuscript and appears to be a composition of the ninth century. It is not a historical document but a fictional romance whose main action concerns a 'love triangle' involving a young prince of Skye called Cano, an Irish girl called Cred and her older husband. The tale shows Cano and his father as members of a high-status Skye family oppressed by Áedán mac Gabráin, who here takes the role of Gartnait's father and eventual slayer. After Gartnait's death Cano flees to Ireland, where he meets and falls in love with Cred. In making Gartnait a son of Áedán the tale gave him a Dalriadan origin, but his name suggests Pictish ancestry. Perhaps he was a man of mixed blood, descended from Picts and Scots, who defied an attempt by Áedán's heirs to impose Cenél nGabráin authority over Argyll and the Isles? Cano, too, bore a name of non-Gaelic origin which seems to be the Pictish equivalent of a Brittonic word *ceneu*, meaning 'whelp', perhaps here with the specific connotation 'wolf cub'.

The chronology of the *Tale of Cano* is awry in its portrayal of Áedán as an enemy of the principal hero. In the Irish annals, which are far more trustworthy than the tale, the activities of Cano and Gartnait occurred long after Áedán's death in 608. One entry refers to the capture of Conamail, son of Cano, in 673, while another notes the slaying of Cano himself in 687. In 690 the annalists mention the death of Coblaith, Cano's daughter. The final entry in this series refers to the killing of Conamail in 705. Reconciling all this data with the *Tale* is a fruitless exercise, chiefly because the story of Cano and Cred is widely acknowledged as a late work of heroic saga and romance. The most that can be said in the present context is that the *Tale* contains a small kernel of truth wrapped in layers of legend. Its hero was evidently a real figure of seventh-century history whose career was summarised by the annalists. From the latter it can be deduced that Cano, son of Gartnait, was a local ruler on Skye who journeyed to Ireland in 668 before returning home after a couple of years to eventually die in 687. Behind these bare facts lay a fierce conflict which culminated in Cenél nGabráin contesting lordship on Skye with a dynasty of Pictish or Picto-Scottish rulers. If the annals are broadly accurate in their depiction of the principal events in this conflict, the struggle for the Isle of Mist was a protracted war spanning half a century.

The Pictish Revolt

At the same time, away in the East, Drust was still reigning over the Picts when Oswiu died in February 670. It is a stark comment on the perils of kingship in those days that Oswiu was the only seventh-century Northumbrian monarch to die peacefully rather than in battle. His son Ecgfrith, by then a young man in his mid-twenties, became not only king of Bernicia but also laid claim to the wider hegemony established by Oswald and Oswiu. This included large tracts of territory west of the Pennines that had formerly lain under the rule of native British kings. Northumbria had conquered these kings and extinguished their power, not by reducing them to tributary status but by expelling them from their lands. When Ecgfrith succeeded Oswiu the area under his direct authority extended as far west as the Solway Firth and south-west to the River Ribble. The Britons who inhabited these lands in what is now Cumbria and Lancashire acknowledged Ecgfrith's overlordship at his accession in 670: there is no record of a revolt by whatever remained of the native aristocracy. The situation further north, however, was rather different. Oswiu's supremacy over his neighbours in Pictavia, Dalriada and on the Clyde had been sustained by a proven military record and by his reputation as the greatest king of his time, but these were personal traits that died with him and did not automatically pass to his heir. Ecgfrith therefore ascended the throne as a novice who had to prove himself as a man of strength and ruthless ambition. Failure would swiftly bring the loss of the 'empire' created by his father and might allow a Pict, Scot or Briton to claim overlordship in the North. It was only a matter of time before the new king's mettle was put to the test. Within a year or two of Oswiu's death the conquered portion of Pictavia under direct English rule rose in rebellion, probably at the instigation of Drust the Pictish overking.

Ecgfrith had no intention of meekly relinquishing his father's Pictish gains, and he responded with a military strike against the rebels. The ensuing campaign was reported by Stephen of Ripon, an English monk who wrote a *vita* of Bishop Wilfrid in the early years of the eighth century. Stephen called the enemy 'bestial Pictish populations' whose unnamed leader 'gathered together innumerable nations from every nook and corner in the North'. This leader, possibly identifiable as King Drust, hoped to free the conquered Pictish districts from English rule or, as Stephen puts it, to liberate them from 'the yoke of servitude'. Hastening north, Ecgfrith led an army of mounted warriors in a rapid advance which soon brought him face-to-face with the rebels. The clash of arms resulted in a significant English victory. According to Stephen, Ecgfrith's soldiers killed 'an immense number of people, filling two rivers with the corpses of the slain, so that – marvellous to relate – the slayers, passing over the rivers dry-foot, pursued and slew a crowd of fugitives'. The two rivers were probably the Earn and the Tay, both of which follow a parallel eastward course before emptying into the sea near Perth, a place not far from the Pictish monastery at Abernethy. The victory confirmed Ecgfrith's hold on his father's gains and ensured that the southern Pictish elites continued to make tribute-payments to Northumbria.

More than one modern historian has suggested that Drust might not have been Ecgfrith's foe but merely a vassal or puppet installed in Pictland by Oswiu. A similar status has been envisaged for Talorcan, but there is no hint in the sources that either of these kings owed their power to an English overlord. Around the time of Ecgfrith's victory, or not long afterwards, Drust was expelled from his kingdom by unidentified opponents for reasons unknown. The Irish annals noted the event at 672, in the early years of Ecgfrith's reign. Further speculation by historians includes a theory that Drust was ousted by internal rivals who deemed him unworthy of kingship after Ecgfrith's victory. Those who regard Drust as a

Northumbrian vassal place his expulsion before the battle and suggest that Ecgfrith's expedition was launched in revenge for the deed. The precise circumstances will never be known. Among the few certainties is that Drust was eventually succeeded by Brude, son of Beli, a man soon to become the most famous Pictish king of the seventh century.

CHAPTER 7
Brude and Ecgfrith

The final quarter of the seventh century opened with a unified Northumbria in a dominant position as the most powerful kingdom in Britain. In the person of Ecgfrith, Oswiu's son, it possessed an energetic warlord determined to build on the conquests of his predecessors. Much of Ecgfrith's authority was inherited from his father Oswiu who, after defeating Penda, had subjugated not only the Mercians in the South but also the Picts and Britons in the North. The Scots, too, were in some kind of tributary relationship with Oswiu. This wide area of authority remained intact when Ecgfrith succeeded to the kingship, because his father's vassal rulers did not yet consider the moment to be ripe for a challenge.

Brude, Beli's son, was one of the kings who paid tribute to Ecgfrith. This burden involved regular offerings of livestock, agricultural produce and other material resources, together with an obligation to provide hospitality to the foreign overlord's tribute-collectors. It was an unequal relationship and could be demeaning for the lesser partner, but it had to be endured until an opportunity arose to change it. Such opportunities usually came when something happened to disrupt the *status quo* by shaking an overlord's grip on his hegemony. For Brude and other northern kings the key moment arrived in 679, in the English midlands, when Ecgfrith fought a great battle with the Mercians near the River Trent. The result was not decisive in a military sense, for it left both sides itching to resume hostilities, but Ecgfrith ultimately emerged as the loser after the Church intervened to defuse the growing tension. His foe in the battle was Aethelred, a younger son of Penda, whose main objective was to wrest back the Mercian province of Lindsey from Northumbrian control. This objective was duly achieved via the terms of a peace accord negotiated by Archbishop Theodore of Canterbury. The treaty left Ecgfrith's hegemony diminished, his domain reduced and his political ambitions in the South effectively curtailed. His grip on the outer fringe of his domain was shown to be breakable. In the borderlands around the Forth-Clyde isthmus, the vassal-kings of the Celtic North began to stir against him.

It was inevitable that the main challenge would come from the Picts, whose recent revolt Ecgfrith had crushed in 672. Having recovered from defeat, they again posed a dangerous and volatile threat to his authority. Under the strong leadership of Brude, Beli's son, they were once again a formidable people. By 679 their elites were longing to take up the sword, regain their lost territories and reassert their independence. Throwing off the burden of paying tribute to Northumbria soon became a priority for Brude, leading him to seek a decisive showdown with Ecgfrith.

The growing antagonism between the two kings incorporated an ecclesiastical dimension whose architect was Theodore of Canterbury. At the beginning of the 680s, the archbishop turned his attention to re-drawing the diocesan map of England, a process that had already seen the removal of Wilfrid as bishop of Northumbria in 678. Wilfrid's huge diocese had been divided by Theodore into the separate bishoprics of Bernicia – with its seat on Lindisfarne – and Deira, with its episcopal headquarters at York. In 681 the archbishop broke the Bernician see into three parts by establishing additional bishoprics at Abercorn and Hexham. Abercorn lay on the southern shore of the Firth of Forth, but the primary responsibility of its first bishop, a Northumbrian called Trumwine, was not the spiritual care of English settlers in Lothian. Instead, Trumwine's designated flock were the conquered Picts of Fife, still languishing under Ecgfrith's direct rule. These communities must have watched the arrival of the new bishop with suspicion, regarding him as a symbol of English domination. On a political level, the church at Abercorn not only gave Ecgfrith's subjection of the Picts an aura of permanence but also implied that it was sanctioned by God. Furthermore, the close proximity of a bishop of the 'Roman' tradition represented a thinly veiled challenge by Theodore of Canterbury to the 'Celtic' churches north of the Tay whose clergy still answered to Iona. The Columban priests who served the spiritual needs of Brude and his people undoubtedly felt threatened by the arrival of Trumwine on their doorstep.

It was at this time that Brude began to flex his military muscle in outlying areas of his kingdom, for the annals mention a siege of Dunnottar in 681, the same year as the establishment of Abercorn. Dunnottar was a coastal promontory fort near the modern town of Stonehaven, a few miles south of Aberdeen. The ruined medieval castle now occupying the site succeeded an earlier stronghold known as *Dun Foither*. In the late seventh century this was probably the residence of a wavering local lord who needed to be firmly reminded of his obligations to Brude, or it may simply have been the base of a dynastic rival who claimed the Pictish overkingship. Brude evidently won the encounter, for in the following year he launched a destructive campaign against Orkney. Like his namesake of a hundred years earlier who, in the presence of Saint Columba, had issued commands to an Orcadian sub-king, Brude regarded these isles as part of his hegemony. He demanded homage from the Orcadians and imposed his will upon them by force of arms. A year later he besieged another outpost of rebels or rivals, the target of his wrath being the hillfort of Dundurn. The strategic position of this place, in the upper valley of the River Earn on a major route from Argyll, made its subjugation essential. It was an imposing fortress whose seventh-century residents were people of wealth and power. Bringing Dundurn to heel strengthened Brude's position within his realm while increasing the flow of tribute and resources to his treasury. Other strongholds no doubt suffered a similar fate during this period of aggression, which saw Brude undertaking a series of military strikes to stamp his authority on peripheral areas of Pictavia.

Ecgfrith, meanwhile, was still nursing a wounded pride after the thwarting of his southern ambitions. He was not the kind of king to suffer such grievances meekly and was soon itching for another contest with Mercia. In 684, within five years of the battle of the Trent, he once more sent his soldiers to war. This time he delegated command to a trusted henchman called Berht, a high-ranking member of the Bernician aristocracy. It was not, however, to Mercian territory in the English midlands that this aggression was directed, but to the midlands of Ireland. The motive behind the campaign is unclear, although several theories have been proposed. One theory suggests that Ecgfrith sought to deter Irish support for his half-brother Aldfrith, a son of Oswiu by a princess of the Uí Néill dynasty of high-kings. Under Irish law, the illegitimate child of this liaison had to be fostered among the maternal kin, which in this case left a potential claimant on the Northumbrian kingship in the care of the ever-ambitious Uí Néill. However, a snippet of information provided by Bede suggests that Ecgfrith and his siblings did not regard their half-brother as a potential rival at all. Bede briefly reported a conversation between Saint Cuthbert and Aelfflaed, Ecgfrith's sister, in the year of the raid on Ireland. In no uncertain terms Aelfflaed disregarded Aldfrith as a viable contender for the Northumbrian throne and seemed to be barely aware of his existence. Assuming that this view was also shared by Ecgfrith, the raid is unlikely to have been spurred by concerns about his half-brother.

Another possible motive for the attack is found in a late and controversial source, the *Annals of Clonmacnoise*, which refers to an alliance between the Irish and the Britons. If such an alliance ever existed in the 680s, and if the Britons in question were in revolt against Ecgfrith, then a punitive raid upon their friends in Ireland could have made some strategic sense. A further hypothesis proposes a religious dimension in which Ecgfrith, with papal blessing, pursued the interests of the Roman Church by terrorising a country where Celtic priests still held spiritual sway. Unfortunately, the sources do not offer any theories of their own and thus it is hard to understand why the attack happened at all. It was certainly regarded as a huge mistake by Ecgfrith's contemporaries. The influential English churchman Ecgbert warned against it, pointing out that the Irish had done no harm to Northumbria, but the warning went unheeded. The venture ultimately backfired and did enormous damage to Ecgfrith's reputation at home and abroad, especially after the callous deeds of his soldiers became widely known. Landing in Ireland, the Northumbrian army rampaged across the plain of Brega, an area whose landscape included the ancient royal sites of Tara and other hallowed places. The English warriors attacked churches and monasteries with a ferocity that shocked observers on both sides of the Irish Sea. After the slaughter and destruction the invaders returned to their ships laden not only with loot but also with many captives, who were taken back to Northumbria as hostages. Even Bede, who was a young Bernician boy of eleven or twelve at the time, wrote later of the 'wickedness' of the campaign and counted it among Ecgfrith's worst sins.

The Battle of Dunnichen

On 26 March of the following year, on Easter Sunday, Ecgfrith and his chief clergymen assembled at York to witness the consecration of Cuthbert as bishop of Lindisfarne. The attendees were a distinguished company headed by Theodore, archbishop of Canterbury, the leader of the English Church. Six other bishops were also present, and one of these was Trumwine of Abercorn, whom Theodore had recently appointed as bishop to the conquered parts of Pictavia. Cuthbert himself had formerly travelled in Pictish lands as a missionary in areas under direct Northumbrian control, although he may have ventured further into territory still ruled by Pictish kings. He had a good grasp of the political situation in the North, and one of his first acts after his appointment as bishop was to urge Ecgfrith not to seek a showdown with Brude. Cuthbert knew that the belligerent son of Oswiu was planning a new northern campaign but had a bad feeling about it and foresaw a disastrous outcome. His advice, like Ecgbert's in the previous year, was brushed aside. Four weeks later, on Sunday 23 April, Ecgfrith visited the monastery of Jarrow beside the River Tyne to witness the dedication of its church to St Paul. The dedication stone, bearing the date and the king's name, can still be seen *in situ* in the wall. Soon afterwards, perhaps within a few days of the ceremony, the Northumbrian army marched to war against the Picts.

Ecgfrith's likeliest route was via the old Roman road known as Dere Street ('The Deira Road') which ran along the eastern side of his kingdom from the Tyne to the Firth of Forth. Although bereft of maintenance for almost 300 years, this ancient highway was still functional. It followed a direct course through Lothian to reach the long-disused Roman fort at Cramond. From there the Northumbrian army would have continued northward to cross the River Forth at the feet of what is now Stirling Castle Rock. To the east lay Fife, which had probably lain under direct English rule since the time of Oswiu. To the north lay the rivers Earn and Tay, both of which the Northumbrian troops crossed via fords in the shadow of an ancient Pictish fortress on Moncrieffe Hill. The invaders now advanced into the heart of southern Pictavia, ravaging and plundering rich agricultural lands. In military terms such ravaging had a twofold purpose: it enabled the confiscation of food supplies for the army while ensuring that the same resources were unavailable to Brude.

Swampy terrain on the east forced Ecgfrith to follow the course of the Tay upstream to its junction with the River Isla. From here, he turned north-east along the great vale of Strathmore, taking a route followed by the modern road from Perth to Forfar. Today this route runs alongside the courses of the Isla and the Dean Water, travelling through a landscape that has changed considerably since the seventh century. The lochs now lying east of Forfar are merely the remnants of much larger stretches of water that would have been encountered by the Northumbrian soldiers. Despite post-medieval efforts to drain Rescobie Loch and Restenneth Loch, the former extent of these features is still discernible on old maps, in place-names and in current patterns of vegetation. In 685 this part of Strathmore was a treacherous landscape of bogs, lakes and pools that would have been difficult to traverse for a large body of warriors marching in unfamiliar territory. Like Agricola before him and Anglo-Norman warlords after him, Ecgfrith led his troops over firmer terrain on the northern side of the Dean Water. Small bands of enemy warriors were seen from time to time, but they faded into the landscape as soon as the English tried to pursue them. The invading army was marching unwittingly into a trap, being drawn deeper into the heart of Pictish territory.

On Saturday 20 May, at around three o'clock in the afternoon, the forces of Ecgfrith and Brude clashed in a great battle. Bede reported the event but does not identify the precise location, although he wrote that the fighting took place in 'narrow passes in the midst of inaccessible mountains'. The Irish annalists called the battlefield *Dun Nechtáin*, 'Nechtan's Fort', a name of Gaelic rather than of Pictish origin. The Picts' name for the place is unknown, but later Welsh texts called it *Linn Garan*, 'Crane Lake', a name almost certainly borrowed from the North Britons. Since the Picts spoke a language similar to Brittonic they, too, probably called the battlefield *Linn Garan* or something very similar. In the twelfth century a Northumbrian monk, Symeon of Durham, gave the English name of the site as *Nechtanesmere*, 'Nechtan's Mire', and this was undoubtedly the name used by his countrymen five centuries earlier.

The battle was basically a clash of foot-soldiers with limited fighting on horseback. Cavalry warfare was not common in the British Isles during this period, despite stylised depictions of armed riders in heroic poetry or on sculptured stones. Horses were valued as high-status possessions, but their main military use was as a means of transporting warriors to a battlefield. There the riders dismounted, leaving their horses in the care of weaponless servants while they themselves formed up in groups to fight on foot. Some leaders may have remained in the saddle to perform certain rituals of warfare: cantering along the line to encourage their men, or riding forth to parley with the enemy. However, when combat commenced it was essentially a melee of infantry against infantry. Swords, spears, axes and shields were the tools of the trade, but there was little or no archery. An indication of the sheer brutality of this type of fighting comes from graves unearthed at medieval battlefields, which show the terrible injuries inflicted by bladed weapons. Such evidence shows the grim reality behind the 'heroic' images of war presented on carved monuments or in battle-poems such as *The Gododdin*. The encounter at Nechtanesmere in 685 would have been a scene of bloody savagery. Its outcome was a great victory for the Picts, for Ecgfrith and nearly his whole army were slaughtered. His loyal bodyguard of chosen warriors fought to the last man, until all were slain around him.

The Site of the Battle

Historians generally agree that the *Dun Nechtáin* of the Irish annals was an ancient fortification on Dunnichen Hill near Forfar. A little below the summit, the broken remnants of a wall were visible in the eighteenth century, but much of the stonework was subsequently removed to be re-used by local people. Quarrying on the site eventually destroyed most of what remained. The hill overlooks, on its south-east side, a boggy field called Dunnichen Moss, in the midst of which a small pond is all that now remains of a more substantial area of water. This was drained in the eighteenth century, but its former extent can be reconstructed by reference to old maps, which show a small loch occupying what is now the 'Moss'. Until recently a consensus of opinion believed that this loch was Symeon's *Nechtanesmere* and the Welsh *Linn Garan*, with the great battle taking place in the shadow of *Dun Nechtáin*. In recent years, however, this view has been challenged by an alternative hypothesis which questions the viability of Dunnichen Moss as the site of Brude's victory. Central to the challenge is the fact that the Moss lies on the opposite side of Dunnichen Hill from Ecgfrith's likely route along Strathmore. In order to reach a battle-field on the hill's south-east flank, the Northumbrian warriors would have been obliged to traverse its southern slopes before finding themselves snared between high ground and an expanse of water or swamp. Such a manoeuvre would have brought the catastrophic consequences lamented by Bede, but it is hard to believe that an experienced warlord of Ecgfrith's calibre could have made this type of elementary mistake. More credible is an alternative theory, which sees the Northumbrian army crossing Strathmore at the head of the Loch of Forfar before marching along the south side of Restenneth Loch to meet Brude's army below the northern slopes of Dunnichen Hill. Accordingly, this theory identifies Restenneth Loch – in its more extensive, pre-modern manifestation – as *Nechtanesmere* or *Linn Garan*. An entirely different location has also been suggested, in a district some fifty miles to the north, at Dunachton near Aviemore on the western edge of the Cairngorms. While this might seem a better fit with Bede's description of 'narrow passes in the midst of inaccessible mountains', it may be too far north to have been a viable objective in Ecgfrith's campaign. Bede was not, in any case, an eyewitness of the event and had to rely on recycled information of the kind available to historians who study the battle today. The geographical contexts he provided for this and other military campaigns may have owed more to dramatic rhetoric and far less to reliable reporting. His main purpose was not to give a precise depiction of battlefield topography, but to show Ecgfrith being trapped and slain by the Picts as divine punishment for his assault on the monasteries of Ireland.

It is curious that the Welsh and English sources associate the battle with a lake or mere, while the Irish annals suggest a hill or hillfort as the key topographical feature. Both traditions can be reconciled if the fighting is envisaged as taking place on low ground between Dunnichen Hill and an older, greatly enlarged Restenneth Loch. A remnant of the latter feature survives as the diminutive Loch Fithie, and this may mark the approximate northern boundary of the battlefield. A likely venue for the main phase of combat is therefore the strip of terrain which once lay between the waters of the loch and the lower slopes of the hill.

The Aftermath

On the day of the battle, Saint Cuthbert was visiting Carlisle where Queen Iurminburg, Ecgfrith's second wife, sat waiting anxiously at a nunnery which her sister governed as abbess. During the afternoon the royal official who administered the city gave Cuthbert a guided tour of the local Roman antiquities, perhaps as a diversion from the tense atmosphere prevailing among the queen's entourage. At three o'clock, when Cuthbert was being shown a finely carved fountain, he suddenly became visibly agitated and lifted his eyes to the sky. 'Oh, oh, oh!' he cried. 'I believe the war is ended and the verdict has been given against our warriors.' Despite being asked to explain his premonition, the holy man would say no more but rushed immediately to Iurminburg, advising her to expect the worst. Within a few days their fears were confirmed by tidings from the North. One of the few survivors of Ecgfrith's army reached Carlisle to bring news of the Pictish victory and to inform the queen that her husband was dead.

Contemporary and later Northumbrian writers regarded the battle as 'wretched and mournful' and as 'a most woeful disaster'. To Bede, it marked a turning-point in the fortunes of Northumbria. 'From this time,' he wrote despondently, 'the hopes and strength of the English kingdom began to ebb and fall away.' He added that the Picts 'recovered their own land which the English had formerly held', while the Scots of Dalriada as well as 'some part of the British nation' also threw off the Northumbrian yoke to recover their independence. In broad political terms this meant that the kings of Pictavia, Dalriada and Alt Clut shook off the burden of paying tribute to an English overlord.

The immediate aftermath had grim repercussions for English settlers north of the Firth of Forth. Northumbrian families who had made their homes in Fife or in other districts seized by Oswiu from the Picts now found their situation untenable. A brutal fate awaited them as Brude's victorious army stormed across the Tay to reclaim the conquered lands. Bede wrote that many of the English in this region 'were either slain by the sword or enslaved or escaped by flight from Pictish territory'. The most high-profile refugee was Trumwine, bishop of Abercorn, who fled with his monks to seek sanctuary in the monastery at Whitby. There he remained to the end of his days, serving God in piety and austerity and never returning to the northern borderlands.

As for Ecgfrith himself, he was soon identified among the slain and borne in honour from the field by Pictish warriors. He never came home to Northumbria, for his body was taken to Iona for burial. This was remarkable and unprecedented: no English king had ever before been interred on the holy island of Saint Columba. The unexpected decision was made by Brude who, as the unchallenged master of the region around the battle, was able to dictate the fate of his enemy's corpse. Ecgfrith's widow and other members of the Bernician royal family might otherwise have chosen a site in Northumbria to be his final resting-place, but the decision was not theirs to make. Aelfflaed, Ecgfrith's sister, jointly governed the monastery at Whitby with their mother, and this was where their renowned father Oswiu lay buried. It is likely that Ecgfrith, too, would have been entombed at Whitby if his kin had been given any say in the matter. Instead, he was conveyed to Iona to rest alongside the kings and saints of the Celtic North. From Brude's point of view this was more than a gesture of goodwill to a fallen foe. It demonstrated his own elevated status as the new overlord of northern Britain, while presenting him as a generous and forgiving Christian ruler.

For Brude the most immediate consequence of victory was that he was no longer obliged to send tribute-payments to Northumbria. The surpluses previously set aside to meet those payments, together with agricultural produce from southern Pictish districts formerly under English rule, were now at his disposal. He diverted these resources to the ongoing task of strengthening his authority, bringing outlying regions of Pictavia more firmly under his control and laying the foundations of the great kingdom that would eventually rise to power in the following century. Beyond the economic gains, it is difficult to assess the political significance of the Battle of Dunnichen. It did not, as some historians believe, prevent an imminent English conquest of the entire Pictish nation: such a venture would have lain beyond even Ecgfrith's wide ambitions. Nor did it extinguish Northumbria's territorial claims around the Firth of Forth. Bede's doom-laden rhetoric makes his countrymen look like a spent force after what he calls the 'woeful disaster' of 685, but this was simply not the case. It is true that Bernicia would produce no great warrior-kings in the following generation, but this was chiefly due to Ecgfrith's childlessness and to the period of dynastic instability that it precipitated. In real political terms Northumbria remained a major power and continued to play an important role in Pictish affairs for many years to come.

The Legacy of Dunnichen

Brude's victory has nevertheless become a famous event in Scottish history. To many people it ranks alongside Bannockburn, Flodden, Culloden and other momentous struggles whose outcomes had far-reaching consequences. Unfortunately, in the absence of contemporary information on the matter, it cannot be elevated to these lofty heights. Its significance should rather be seen in the narrow context of political rivalries in the late seventh century. To Bede it was a decisive battle. To his contemporaries in Pictavia it must have seemed equally important, although their lack of a literary culture deprives historians of a Pictish account of the battle. Some modern observers believe that the triumph was instead immortalised by skilled artisans who commemorated Brude's achievement in stone. The sculptured object in question is an upright slab, some seven feet in height, standing today in the kirkyard at Aberlemno. To the south-east, less than four miles away, lie Dunnichen Hill and the reed-grown meadows where Restenneth Loch formerly lay.

The stone is one of several monuments in the vicinity of Aberlemno, but it is by far the most striking of the group. On one side it carries a large cross of intricate workmanship. The other side shows two of the enigmatic Pictish symbols at the top: a triple-disc and a notched rectangle with Z rod. Beneath these are small cameos of warriors engaged in combat, with the action arranged in three horizontal sections or 'registers'. The upper register shows two horsemen, one pursuing the other. The fleeing rider wears a helmet with a long nose-guard, while his pursuer is bare-headed and long-haired, and brandishes a sword. Beneath these two a middle register depicts three long-haired infantrymen confronting another helmeted horseman, who threatens them with a spear. Finally, in the lower register, two horsemen face each other in combat while a helmeted warrior on foot – the largest figure in the sequence – is devoured by a raven.

The precise date of this unique monument's creation is unknown, but the style of sculpture belongs to the eighth century. The helmets worn by four of the carved figures look like crude representations of a type of military headgear associated with warriors of the Early Historic period. By far the most striking example of this design is the Coppergate Helmet, an eighth-century Northumbrian artifact recovered during archaeological excavations at York. The depiction of similar helmets on the Aberlemno stone has been seen as evidence that the monument was erected to commemorate the Battle of Dunnichen. The carved scenes have thus been interpreted as a visual record of the event in the same way that Bede's text provides a written narrative, the bare-headed warriors being seen as Picts fighting helmet-wearing Englishmen. Some historians take these identifications further by using the sculptor's placement of the figures to reconstruct the actual course of the fighting, despite the monument being an abstract and stylised work of art.

There are, however, major difficulties in believing this stone to be a commemoration of the Battle of Dunnichen. One problem is the date assigned to the sculpture by art historians, who suggest that the monument was created no earlier than the eighth century. The style of carving means that a date around the middle of the century – two generations after Brude's victory – seems most likely. Doubts have arisen about the style of attire worn by the presumed 'English' warriors, chiefly because archaeologists do not believe that helmets of the Coppergate type were available in seventh-century

Northumbria. The main argument for believing that the Aberlemno stone commemorates the battle of 685 rests on its proximity to Dunnichen, but this is hardly conclusive and need be no more than a coincidence of geography. In every major aspect of its artistic and archaeological contexts, the monument should commemorate an event of the eighth century rather than of the seventh. Possible alternatives from the decades after 700 do in fact exist, most notably a series of victories achieved by the Pictish king Óengus, son of Fergus, against Dalriada and Alt Clut between 734 and 756. It is possible that one of these battles inspired the scenes carved on the monument in the kirkyard at Aberlemno.

A quite different memorial, in the form of a poem, was created to celebrate the outcome of the Battle of Dunnichen. Only a portion survives, as six lines of verse preserved in an old Irish manuscript. This fragment is all that remains of what may once have been a long heroic poem in praise of Brude's victory. The lines are attributed to an Irish priest called Riaguil who dwelt among the Picts at the time of the battle, but the original composer is more likely to have been a Pictish bard whose name is now forgotten. Bards were important members of a king's entourage, their task being to proclaim their patron's fame and status at ceremonial gatherings. In carefully constructed verses they recited heroic poetry in praise of the king's past deeds, thereby fulfilling what was essentially a 'public relations' role. The following verse, although credited to Riaguil, was probably the work of a bard at the royal court of Pictavia.

> This day Brude fights a battle for the heritage of his
> grandfather.
> Unless the Son of God wishes otherwise, he will perish in it.
> This day Oswiu's son has been killed in battle against
> blue swords.
> Although he did penance, it was penance too late.
> This day Oswiu's son has been killed, who had the black
> draughts.
> Christ has heard our prayers, that they should save Brude
> the Brave.

The mention of 'blue swords' may be a stylised reference to oxidation resulting from re-heating iron blades to make them stronger, unless it refers simply to the bluish hue of steel. The 'black draughts' associated with Ecgfrith are the deep, gaping wounds from which he died on the battlefield. More intriguing is the claim that Brude fought 'for the heritage of his grandfather', which implies that the Pictish king's ancestry gave him an additional motive or objective. Unfortunately, the poet does not say which grandfather is being referred to. Brude's paternal grandfather – his father's father – was Neithon, king of the Clyde Britons, but the maternal grandfather is unknown. No source names Brude's mother but, given that she gave birth to a Pictish king, she was a lady of Pictish royal blood. It was therefore her father – rather than Neithon of Alt Clut – for whose 'heritage' her son fought at Dunnichen. The heritage was surely the district being menaced by the Northumbrian army on the day of the battle. Perhaps this area had once belonged to Brude's maternal grandfather who, as well as being the father of a royal princess, was also patriarch of a family in which male children were groomed as potential overkings of Pictavia. This family may have ruled the lands around Dunnichen Hill as the lords of Circinn, the

Front   Back

Figure 5. Horseman and Pictish symbols on a stone from Meigle, Perthshire, now housed in the local museum. Reproduced from J.R. Allen and J. Anderson, *The Early Christian Monuments of Scotland* (1903).

ancient province which is now the county of Angus.

In c.830, the Welsh author of the *Historia Brittonum* presented his own comments on the Northumbrian defeat: 'This Ecgfrith is he who made war against his *fratruelis* ('cousin') Brude, the king of the Picts. There he perished with all the best of his army, and the Picts with their king were the victors. The Northumbrians have never managed to exact tribute from the Picts since the time of that battle which is called the Strife at Linn Garan.' This summary was based on Bede's, but it includes the curious information about a blood relationship between the two kings. Modern historians have puzzled over the truth of this alleged kinship but have not yet reached any consensus on the matter. Central to the debate is the Welsh author's use of the Latin term *fratruelis*, which had a fairly precise meaning in denoting male cousins who were the sons of siblings. However, expert opinion is divided on whether these siblings were male or female. In late Roman times *fratrueles* usually denoted cousins who were sons of brothers but, by the early seventh century, it could also mean cousins whose mothers were sisters. Various explanations have been put forward to explain how this relationship might be applied to Brude and Ecgfrith, mainly by reconstructing hypothetical royal genealogies. Some of these reconstructed 'family trees' are based on Pictish matrilineal succession, while others devise alternatives which consciously seek to disprove the matrilineal theory. One hypothesis sees Brude as a grandson or great-nephew of the Pictish king Talorcan whose father, Eanfrith, was Oswiu's elder brother and thus an uncle of Ecgfrith. Making Eanfrith the ancestral link between the two Dunnichen protagonists works well with the matrilineal hypothesis but falls foul of chronology by placing Brude two generations later than Talorcan. A different theory sees Brude's mother, like Ecgfrith's, as a daughter of Edwin of Deira. This idea presents the unlikely scenario of Brude, whose father was certainly Beli, king of the Clyde Britons, being the child of two non-Pictish parents. Even setting aside the notion of matrilineal succession it is hard to give credence to a theory which gives Brude no Pictish parentage at all. The many uncertainties about who married whom during this period of shifting political allegiance and inter-dynastic marriage mean that the truth of the matter continues to remain elusive. All that can be said with certainty is that the author of the *Historia Brittonum* saw nothing improbable in the idea of Brude and Ecgfrith being *fratrueles* or cousins in some sense, even if this kinship was once or twice removed.

Brude died in 693, ending his life peacefully and naturally rather than in the grim fray of battle. His body was brought to Iona where Abbot Adomnán, stricken by grief, decided to hold an all-night vigil beside the corpse. According to legend, the vigil was almost over and dawn was breaking when the Pictish king began to show signs of life. By morning the dead eyes had opened in the presence of a horrified bystander. This fellow, described in the legend as 'an unsympathetic member of the faithful', warned of dire repercussions if the process was not halted immediately. 'If, as seems likely,' he said, 'the dead are being raised by Adomnán, I declare that no cleric will be appointed abbot to succeed him unless he too raises the dead.' Adomnán's response was given with calm understatement: 'Some implications may indeed be involved here.' After giving the matter due consideration he added: 'If it be more appropriate, let us therefore utter a blessing over this body, in the interests of Brude's soul.' To the relief of the bystander, the sorrowful abbot halted the resurrection and let fate take its course. In a slightly different version of the legend, Adomnán grieved beside the corpse before blessing Brude's soul. He then noted the irony of a powerful and wealthy monarch being entombed in nothing more ostentatious than a wooden coffin: 'It is strange that, after he has been king of the North, a hollow stump of withered oak should be about the son of the king of Dumbarton.' Behind these stories is the solemn occasion of Brude's burial in the monastic graveyard on Iona. This hallowed site, which already held the bones of Ecgfrith, now became the final resting-place of the proud victor of *Dun Nechtáin*. Within eight years of their great clash of arms, these two mighty warlords were reunited in peace on the holy island of Columba.

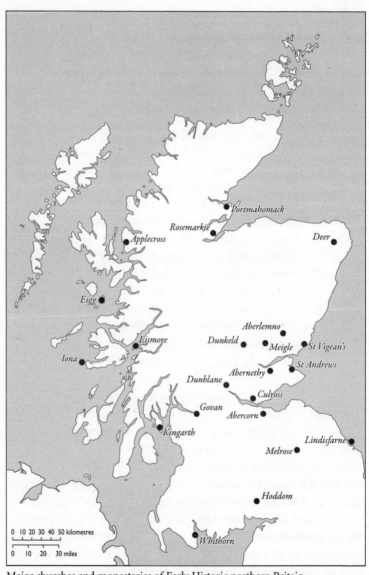

Major churches and monasteries of Early Historic northern Britain.

CHAPTER 8

Reformers and Rivals

The political situation at the end of the seventh century showed how far the Picts had come since their first appearance as barbarian enemies of Rome four centuries earlier. In the 290s the *Picti* were portrayed as uncouth savages whose frenzied raids disturbed the peace of the Empire. In the 690s they presented the rather different image of a people in transition, a maturing nation with deep roots in the past but showing a willingness to adapt in a rapidly changing world. The days of their isolation on the margins were over. As the eighth century dawned, it found them playing a central role in the political and religious developments happening at that time. All over the British Isles, kingdoms were looking less like groups of barbarian tribes and more like well-organised states whose monarchs were steadily exerting a tighter hold on their domains. The spiritual leaders – the bishops and abbots of Christianity – were drawing closer to their secular counterparts – the kings – and were playing major roles in secular affairs.

On the political front the Picts could breathe a little easier, having survived the threat of conquest by aggressive English warlords. That particular menace now lay buried with Ecgfrith's ambitions in the mires around Dunnichen and was never to rise again. Northumbria's new king was the intellectual Aldfrith, Ecgfrith's half-brother and an unlikely candidate for royal power. Having spent much of his early life with religious communities in Ireland and Iona, he was better known as a monk and scholar. He had neither the desire nor the ability to restore English supremacy over the Picts, Scots and Britons. On the contrary, his elevation to the Northumbrian kingship was accomplished with the assistance and approval of his predecessor's former vassals. He was the preferred candidate not only of the Gaelic West but also of Brude, Beli's son, the victor of Dunnichen. Installing as Ecgfrith's successor an Iona-educated prince with Celtic sympathies gave the Scots and Picts an effective means of neutralising English territorial ambitions, at least for a while.

Religious Reform: Adomnán and Curetán

After Brude's death in 693 the Pictish overkingship passed to a prince called Taran, who was probably Brude's sister's son. Taran was ousted in an internal power-struggle four years later and succeeded by another Brude, a son of Derile. Soon after his accession, perhaps within a few months, the new King Brude bore witness to one of the great ecclesiastical gatherings of the early medieval period. The Irish annals noted the event under the year 697: 'Adomnán went to Ireland and gave the Law of Innocents to the peoples.' This brief entry masks the huge significance of the occasion, which took place at the monastery of Birr in County Offaly. It was here that Adomnán, abbot of Iona, summoned a great synod. Unlike the similar meeting at Whitby three decades earlier, the Synod of 697 was essentially a gathering of the key figures of Celtic Christianity. Representatives from the churches and monasteries of Ireland, together with delegates from Iona and its *familia* of satellites, assembled at Birr to discuss matters of profound importance for religious and secular leaders alike. Alongside the bishops, abbots and priests stood an impressive array of kings, many of whom had travelled far to attend the gathering. A long list of attendees and witnesses has survived and, among the names of numerous Irish kings and clerics, the list mentions 'Brude, Derile's son, king of Pictavia'.

The synod is most famous for producing one of the four great religious laws of Ireland, the Law of Innocents, otherwise known as

Cáin Adamnáin ('Adomnán's Law'). This placed a sacred obligation on kings and other lords to ensure the exemption of women, children and priests from the ravages of warfare and from military service. Transgression of the law would incur a large fine payable to Adomnán's churches in Ireland. A detailed discussion of *Cáin Adamnáin* does not belong here, but it is worthwhile to consider its implications. First, the great synod at Birr demonstrated the enormous power and influence of Adomnán, even in regions far from his headquarters on Iona. Summoning the kings of almost every Celtic realm to a meeting, and persuading them to attend in person (or at least to bear witness *in absentia*), was a huge achievement. Second, the inclusion of the name of Brude, son of Derile, in the list of witnesses shows the enduring authority of the Columban Church in Pictavia and its status in the eyes of the royal kindreds there. Third, the presence of a Pictish delegation at Birr signalled that the provisions of *Cáin Adamnáin* were intended to apply in Brude's kingdom, just as the king's witnessing of the Law showed that he promised to abide by its terms. English kingdoms, such as Northumbria, were excluded from the synod, which was essentially a Celtic affair. One Englishman, however, was certainly present: Ecgbert, the Northumbrian cleric who had warned Ecgfrith against the raid on Ireland in 684, attended the gathering in his capacity as bishop of Mayo. His close connections with the Columban Church were soon to have a profound effect on Pictish religious and political affairs.

Brude, Derile's son, might not have attended the synod in person but his interests were represented there by Bishop Curetán, abbot of the monastery at Rosemarkie in Easter Ross. Today Rosemarkie is best known as the location of Groam House, home to a fine collection of Pictish sculpture, but in Curetán's time it was a major ecclesiastical centre of Pictavia. The royal and international connections of its abbot in 697 show that Christian communities in Fortriu and elsewhere north of the Mounth were by no means isolated from those further south. The presence of Rosemarkie's abbot at the Synod of Birr, as a companion or emissary of the Pictish overking Brude, illustrates how even a remote monastery on the windswept North Sea coast could forge and maintain effective links with Iona. Brude's choice of Curetán as his ecclesiastical representative suggests that Rosemarkie was at that time the chief bishopric of Pictavia.

Adomnán surely knew Curetán personally, even before the Pictish bishop's attendance at Birr. During Adomnán's long tenure of the abbacy of Iona, from 679 to 704, he is likely to have visited the Columban churches east of Druim Alban, and several traditions associate him with specific sites. Across the former Pictish lands he is still remembered in place-names and church dedications incorporating *Ernan*, *Eunan* and other variants of his name, some of which might be due to the activities of his disciples if not actual visits by himself. In Atholl there is a noticeable cluster of such place-names, including several 'lost' examples retrievable only from medieval charters and similar land-holding documents. The name of Curetán, too, is found among old Gaelic place-names in former Pictish territory, chiefly in Glen Urquhart and other lands around Loch Ness. In this general area the name *Cladh Churadáin* ('Curetán's graveyard') is found at four separate sites, together with *Tobar Churadáin* ('Curetán's Well') and *Suidhe Churadáin* ('Curetán's Seat'). This saint is in fact a rather mysterious figure, despite his importance as a delegate at the Synod of Birr. Medieval Scottish tradition believed that he had an alternative name, *Boniface*, derived from the Latin *Bonifatius*. A famous pope bore this name in the early seventh century and could have been the inspiration behind Curetán's adoption of it as an alternative name or surname. This was by no means an unusual practice: an English priest called Berhtgisl, who served as bishop of the East Angles between 652 and 669, took Boniface as a surname. The Scottish saint called Boniface is associated with church dedications to Saint Peter, and this might point to Curetán harbouring 'Roman' sympathies if he and Boniface were indeed the same person.

In the late seventh century it was not unusual for a 'Celtic' priest to campaign on behalf of the 'Roman' way of doing things. The great Adomnán himself favoured Rome's ecclesiastical practices over those of the Celtic churches and tried to persuade Iona to reform its customs. Curetán may have shared the same view, taking the papal surname Boniface while campaigning to reform Pictish Christianity on behalf of Rome and at the expense of Iona's influence. Church dedications and old traditions locate the labours of Boniface in Angus, but the medieval cult of Curetán lay further north in the area around Rosemarkie. This suggests that Curetán-Boniface spent most of his career in southern Pictavia before retiring to Easter Ross and dying there. His cult was in existence at Rosemarkie before the end of the twelfth century but remained fairly small and localised. It spread outwards to be reflected in place-names such as *Cladh Churadáin*, but it is possible that these sites were already associated with Curetán during or soon after his lifetime. Stone sculpture of the eighth and ninth centuries at Rosemarkie is testament to the presence of a vibrant ecclesiastical community in the Pictish era, a community whose origins are likely to be found in the 'Roman' reforms of Curetán-Boniface rather than in the context of earlier missions from Celtic Iona.

Religious Reform: Nechtan and Ceolfrith

In 698, the year after the Synod of Birr, hostilities broke out again between Northumbria and the Picts. A battle was fought in the borderlands around the Firth of Forth in which an English leader called Beorhtred, son of Beornhaeth, was slain. Beorhtred was not a king but a royal ealdorman with responsibility for protecting the northern frontier. His name looks similar to the name borne by the warlord *Berht* who led Ecgfrith's attack on Ireland fourteen years earlier. *Berht* was a shortened form of *Beorhtred*, and both names perhaps belonged to the same man or to two individuals who were close kinsmen. Beorhtred's death suggests that the battle of 698 was a Pictish victory. Its occurrence speaks of renewed tension between the two peoples, but the aggressors on this occasion were less likely to have been English. The Northumbrian king, Aldfrith, was a pious ex-monk and a renowned bookworm rather than an ambitious conqueror. He ruled his kingdom within what Bede termed 'narrower bounds' and chose not to follow in the expansionist footsteps of his predecessors. It is therefore no surprise to find him delegating military responsibilities to subordinates like Beorhtred. The battle of 698 was surely instigated by Brude, Derile's son, who had good reason to revive the dormant hostility between Northumbria and the Picts. As a new and untried king, he needed to demonstrate his strength and probably selected his southern neighbour as a suitable target.

Adomnán of Iona died in 704 and was followed a year later by Aldfrith, king of Northumbria, whose son and successor Osred was still a young boy at the time. Brude, son of Derile, died in 706 and was succeeded by his brother Nechtan, one of the most important of all Pictish kings. The early years of Nechtan's reign were marked by sporadic outbreaks of warfare on the northern and southern frontiers. A likely context for this strife would be a renewal by Nechtan of the consolidation of Pictavia undertaken by Brude, son of Beli, in the 680s. The targets were enemies on the periphery of Pictish territory, including rebels in Orkney whom Nechtan defeated in 709. Non-Pictish foes included the Northumbrian English who, in 711, defeated an army of Picts in the district of Manau. The victor on this occasion was Beorhtfrith, presumably a kinsman of the ealdorman Beorhtred who had died in the border clash of 698. The repeated occurrence of these similar-sounding names implies that a family of Northumbrian aristocrats was entrusted with the hereditary role of guarding the Pictish frontier, an area which clearly remained unstable in the decades after the battle of Dunnichen. The annals name one Pictish casualty in the defeat of 711: Finguine, son of Deleroith, who 'fell by premature death'. Finguine was a warlord of noble or royal blood to whom King Nechtan gave responsibility for military leadership on the southern fringes of Pictavia. He may have been Beorhtfrith's Pictish counterpart as march-warden in the troubled borderlands around the Firth of Forth.

Nechtan desired stability and began to consider making peace with Northumbria. After his defeat at Manau in 711, the old tensions still simmered, prompting him to seek a diplomatic solution before

Figure 6. Cross-slab with Pictish symbols on a stone from Glamis, Angus.
Reproduced from J. Anderson, *Scotland in Early Christian Times* (1881).

hostilities flared again. His diplomacy went hand-in-hand with an approach to the English clergy that he made as royal patron of their Pictish counterparts. In a letter addressed to Ceolfrith, abbot of the dual monastery of Wearmouth-Jarrow, Nechtan asked for advice on certain ecclesiastical matters. In particular, he stated his intention to bring his churches into line with the 'Roman' method of calculating the date of Easter Sunday, which had been adopted throughout Northumbria after the Synod of Whitby in 664. To achieve this, however, he had to convince the bishops and abbots of his kingdom that they should change their old ways. At that time, the churches of Pictavia still followed Iona in using archaic Celtic practices, including the obsolete method of calculating Easter and a strange form of tonsure. This style – which left the front of the scalp completely bare – was regarded by English clerics as archaic and heretical. In England, as elsewhere in Western Europe at that time, the accepted style was the 'Tonsure of Saint Peter' – a band or crown of hair encircling a shaved scalp. This is the style most commonly associated with medieval monks. The origin of the Celtic style is unknown, but it was certainly ancient and may ultimately have had druidical origins. The Columban clergy of Iona and Pictavia therefore differed from their brethren in England, Ireland and Europe not only in their Easter calculations but also in their physical appearance. During his abbacy of Iona, the great Adomnán himself had tried to persuade the monks to adopt 'Roman' ways but, despite his authority, they resolutely adhered to their old traditions. Their Pictish colleagues across the Spine of Britain continued to follow suit.

Nechtan was a man of great learning who had diligently studied the ecclesiastical literature relating to the Easter controversy. He was, however, first and foremost the king of a powerful and warlike people who faced potential enemies on every border. His letter to Ceolfrith was sent on a religious pretext but, in political terms, it represented a communication from one sovereign kingdom to another with whom it had recently engaged in warfare. It was therefore sent in the context of – and as a component of – a wider diplomatic process that Nechtan hoped would bring a final end to the conflict between Pictavia and Northumbria. Ceolfrith's reply, in which he provided justification for adopting the 'Roman' Easter and the Petrine tonsure, was likewise a diplomatic as well as a religious response. It was probably composed in consultation with the young Northumbrian king Osred, Aldfrith's teenage son, who was more than willing to make peace with the Picts. Both Nechtan's original letter and Ceolfrith's reply represented the religious component of a broader peacemaking process between the two kingdoms. This broad perspective can be seen in the following words, addressed to Nechtan, which appear at the end of the letter sent to him from Jarrow: 'May the grace of the eternal King keep you in safety to reign for many years and so bring peace to us all.'

The text of Ceolfrith's letter to the Pictish king is preserved in Bede's *Ecclesiastical History*. The original may even have been composed by Bede himself at the monastery of Jarrow, where he had lived as a monk since childhood. As one of the foremost scholars of his generation, Bede was well-equipped to provide the Biblical quotations and ecclesiastical references required by Ceolfrith as justification for adopting the 'Roman' system. The resulting document certainly pleased the Pictish king and convinced him that he was right to persuade the clergy in his realm to abandon their archaic Celtic ways. With the letter from Wearmouth-Jarrow came English craftsmen, sent by Ceolfrith, whose task was to build a church of stone 'after the Roman fashion' and in accordance with a specific request from Nechtan. This church was dedicated to Saint Peter, chief of the Apostles, but its precise location remains a mystery. One candidate is the church at Meigle in Angus, which not only bears a dedication to Saint Peter but also occupies an ancient ecclesiastical site. In Pictish times it was known as *Migdele*, and its antiquity as a religious centre with royal associations is indicated by the fine collection of richly carved stones currently housed in the adjacent museum. Meigle might indeed mark the site of Nechtan's stone church but it is not the only candidate. Another is Restenneth, near Forfar, where the lost place-name *Egglespether*, 'Saint Peter's church', appears in a medieval charter and could relate to the site where the twelfth-century priory now stands. The form *Egglespether* might preserve an original Pictish name bestowed in the eighth century to denote Nechtan's English-built foundation. If so, then the latter may lie beneath the ruins of the priory, in a location that would have been hugely symbolic for Picts and Northumbrians alike. Somewhere close by, in the shadow of Dunnichen Hill, the greatest battle ever fought between the two nations took place in the spring of 685. However, an equally symbolic site – for similar reasons – is the parish church at Aberlemno, to which the name *Ecclespether* may have been attached in early times.

Bede described the scene at Nechtan's court when Ceolfrith's reply was received. The document was read aloud in the presence of the king and his 'assembled leaders', who included not only important aristocrats but also various 'learned men'. The latter were clerics of high status, namely the bishops and abbots of the Columban Church in Pictavia. Such men were able to understand Latin – the language of ecclesiastical discourse – and so, perhaps, was the king. But the noblemen of his entourage needed to hear the letter read aloud in their own language. The Latin text was duly translated into Pictish for their benefit and, after due consideration, the king gave his reaction. Bearing in mind that the 'assembled leaders' undoubtedly included older Picts who had taken part in the victory at Dunnichen, Nechtan's response is unlikely to have happened in the way described by Bede, who wrote triumphantly that the Pictish king 'knelt down, thanking God for having made him worthy to receive such a gift from England'. Given the recent hostility between the two kingdoms, it is likely that Nechtan's true reaction was rather more measured and sober.

After receiving the letter, the king sent instructions to clergymen in every part of his realm, informing them that they must now compute the date of Easter according to the 'Roman' method. Alongside this decree went a requirement for them to tonsure their hair in the manner of a circular crown and to abandon the ancient Celtic style. The fact that Nechtan's instructions were adopted throughout his kingdom shows the extent of his control over ecclesiastical as well as political affairs. He was a charismatic and confident king who regarded the religious elite as his subordinates and as men who should obey his commands. In cultural and artistic terms, his realignment of the Pictish Church coincided with a new style of monumental sculpture: the upright stone slab with an elaborately carved cross on one side. The vibrant style of craftsmanship on these monuments reflects the energy and vigour of Christianity in Pictavia in the wake of his reforms. Similarities between the new sculptural techniques and those of Northumbria indicate the presence or influence of English craftsmen. Further Northumbrian influence may have led to the veneration not only of Saint Peter but also of Saint Andrew, to whom the monastery at Hexham in the Tyne Valley was dedicated. It is possible that a church and cult-centre associated with Andrew were founded by Nechtan on the coast of Fife where the cathedral city of St Andrews stands today.

Alongside the religious changes, there came a formal end to hostilities between Northumbria and the Picts. Bede refers to this as a *foedus pacis*, a peace treaty, and it was still in place when his *Ecclesiastical History* was published in 731. The treaty originated during the period of communication between Nechtan and Wearmouth-Jarrow and was one of a bundle of conciliatory gestures, which included Ceolfrith's advice and the loan of English stonemasons. The political and religious negotiations were closely interwined, eventually producing the non-aggression pact and Nechtan's commitment to bring the Pictish Church into line with 'Roman' practice. From a wider perspective, this meant a swift termination of Iona's influence in Pictavia.

The key players in the various negotiations represented the secular and spiritual hierarchies of the two kingdoms. Nechtan was the main secular figure on the Pictish side, while the young king Osred and his advisers represented Northumbria's political interests. Ecclesiastical aspects of the peacemaking process were directed, on the English side, by Ceolfrith and his monks, with Bede himself perhaps acting as chief scribe. Their main Pictish counterpart may have been Curetán of Rosemarkie, who had previously represented Nechtan's brother Brude at Adomnán's great synod of the Celtic churches in 697. Like Adomnán, Curetán was probably an advocate of 'Roman' ways and thus sympathetic to Ceolfrith's views. Another Northumbrian cleric who shared the same opinions was Ecgbert, a co-attendee at the Birr gathering in his role as abbot of the Irish monastery of Mayo. In 712, at a time when Nechtan was making his first diplomatic approaches to Northumbria, Ecgbert became bishop of Iona. His new role brought him into direct contact with the Pictish clergy, all of whom at that time still acknowledged Iona's authority in important matters. Ecgbert must have known Curetán from their attendance at the synod of 697, and would have regarded him as a key ally in bringing Pictish Christianity into conformity with 'Roman' ways. As bishop of Iona, Ecgbert would have made periodic visits to King Nechtan, who probably used Curetán as an intermediary. It is equally likely that Ecgbert was also a key link in the communication between Nechtan and Ceolfrith. This widely travelled Englishman's greatest achievement came some years later, in 716, when he finally persuaded the brethren of Iona to abandon their old Celtic customs and fall in line with Rome. Despite this, some priests were reluctant to make a rapid change. Among the Pictish churches, this meant that the reforms imposed by Nechtan were not implemented as quickly as he might have wished. In 717 his frustration boiled over and he expelled the remaining Columban clerics from his realm.

Dynastic Crisis in Pictavia

With peace assured on his southern frontier, Nechtan was free to turn his attention to a growing problem closer to home, where strife was brewing among rival royal factions. The first sign of trouble came in 713 when his brother Ciniod, son of Derile, was killed. Ciniod's slaying may have been an act of murder by Talorcan, son of a certain Drostan and half-brother to Derile's sons. Talorcan ruled the province of Atholl as a sub-king under the overkingship of Nechtan but nurtured high ambitions of his own. The murder of Ciniod, a likely heir in the event of Nechtan's death, opened the possibility of succession to rival claimants such as Talorcan. In a clear demonstration of royal authority Nechtan ordered the imprisonment of Talorcan, who was not heard of again for almost twenty years.

Ironically, Nechtan's success in stabilising his southern border with an Anglo-Pictish peace treaty may have led to murmurs of discontent among his aristocracy, some of whom had recently fought his new English friends on the plains of Manau in 711.

Among the royal entourage were older noblemen who had tasted victory at Dunnichen in 685, together with other veterans who had battled Northumbrian armies in the intervening years. These grizzled warlords may have resented Nechtan's conciliatory attitude. To them, the rapprochement with an old enemy might have looked like an act of surrender, a truce too far. It certainly raised the spectre of a gradual infiltration by English culture and ideology. To the Pictish nobility, this probably seemed rather less palatable than the Gaelic cultural influences to which it had already been exposed for more than 100 years. Gaeldom had long held a foothold in Pictavia through the activities of the Columban Church but, with Iona's influence now curtailed by Nechtan's religious reforms, the Picts faced the prospect of being drawn closer to their recent foes.

Within a few years the shadow of dynastic upheaval began to fall on Nechtan's kingdom. Rivals emerged to challenge his authority and, in 724, he withdrew from the kingship to become a monk. Although this seems broadly consistent with Bede's portrayal of Nechtan as a religious zealot, he is unlikely to have surrendered his crown willingly. On the contrary, subsequent events suggest that he entered monastic life under duress. He was replaced as king by a man called Drust, whose son was promptly captured and bound by another rival faction. In the ensuing uncertainty Nechtan was hauled out of monastic retirement to become the bound prisoner of Drust, who presumably blamed his predecessor for the treatment meted out to his son. Drust himself was soon toppled from the kingship by a third rival called Alpín. This freed Nechtan from captivity, but he chose not to return to the religious life and instead plunged headlong into the maelstrom of dynastic strife. The brief reign of Alpín witnessed further turmoil, in which several rivals for the overkingship jostled each other for position. Foremost among these were Drust, Alpín and Nechtan, together with a newcomer on the political stage: an ambitious prince called Óengus, the son of Fergus.

In 727 Óengus toppled Alpín to set himself up as the paramount king. He then marched to war against Drust, upon whom he inflicted three successive defeats. Neither Drust nor Alpín were beaten decisively, for both quickly returned to the fray. In 728, at *Monid Chroibh*, the forces of Alpín and Óengus fought a battle in which Alpín's son was killed. The setting was Moncrieffe Hill, three miles south-east of Perth. Here, the remains of a stone-walled enclosure show that the site held high status in prehistoric times. In the Early Historic period, it still held an aura of ancient power and provided a suitable backdrop for a mighty clash of arms. The battle took place not on the hill itself but on the lower ground at its feet, close to an important ford on the River Earn. It was a major victory for Óengus, enabling him to substantially reduce the threat posed by Alpín. Hostilities continued to rage, rendering the Pictish over-kingship meaningless as long as rival claimants competed for it. The balance shifted when Óengus and Nechtan joined forces in an effort to crush Alpín once and for all. Within a few months of the Battle of Moncrieffe, the new allies routed Alpín's army at *Caislen Credi*, an unidentified fortress. This crushing defeat effectively removed Alpín from the contest and resulted in the transfer of his lands and military resources to Óengus, who was left in a strong position but still lacked the ultimate prize. In dynastic terms the real beneficiary was not Óengus but his ally, Nechtan, who regained the over-kingship after the Pictish nobility finally disregarded Alpín's claim.

At the start of the following year, 729, three of the four rivals still remained: Nechtan, Óengus and Drust. The final scenes in the drama were played out during the ensuing months, beginning with a great battle between the forces of Óengus and Nechtan at a place called *Monith Carno*. The location of this battle, like that of *Caislen Credi*, cannot be pinpointed, but the name indicates a prominent *monadh* or hill. The result was decisive: the forces of Óengus vanquished Nechtan's army and slew three *exactatores*, 'tribute-gatherers'. These men were of sufficient importance to be named by the Irish annalists and were therefore not merely a trio of lowly royal servants. Their identification in the annals confirms their high status and suggests that their deaths were related to the outcome of the battle, or perhaps to its cause. The bone of contention may have been a refusal by Óengus to acknowledge Nechtan's status as senior partner in their alliance, if indeed the agreement was still intact.

Óengus seemingly made his move when the overking's *exactatores* came to demand an appropriate gift of tribute.

Nechtan survived the defeat, but it shattered his military reputation and ended his reign. He departed from the political stage, never to return. Given his earlier fondness for religious matters it is likely that he returned to a life of monastic retirement. His exit left Drust as the last remaining challenger to Óengus, who now stood poised on the brink of supremacy. The last act in the long and bitter conflict was played out at *Druim-Derg-Blathuug*, 'The Red Ridge of *Blathuug*' on 12 August 729. Some historians envisage this encounter taking place on the southern slopes of Blath Bhalg, a large hill six miles east of Pitlochry, but the suggested location is extremely remote and seems an unlikely venue for an important battle. Better candidates exist at Drumderg, a low ridge rising above farmland five miles north of Blairgowrie, or in the valley of the River Isla at the feet of the mountain Druim Dearg. Wherever the battle was fought, its outcome was catastrophic for Drust, who was defeated and slain. His demise gave final victory to his opponent and brought closure to the years of dynastic strife. The various factions among the Pictish royal kindreds acknowledged Óengus as their new overking and bowed to his authority. No other rivals stepped forward to deny his right to rule, which now lay beyond challenge or doubt. The frontiers of Pictavia did not, however, mark the limits of his ambition. His eyes roved elsewhere, to the land of the Scots on the far western coast, and his war-hardened henchmen began to sharpen their swords. Marching beneath his banner, the Picts would soon reach the zenith of their military power.

CHAPTER 9
The Warlord

In his description of northern Britain in 731, Bede offered a picture of relative calm and stability. Northumbria, his own homeland, lay at peace with her neighbours, even with Mercia, which was then the most powerful English realm. The Mercian king, Aethelbald, held all lands south of the Humber under his sway. Northumbria herself controlled a large swath of territory west of the Pennines and north of the Solway Firth. Beyond what is now Ayrshire the English frontier marched with the southern border of Alt Clut, the last remaining kingdom of the North Britons. The Clyde kings regarded their Northumbrian counterparts as rivals for mastery of the Lowlands but seemed disinclined to make war against them at that time. In the far north-west, on the coastlands of Argyll, the Scots of Dalriada likewise showed no aggression to Northumbria and seemed – in Bede's view – to be 'content with their own territories'. East of Druim Alban the Picts, under their new overking Óengus, still maintained a treaty with the English. Bede was thus able to end his book on an optimistic note, rejoicing in 'these favourable times of peace and prosperity'.

To an elderly English monk living in quiet cloisters beside the River Tyne, the outside world might indeed have seemed calm and secure. This was not, however, a perspective shared by Bede's contemporaries in the monasteries of Dalriada. The view from their own windows looked rather different. For nearly thirty years the Scots had been racked by dynastic conflict, as the royal kindreds of Kintyre and Lorn competed for the overkingship of Argyll. Amid these bitter internal wars, the Scots were obliged to meet the Clyde Britons in battle on two occasions, both of which resulted in defeat for the warbands of Alt Clut. The key players in the Dalriadan kin-strife were Selbach of Cenél Loairn, whose chief stronghold lay at Dunollie near modern Oban, and the descendants of Áedán mac Gabráin. In 731 the Cenél nGabráin kingship was held by Eochaid, a great-grandson of Domnall Brecc, who ruled as paramount king of Dalriada from 726 until his death in 733. Selbach of Cenél Loairn died in 730, but his political ambitions were continued by his belligerent son Dungal, who launched an attack on Cenél nGabráin territory in the following year. The target was *Tairpert Boittir*, a frontier fortress at Tarbert in Kintyre, which Dungal captured and burned.

It was around this time that Óengus, king of the Picts, had his first military clash with Dalriada. His son, Brude, met a force of Scots in battle and emerged victorious. The defeated warlord was Talorc, a man with a Pictish name but with an ancestry linking him to Cenél nGabráin. His mother was probably a Pict or a half-Pict, but his father bore the Gaelic name Congus and was a great-great-grandson of the mighty Áedán. Brude's victory forced Talorc to flee to Kintyre where his distant kinsman Eochaid still reigned as overking of Dalriada. With no record of Brude pressing home his advantage after the battle, it would seem that his father had no immediate plans for a sustained military campaign in the West. A few months later, Brude departed from Pictavia for a quiet life in an Irish monastery on Tory Island off the coast of Donegal. There he contemplated a religious career while taking a break from the cares and perils of the secular world.

In 732 the annalists noted the death of the former Pictish overking Nechtan, son of Derile, an event that would have been marked by considerable grief in Northumbria as well as in Pictavia. At the court of King Óengus, however, the news may have been greeted by a sigh of relief at the departure of an old adversary. With the passing of Nechtan, the position of Óengus as undisputed king of the Picts was even more secure. Having proved himself a competent warlord in a series of battles against his rivals, he was rightly regarded by his contemporaries at home and abroad as a formidable foe when provoked to anger. Only a bold, rash or foolhardy adversary would dare to stir his wrath. Far away in Argyll, among the Scots of Cenél Loairn, such a man now stepped forward in the person of Dungal, son of Selbach.

Nechtan had been dead for barely a year when Dungal led a warband across the sea to the coast of northern Ireland. The political context was probably an offer of military aid by Cenél Loairn to an Irish king in a local war. From a Pictish viewpoint, this distant venture was of little concern until Dungal began to direct his aggression against offshore sites. One of these was the monastery on Tory Island where Brude, the son of Óengus, was living in peace as a guest of the brethren. With complete disregard for Adomnán's Law of Innocents, this holy place was attacked by Dungal's warriors. To make matters worse, its special status as a sanctuary was brutally violated when the raiders identified Brude among the monks. To the horror of his hosts the Pictish prince was dragged out by the Scots and taken captive.

News of the outrage reached Óengus at the royal court of Pictavia. His immediate reaction can probably be imagined. Requests for the release of his son were no doubt sent west over Druim Alban but were rebuffed by the Scots. Prince Brude was clearly a valuable prisoner and his captors were in no hurry to give him back. Perhaps they hoped to gain territorial concessions from Óengus, or pledges of peace, in exchange for his son's freedom? The Pictish king's response was a full-scale invasion of Argyll. The principal targets were the leaders of Cenél Loairn – namely the devious Dungal and his henchmen – but a mood of fear spread throughout Dalriada as a whole. In Kintyre the Cenél nGabráin prince Talorc – defeated in battle by Brude in 731 – was handed over to the Picts by his own kin. If the desperate gesture was meant to appease Óengus it evidently worked: Talorc was executed by ritual drowning and the Pictish warbands launched no assaults on Kintyre. The brunt of the invasion was borne solely by Cenél Loairn, and the outcome was never in doubt. Dungal was wounded in battle at the unidentified fortress *Dun-leithfind*, which the Picts captured and destroyed. Fearing for his life Dungal took no chances and fled far away, crossing the sea to seek refuge in Ireland.

Óengus next moved against the important Cenél Loairn stronghold of Dunollie. It was near this place that he captured and bound a Pictish exile: Talorcan, Drostan's son, the half-brother and former rival of Nechtan, son of Derile. Talorcan had been the provincial king of Atholl during Nechtan's overkingship but had been imprisoned in 713. At some point thereafter he had sought refuge in Dalriada, in the sub-kingdom of Lorn among Selbach's kindred. Although his ambitions for power in his homeland were effectively extinguished, he was still a Pictish prince. To Óengus such a man posed a potential threat and had to be suitably neutralised but, with a major military campaign already under way, a decision on the exile's fate was postponed for a while.

The annals do not record a Pictish attack on Dunollie, but it was a strategic site unlikely to have been ignored by Óengus. It either surrendered to him or was besieged and taken. By then, the kingship of Cenél Loairn had already passed from the exiled Dungal to his cousin Muiredach. The release of Brude from captivity occurred around the same time, perhaps as a token of Muiredach's submission. At this point Óengus may have felt that his main objectives had been achieved: Dungal had been forced to flee and his successor was now a tribute-paying vassal. However, the final phases of the drama had yet to be played out. Dungal sneaked back from Ireland to rejoin his kindred, thereby provoking a new round of hostilities which saw Óengus rampaging through Lorn. His army seized the great royal fortress of Dunadd and burned an unidentified place called *Creic*. It may have been at Dunadd that Dungal was finally captured and put in chains, together with his brother Feradach. What happened to Dungal after he fell into Pictish hands is unknown, but his fate is unlikely to have been pleasant. Feradach, on the other hand, was sent to Pictavia as a high-status hostage, a trophy of war, and it is in this guise that he reappears at a later date. Even with Dungal's removal, the war raged on. A Pictish army under the command of Talorcan, brother of Óengus, defeated Dungal's cousin Muiredach, king of Cenél Loairn. The encounter probably took place near Loch Ederline, south-east of Dunollie, and resulted in the deaths of many Dalriadan nobles. Muiredach himself survived the battle but fled with the remnants of his warband and nothing more is heard of him.

Óengus was now effectively the overlord of Dalriada. The power of Cenél Loairn was temporarily broken, and there is no record of Pictish conflict with Cenél nGabráin or any other kindred. The various elite groups among the Scots had little choice but to accept Óengus as their patron. Within a year of his triumph, however, the Pictish king tasted grief and bereavement at the passing of his son. No link between Brude's death and a particular battle is made by the sources, so the cause may have been illness or accident, although time spent as Dungal's prisoner is unlikely to have improved the prince's health.

With the Scots laid under a yoke of subjection and with the wealth of Argyll heading east in regular tribute-payments, Óengus stood at the height of his power. For the next few years no more warfare involving his armies is recorded in the sources. From 736 to 740 he ruled in peace as overlord of all territory north of the Forth-Clyde line. During this period of relative calm he may have deployed some of his treasury towards religious ventures, perhaps endowing a new church at St Andrews or refurbishing an earlier church at the site. The only violent event known from these years was the slaying of Talorcan, Drostan's son, the exiled former king of Atholl taken captive near Dunollie during the war against Cenél Loairn. In 739 this forlorn relic of Pictavia's dynastic wars was executed by ritual drowning.

The Pictish war-sword was drawn again in the year following Talorcan's death. His half-brother Nechtan's treaty with Northumbria finally collapsed, after preserving an uneasy peace for almost three decades. At that time the northern English were ruled by Eadberht, an ambitious and warlike king, whose chief concern was the growing power of Mercia. His relationship with the Picts had already cooled because of a newly forged alliance between Óengus and the Mercian king Aethelbald, an agreement which may have included support by both kings for an exiled rival of Eadberht.

This inevitably led to a breakdown of the old peace-pact forged by Nechtan and warmly praised by Bede. Hostilities broke out between the two sides in 740 when Óengus crossed the River Forth to raid Eadberht's northern frontier in Lothian. At the same time, Aethelbald of Mercia attacked Northumbria from the south before leading his army on a destructive rampage. The outcome of the fighting between Eadberht and Óengus is unknown but, with the Mercians taking advantage of the situation, the Northumbrian king probably made a temporary peace on both fronts by acknowledging the superiority of the allies. A payment to the royal treasury of Pictavia, with another heading south towards the midlands, no doubt saved Eadberht's kingdom from further ravaging.

After this brief conflict Óengus turned his attention elsewhere. In 741 he again marched across Druim Alban to attack the Scots, presumably because they had defaulted on tribute-payments. He crushed their defiance during a campaign described by the annalists as *Percutio Dalriatai*, 'The Smiting of Dalriada'. It was to be his last war in the Gaelic West. Within a few years his predatory instincts sought new territory to conquer and new enemies to fight. These were the Clyde Britons, a people whose apparent absence from the annals in the first half of the eighth century disguises the fact that they were still a major northern power. Óengus confronted them in the mid-740s but, for the first time in his career, he met an enemy capable of halting his ambitions. The first battle occurred in 744, but neither the site nor the outcome are known: it may have been an initial foray by Óengus to test the military strength of Alt Clut. Six years later, at a place recorded in the sources as *Mocetauc*, a Pictish raid was repulsed by an army of Britons led by their king Teudubr. The site of the battle lay at Mugdock, below the valley of Strathblane, on an important north-south route followed today by the A81 highway between Glasgow and Aberfoyle. The Picts were led by Talorcan, brother of Óengus, whose martial reputation had been sealed by his victory over Cenél Loairn in 736. At *Mocetauc* in 750, this redoubtable Pictish commander perished at the hands of Teudubr's warriors. So noteworthy was the Clyde king's victory that it was noted in the Irish and Welsh annals as well as in the *Anglo-*

Figure 7. Mounted Pictish warriors on a stone from Benvie, Angus, now housed in Dundee Museum. Reproduced from J.R. Allen and J. Anderson, *The Early Christian Monuments of Scotland* (1903).

Saxon Chronicle. From a Pictish standpoint it was a disaster, a view shared by the Irish annalists who ominously observed 'the ebbing of the sovereignty of Óengus'.

Great warlords rarely relinquish their power willingly or give up their reputations without a fight. A rival Pictish faction, hoping to exploit the uncertainty after *Mocetauc*, attempted to topple Óengus from the kingship but found him unwilling to move aside. In a battle at *Asreth* – an unidentified place in the province of Circinn – these rivals were duly chased off the field. Nor was Óengus ready to curtail his expansionist ambitions or surrender his status as supreme ruler of the North. As well as being a renowned general, he was also a shrewd politician who chose his friends and allies carefully. He had previously forged an alliance with Aethelbald of Mercia, the overlord of southern and midland Britain, and this was presumably still in place. The agreement was not confined to a mutual interest in restricting the power of Northumbria and was useful in other ways, such as presenting a formidable united front to potential challengers. This unity was seen when the West Saxons rebelled in 750, the cause of their grievance being the joint dominance of Aethelbald and Óengus. Nevertheless, during the next few years Óengus made peace with the Northumbrian king Eadberht and solicited his support for a new campaign of aggression against Alt Clut. Working together, these two former foes began to lay plans for a combined assault on the Britons.

Eadberht's expanding hegemony already encroached on districts close to the southern border of Alt Clut. In 750, for example, he had seized the Ayrshire plain of Kyle from Britons who were either neighbours or vassals of the Clyde kings. In 756 he attacked Clydesdale from the south while Óengus launched a simultaneous assault from the north. The royal fortress of the Britons at Dumbarton was besieged and their king Dyfnwal, son of Teudubr, was forced to sue for peace on 1 August. The campaign appeared to be a military triumph for the allies, but their victory was short-lived. On 10 August, as the Northumbrian army marched homewards, it was ambushed and slaughtered by an unidentified force. The Picts were possible culprits but they, too, were marching back to their own lands when it occurred. Perhaps they took a detour to inflict a treacherous blow on their unsuspecting allies? Alternatively, the English column may have been attacked by a warband of Clyde Britons bent on avenging their king's submission nine days earlier.

After returning home from the Dumbarton campaign, Óengus made no further attempt to impose his authority on his neighbours. He was still overking of Pictavia and retained some kind of dominance over Dalriada, but his days of glory and conquest were ending. He died in 761, having ruled for more than thirty years. No other Pictish king achieved so much on the battlefield, nor subjected so much territory to his dominion. In the eyes of his enemies he was regarded as a voracious predator who lived by the sword. 'From the beginning of his reign right to the end he perpetrated bloody crimes, like a tyrannical slaughterer,' declared one English source. Similar sentiments were no doubt voiced by the Scots and Britons when they learned of his death. He was, however, more than just a ruthless warlord. Through sheer force of will he extinguished the dynastic strife of the 720s to unite the various Pictish factions under his authority. His reign saw his people standing tall as undisputed masters of the North.

Two famous monuments may commemorate the achievements of Óengus. One is the St Andrews Sarcophagus, a richly carved stone shrine featuring Biblical scenes and other motifs. The sculpture is dominated by a large human figure, a representation of the Israelite warrior-king David slaying a lion. Some historians believe that this is an image of Óengus himself and that the Sarcophagus once contained his body. The other monument is the cross-slab in the kirkyard at Aberlemno, previously described in Chapter 7. Although the weight of tradition associates this stone with the nearby Battle of Dunnichen in 685, an equally plausible context is one of the military successes attributed to Óengus. The stone was erected in the eighth century and its finely sculpted battle-scene might depict a victory over Cenél Loairn in the 730s, or over the Britons twenty years later. Above the scene is a carved symbol – a notched rectangle with Z rod – which might even represent the name *Óengus*.

The Aberlemno cross-slab may be an epitaph carved in stone, but another memorial to Óengus survives in literature, as a fragment of heroic poetry from ninth-century Ireland. In this verse the poet refers to Alba, a contemporary name for Scotland, but his words hark back 100 years earlier to the era of Pictish ascendancy:

Good the day when Óengus took Alba,
hilly Alba with its strong chiefs;
he brought battle to palisaded towns,
with feet, with hands, with broad shields.

CHAPTER 10
East and West

After the death of Óengus, son of Fergus, in 761 the Pictish over-kingship passed to his brother Brude. Within two years Brude died and was succeeded by Ciniod, son of Feradach. The new king's father was a Scot from Dalriada, the brother of Dungal of Cenél Loairn who had fought against Óengus thirty years earlier. Both brothers had been captured by the Picts in 736 and put in chains. Dungal was presumably executed, but Feradach was brought back to Pictavia as a high-status hostage. At some point during his captivity he sired a son on a Pictish princess. Ciniod, the offspring of this union, was therefore a half-Pict with Cenél Loairn blood in his veins. It is likely that his mother was a sister of Óengus and Brude. Under a system of matrilineal succession this would have made Ciniod the nephew ('sister-son') of two previous kings and therefore a legitimate heir.

The hard-won sovereignty obtained by Óengus over the Scots evaporated in the years following his death. In 768, an army led by Áed Find ('Áed the White'), king of Cenél nGabráin and overking of Dalriada, advanced into Fortriu to fight a battle with Ciniod. Áed Find had gained the kingship of Cenél nGabráin during the period of Pictish supremacy and had ruled initially as a tribute-paying client. With Óengus now gone he was free to offload the burden of tribute and pursue his own political ambitions. A show of military strength in the Pictish heartlands was as good a way as any to reassert his dynasty's independence. The campaign signalled the resurgence of the Scots and marked a turning-point in the fortunes

Centres of power: fortresses and royal residences.

of Cenél nGabráin. Although it brought Áed no permanent territorial gains east of Druim Alban, it dented Pictish hopes of restoring the supremacy won by Óengus. After 768 the sources show no more outbreaks of hostility between East and West until the middle of the next century, when an alleged descendant of Áed claimed the overkingship of Pictavia.

Ciniod died in 775 and was succeeded by two obscure kings whose reigns were uneventful. A period of uncertainty ensued and, by 780, the overkingship was lost in a new outbreak of dynastic strife between the Pictish royal families. The situation demanded a strong individual, a figure in the mould of Óengus, who could reunite the competing factions. No such figure emerged, so the Picts divided into – or perhaps reverted to – a partitioned hegemony ruled separately by two overkings. The provinces or sub-kingdoms north of the Mounth were ruled by Talorcan, son of Drostan, while southern Pictavia acknowledged the claim of another Talorcan, a son of Óengus, who bore the curious nickname *Dubthalorc* ('Black Talorc'). The dynastic upheavals of this time were so acute that the system of matrilineal succession was severely disrupted, thereby allowing Black Talorc to claim the overkingship. As the son of a previous overking he should not have been eligible under the rules of matriliny. The same can be said of his son Drust, who succeeded him in 782. Within the next few years, however, the divisions between the royal dynasties of north and south were healed, and the unity of Pictavia was restored under the rule of a single paramount sovereign. This was either Drust himself or his successor, whom the Pictish king-list wrongly identifies as a Dalriadan prince called Conall, son of Tadg. The presence of a Scot in this part of the list is an error – perhaps a deliberate one – on the part of the compiler. By inserting Conall's name at this point the compiler hoped to give an impression of close links between East and West in the late eighth century. In reality, Drust's successor as overking of Pictavia was Constantine, son of Fergus, who – like Drust himself – was a grandson of the mighty Óengus. Neither of these men would have been eligible to rule if the matrilineal system had remained intact.

Constantine

Conall, son of Tadg, was not Constantine's predecessor in the Pictish overkingship but his enemy in war. In 789 the armies of the two men fought a battle from which Conall narrowly escaped alive after suffering a major defeat at Constantine's hands. The Irish annalists thought that this battle was fought between two Pictish factions, of which one was led by Conall, despite the likelihood that he was a Scot. To some historians the idea of Conall being a Pict fits neatly with another anomaly in the sources, namely Constantine's appearance in the Dalriadan as well as in the Pictish king-list. This has often been seen as an indication that he ruled the Scots and Picts simultaneously. From this viewpoint, Constantine's clash with Conall could be seen as consistent with his involvement in the dynastic politics of both peoples. This interpretation of the data looks doubtful and is not the only one available. Both Constantine and Conall may have had Picts in their warbands at the battle of 789, but the former's presence in the Dalriadan king-list is as erroneous as Conall's appearance in its Pictish counterpart. The two overkingdoms would indeed be joined together under one monarch in the following century but not, perhaps, as early as the closing years of the eighth. In the late eighth century, the Scots were trying to resist a renewal of the Pictish dominance imposed by Óengus in the 730s. In the person of Constantine, son of Fergus, they faced a similarly formidable adversary.

Constantine reigned for more than thirty years until his death in 820. He bore an unusual name that was especially rare within a northern context. Its use among royal families had previously been confined to Dumnonia, a territory encompassing Devon and Cornwall. After the Roman period, this kingdom passed under the rule of native Britons, who held it for more than 400 years against inexorable Anglo-Saxon pressure. Two Dumnonian kings bore the name Constantine in homage to the memory of Constantine the Great, who vanquished his rivals to become the first Christian emperor of Rome. During the early eighth century, the name was borne by a pope and by a Byzantine emperor whose reign – from

741 to 775 – encompassed the year of the Pictish Constantine's birth. The name therefore had strong associations with martial prowess, imperial authority and Christian piety. Bestowing it upon a child who was destined to be a candidate for the overkingship of Pictavia was a deliberate political act on the part of his family, who clearly hoped for great things to come.

It was during Constantine's reign that Forteviot in the lower valley of the River Earn was chosen as the site of a royal palace. Prior to its construction a church had been established somewhere in the immediate vicinity, but no trace survives in the modern landscape. This church probably originated in the eighth century as a royal chapel and major ecclesiastical centre. A fragment of a stone arch, decorated with human and animal figures, was discovered in the early nineteenth century on the nearby riverbed of the Water of May. This unique example of Pictish architectural sculpture is the sole surviving relic of the lost church at Forteviot. Art historians attribute the fragment's style of carving to the early ninth century, which suggests that the arch was added to the fabric of an existing structure during the later years of Constantine's reign. Three figures are depicted on the fragment, the larger of these possibly identifiable as Óengus II, Constantine's brother and successor, or even their grandfather, the great warlord Óengus. An alternative interpretation of the arch is that it was not part of a church but belonged instead to a private royal chapel inside the palace complex.

Forteviot's position in low-lying terrain places it in sharp contrast to the hillforts of the sixth and seventh centuries. Strongholds such as Dundurn and Dunadd were built on imposing rocky outcrops from whose summits they could frown down on a landscape that they physically dominated. The lofty height of these places symbolised the high status of their occupants and bestowed an aura of supremacy. The military aspect of hillforts was immediately obvious, but their natural defensive capabilities were further enhanced by the addition of stone ramparts. In contrast, the royal residence at Forteviot presents an altogether different character. It was not located on a site conducive for defence and would not have survived a sustained assault. Instead, it looks like an abode for people who wanted to dwell in a comfortable setting among green pastures rather than in a windswept fortress on top of a craggy hill. The hillforts of the Early Historic period often succeeded much older strongholds, which gave them an air of ancestral authority. The absence of this kind of aura at a newly built site such as the palace of Forteviot meant that its occupants had to look elsewhere for useful links with ancient power. This is why the palace was deliberately located next to an impressive 'ritual landscape' of prehistoric henges and barrows, whose connections with powerful ancestors could not be questioned. The new centre of Pictish royalty thus received a stamp of legitimacy and a suitable whiff of antiquity from its proximity to monuments of the remote past. Its primary function was unlikely to have been as a permanent residence for Constantine, but rather as one among a defined network of sites favoured by the king and his entourage. The peripatetic or itinerant nature of Early Historic kingship required the establishment of such networks so as to provide temporary or seasonal dwellings for royal entourages during their formal 'circuits' or tours of the kingdom. Interestingly, the presence of what might be a carved representation of the Paschal Lamb on the Forteviot Arch suggests that the palace there may have been a preferred location for the royal family's celebration of Easter.

Vikings

In the final decade of the eighth century a new people arrived on the shores of Britain, a people with whom the fates of Picts and Scots alike were to become inextricably entwined. These newcomers, the Vikings, were destined to have a profound effect on the shaping of medieval Scotland. They hailed from the fjords and sea-coasts of Scandinavia and were the foremost sailors of their age. Their attacks on Britain were first noticed by contemporary chroniclers when a raiding party attacked the Northumbrian monastery on Lindisfarne in 793. These raiders were Norsemen or Northmen – natives of Norway – and had absolutely no interest in the sanctity of Christian churches. They were pagans who worshipped their own gods. Their targets in the early phase of raiding were exposed sites sundered from the mainland, and it was not long before they turned their attention to the myriad islands of Argyll. In 795 the Irish annals noted the plundering of Irish monasteries and, in the same year, the heathens attacked the heart of Celtic Christianity on Iona. Like Lindisfarne and other island monasteries Iona was extremely vulnerable, having no defences and no protection. Such places presented soft targets to the Vikings. Precious objects of gold and silver, together with livestock and foodstuffs, offered easy pickings for shiploads of heathen marauders. The unarmed monks and nuns could offer little resistance against iron swords and axes. Those who did not escape to safety were borne away in longships to be sold as slaves.

The attacks continued for many years and, in 806, the brethren of Iona were butchered in a single raid. With Viking fleets holding mastery of the seaways, the kings of Dalriada could do little but defend their coasts as best they could. Under the relentless stress of those times a dynastic crisis was almost inevitable and, amid the confusion, Constantine of Pictavia installed his son Domnall as overking of the Scots. How this was achieved – whether by military force or political marriage – is not revealed by the sources, but it marked a significant change in relations between East and West. Domnall's reign in Dalriada, while representing some measure of imposed sovereignty by Constantine, was a big step towards unifying the two peoples as a single nation. Gaelic culture and customs had already permeated Pictavia through the influence of the Columban Church, but the process was now given a boost. The eastern and western overkingdoms, ruled as respective hegemonies by a Pictish father and son, inevitably drew closer together in political matters at dynastic level, and in social matters at the level of the aristocratic elite. A corresponding increase in communication across Druim Alban may be envisaged at this time, accompanied by the growth of bilingualism and an exchange of cultural traditions. This undoubtedly began as a two-way process, with influences passing to and fro between the two realms. After a while it became increasingly uneven, a one-way movement which led to the slow erosion of Pictish culture and its replacement by a Gaelic counterpart.

Constantine died in 820 and was succeeded by his brother, Óengus II. At that time the Picts and the Scots still lay under the authority of one family because Domnall, Constantine's son, remained overking of Dalriada for a further fifteen years. Gaelic influence on the upper strata of Pictish society continued, its most visible aspect being an artistic tradition which produced new styles of sculpture. In Argyll itself the ever-present threat of Viking raids created a feeling among the nobility that their homeland was no longer a safe place to be. After 800, the frequency and intensity of the attacks increased. Despite the scenario of random, opportunist raiding presented by the sources, it is possible that the Viking warbands had not in fact sailed to Britain as pirate gangs but had arrived primarily as armies of occupation. Mainland Pictavia with its North Sea coastline was a convenient objective for Scandinavian fleets of the early ninth century, while Orkney and Shetland had probably been targeted even earlier. Both Constantine and his brother Óengus are likely to have defended their homeland against the heathens, although the ensuing encounters are unrecorded. The death of Óengus in 834 preceded that of his nephew Domnall by one year, their demise shaking the growing political unity of East and West. But the Pictish overlordship of Dalriada was by then too well-established to dissolve completely, and the next paramount king of the Scots ruled as the vassal of an eastern sovereign. His name was Áed, son of Boanta, and his Pictish patron was Drust, son of Constantine, the nephew and successor of Óengus II. Against the Viking menace these two kings tried to present a united front, but the tides of fate were about to engulf their realms in catastrophe.

Religious Developments

A little way above the north bank of the Earn, and across the river from the palace at Forteviot, there stood until recently a free-standing cross of sandstone. It was carved and erected in the early ninth century and is one of the most remarkable examples of Pictish sculpture. Standing nearly 2.5 metres high and with a span of 1 metre, it is an imposing and impressive monument whose fame is richly deserved. Its former location on a hillside above Dupplin Castle gave it the name by which it is known today: the Dupplin Cross. In 1998 it was moved from its original setting to be studied and restored at Edinburgh before being returned to Strathearn in 2002. It currently resides in the medieval St Serf's Church at Dunning on the valley floor. Relocation to a safe environment has ensured that the monument's unique carvings are now not only protected from the elements but are also more accessible to the public.

The shaft and arms of the cross bear intricate carvings of spirals, interlace and other patterns, together with humans, beasts and birds. The arcane Pictish symbols that are such a feature of earlier sculpture are completely absent. On one side of the shaft, below the arms, a square panel shows the image of an equestrian figure wearing a moustache and carrying a spear. Beneath him four spear-armed warriors march in close array, while two more appear in similar form on another side. On the western face a second square panel bears faint traces of an inscription, the first line of which begins with a name: *Custantin filius Fircus*. This imposing monument is clearly a memorial to Constantine, son of Fergus, and the mounted figure is in all likelihood a representation of the king. It may have been commissioned by Constantine himself, or by someone who sought to commemorate him in this way. The probability that the sculptural style can be precisely dated to the 820s strongly suggests that the patron was Constantine's brother and successor Óengus. References to a similar cross at Invermay near Forteviot show that the Dupplin monument was not unique. It is, however, the only one of its kind to survive, for it is quite different from the free-standing crosses of Ireland and Argyll. Its purpose was to display the power, prestige and Christian affiliations of a confident royal dynasty for whom the old symbols of pagan ancestors no longer held any significance.

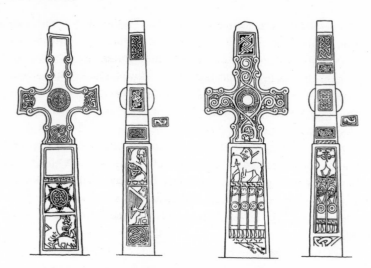

Figure 8. The Dupplin Cross, erected in commemoration of the Pictish king Constantine, son of Fergus. Reproduced from J.R. Allen and J. Anderson, *The Early Christian Monuments of Scotland* (1903).

Constantine's reign coincided with the beginning of a renewed Pictish interest in Columba. Iona was beset by Scandinavian raiders, but its founder's memory was making a comeback in the East. In the previous century the Columban Church had been rejected by Nechtan, son of Derile, and its personnel had been compelled to leave. A hundred years later, in a climate of closer cultural links between Picts and Scots, pro-Gaelic trends were again finding favour. The new *rapprochement* was symbolised by Constantine's patronage of the first church at Dunkeld, a place more commonly associated with the reign of Cináed mac Ailpín three decades later. Cináed was the king who transferred relics of Columba from Iona to Dunkeld after seizing power in Pictavia during the 840s. He developed a major ecclesiastical centre around Constantine's earlier church, which had itself been deliberately sited at a location of great significance. Dunkeld lay in a strategic setting and had traditional associations with the ancestors of the Picts. Constantine's church – and Cináed's later structure – lay beneath the medieval cathedral beside the wide waters of the River Tay. To the west, where the present town spreads out along the riverbank, a prominent hill called King's Seat dominates north-south communication along this part of the valley. Upon this height in prehistoric times stood the Fort of the Caledonians, a stronghold of ancient power whose looming presence bestowed great prestige on the Christian settlement nestling below.

During the second decade of the ninth century Cellach, the abbot of Iona, decided to remove Columba's bones to Kells in Ireland, where an enlarged monastery had been built over a ten-year period between 804 and 814. Kells was selected as the new headquarters of the Columban monks because it offered a safer location for the earthly remains of their founding father. The decision to abandon Iona was made because of the island's exposed position in the face of continuing Viking raids. Cellach approached Constantine to discuss a possible division of the bones, and it was agreed that a portion of the precious relics would remain in northern Britain. Both abbot and king clearly regarded Dunkeld as suitable for this purpose, its inland location rendering it less vulnerable to attack than an offshore site in Argyll. For some reason, however, the division and movement of the bones did not occur in 814, when Kells was completed, nor between then and the death of Constantine in 820. In fact, the respective transfers of relics to Pictavia and Ireland did not take place until 849. This poses something of a mystery, for Iona was still being raided by Vikings until the mid-820s, but the sources are silent on the reason for the delay.

Constantine's brother and successor Óengus II is credited with developing another of the great ecclesiastical sites of medieval Scotland. Old traditions name him as the first patron of the Church of Saint Andrew at Kilrymont on the coast of Fife. Today this place is better known as St Andrews, but its importance certainly pre-dates the career of Óengus II. Rather than being its founder, he was probably responsible for its development as a major church and cult-centre. Before his time it already had royal associations which extend back into the reign of his grandfather and namesake

Óengus, the renowned warrior-king who died in 761. The place-name Kilrymont derives from *Kinrymont*, which is Gaelic *Cenrigmonaid*, meaning 'the end of the king's hill'. In this context the term *monadh* denotes not a prominent peak but an area of upland grazing while the middle element *rig* corresponds to Gaelic *ri* ('king'). Other place-names in the vicinity imply the presence of wild boar, and it is likely that Pictish kings had formerly used the area as a hunting-ground. The earliest Christian settlement at *Cenrigmonaid* was a monastery which certainly existed before the middle of the eighth century. The Irish annals noted the death of its abbot in 747 during the reign of Óengus I, but its original founder may have been Nechtan, son of Derile. The dedication to Saint Andrew may date from Nechtan's time, but nothing is heard of this monastery between 747 and the reign of Óengus II seventy years later. Under the patronage of the younger Óengus the site was enhanced to become a shrine where genuine relics of the Apostle were allegedly housed.

In the twelfth century a foundation-legend was created by the monks to provide a suitable history for their church and for the cult that grew around it. The legend contains much fanciful material, but it preserves a nucleus of truth and gives an interesting portrayal of Óengus II. It introduces a priest called Regulus or Rule, who is described as travelling to Britain with Andrew's sacred bones. On reaching Pictavia, Regulus met Óengus who granted land at Kilrymont for the foundation of a church, which in later centuries developed into the great cathedral of Scotland's patron saint. The legend appears to derive from an original story composed in the mid-ninth century to enhance the site's status under the patronage of Óengus II. A dedication to Andrew prompted the creation of an exotic but wholly fictional story about the Apostle's remains being brought to Pictavia from their repository at Constantinople. The figure of Regulus is likewise a fiction, but the core facts of the tale depict an important event from the reign of Óengus II, whose image was suitably enhanced by association with Andrew.

The Pictish royal church at St Andrews has not survived, but it lay between the cathedral and the area known today as Kirkhill.

Burials of ninth-century date have been found nearby, but the most spectacular discovery was the stone sarcophagus unearthed in 1833 and currently displayed in the cathedral. This stunning example of Pictish art was created as a box-shrine to hold the relics of an important person closely associated with St Andrews. It belongs to the period 750–850 and was designed for display in a prominent position inside a royal church, the patron who commissioned it undoubtedly being a king. Those who came to view the sarcophagus were able to walk around its four richly carved sides and would have understood the significance of each portion of the sculpture. The objectives behind its creation and display were obviously political, but the identity of the king who commissioned it is unknown. Equally obscure is the question of whom it commemorated, although a plausible candidate is the warlord Óengus I. This would mean that the sarcophagus was his lasting memorial, probably commissioned by his grandson and namesake Óengus II as an appropriate focus for the new religious house of their dynasty.

The Disaster of 839

Óengus II died in 834 and was succeeded by his nephew Drust, who may have shared the Pictish overkingship with a certain Talorcan, son of Wthoil, although the nature of this arrangement is unknown. If a two-part division of Pictavia still persisted, then Talorcan perhaps ruled north of the Mounth. Within a few years both he and Drust were gone and a single overkingship was restored by Eoganán, a son of Óengus II. In Dalriada the vassal-king Áed, son of Boanta, continued to accept Pictish overlordship and acknowledged Eoganán as his new patron. The successions of Eoganán and Drust represented a break with the old matrilineal custom, because their fathers had also been kings. Father-to-son inheritance is a key feature of patrilineal succession but is often absent from matrilineal systems where a man is normally succeeded by the son of his sister or by his own womb-brother. Father-to-son succession was rare

Figure 9. St Orland's Stone, Cossans, near Kirriemuir. Reproduced from J.R. Allen and J. Anderson, *The Early Christian Monuments of Scotland* (1903).

among the Picts and did not appear until the late eighth century, at a time when Gaelic customs were making inroads into many areas of society and culture. The elevation of Drust and Eoganán as kings indicates that the influence of the Scots, among whom patrilineal succession had always prevailed, was starting to gain momentum as the ninth century progressed.

In Dalriada the fate of Áed, Boanta's son, was ultimately bound up with the fortunes of his liege-lord Eoganán. The two kings mustered a united host of Picts and Scots for a decisive showdown with the Vikings. In 839 this combined army encountered a force of Scandinavian marauders and made a stand against them. The ensuing clash of arms was one of the most decisive battles of the period and, although its precise location is unknown, its outcome is not in doubt. It was nothing less than a catastrophic defeat for Eoganán and Áed, both of whom were slain alongside large numbers of their warriors. This was a dark hour for Scots and Picts alike, the disaster depriving both peoples of their kings and heralding a period of crisis. In Pictavia the situation remained extremely bleak. The victorious Vikings plundered freely and did as they pleased, knowing that the native leadership was broken. Eventually they departed, returning to their ships laden with booty and captives. They left behind a severely weakened kingdom, a shattered aristocracy and a demoralised population.

Meanwhile, in Dalriada, a period of dynastic confusion followed the disaster of 839. Later tradition intruded a man called Alpín into the overkingship of the Scots at this time. In medieval Scottish texts he appears as a grandson of Áed Find and thus of Cenél nGabráin descent. One portion of his story shifts him from Kintyre to Galloway, where he fights against indigenous 'Picts'. In reality, he is little more than a shadowy figure whose origins are wrapped in mystery. He would be fairly unremarkable had he not fathered Cináed mac Ailpín ('Kenneth Macalpine'), one of the most important and controversial figures in early Scottish history.

CHAPTER 11

Twilight of the Picts

Now we shall tell briefly how the very powerful
Pictish race disappeared after so many victories.

Gerald of Wales, *c.*1190

The great Viking victory of 839 caused major disruption not only in Pictavia but also in Dalriada, where the death of Áed Boanta in the battle left the Scots without a king. In the wake of the disaster, Cináed mac Ailpín eventually emerged as Áed's successor. Whether Cináed seized the vacant overkingship by force or was nominated as ruler of Argyll by a Pictish overlord is unclear. He was undoubtedly a man of energy and ambition, but neither his true ancestry nor the details of his career are retrievable from the web of traditions surrounding him. Scottish chroniclers of later times associated him with Cenél nGabráin and constructed a lineage tracing him back to the seventh-century king Domnall Brecc. This kind of tampering with royal genealogies was common practice in medieval times because it offered an easy way to justify a king's right to rule by giving him an impressive 'family tree'. When employed retrospectively a fictional genealogy was useful to a king's descendants in asserting their own legitimacy in times of dynastic strife. In Cináed's case the later traditions have obscured his true origins so completely that modern historians are unable to say whether he was a Scot or a Pict.

Whatever his ethnic heritage or preferred ethnic affiliation

Cináed's claim on the overkingship of Dalriada was accepted by the Scots. This means that their royal kindreds, warrior aristocracy and ecclesiastical elite acknowledged his right to rule. He presumably held power on the mainland, perhaps in Cenél nGabráin territory, but it is likely that many offshore territories were already controlled by Viking warlords. Cináed and his contemporaries knew that the extensive Dalriada of earlier times was no more. The Hebridean islands formerly under the hegemony of overkings based in Lorn or Kintyre had fallen into Scandinavian hands and would not be regained by Scottish monarchs until much later in the medieval period. When Cináed succeeded to the kingship vacated by Áed, son of Boanta, in 839 he came to power as ruler of a much-reduced domain.

Gaels in the East

Cináed has long occupied a special place in Scottish history: he is credited with unifying the Picts and Scots as a single nation. Whether he should really be seen as the architect of such an impressive political feat is a matter of debate. The Irish annalists noted his death in 858 and described him as *rex Pictorum* ('King of the Picts') but failed to say how, when or why he acquired this title. Since other sources agree that he ruled Pictavia for sixteen years, a simple subtraction pinpoints 842 as the beginning of his reign in the East. To explain his emergence as king of the Picts a tale of conquest was formulated in later times. Twelfth-century writers such as Gerald of Wales, whose words appear at the beginning of this chapter, promoted a dramatic vision of conflict in which Cináed defeated the Picts in battle before annexing their lands. This version of events is disputed by modern historians, many of whom interpret *rex Pictorum* as meaning that Cináed arrived in Pictavia not as a conqueror but as a legitimate candidate for the Pictish overkingship. For such a claim to be acceptable to the Picts, he presumably had Pictish ancestry, perhaps through his mother if his father Alpín was a Scot from Kintyre. It is possible, of course, that

Cináed himself was a full-blood Pict whose true heritage lay not among Cenél nGabráin but among the Pictish royal kindreds. Perhaps his alleged Dalriadan ancestry was devised by later writers who wished to make him appear 'Scottish' rather than Pictish? Supporters of the idea of a half-Pictish or full-Pictish Cináed point out that his name is a Gaelic variant of *Ciniod*, a name borne by two Pictish kings. The same can be said of his father's name, which seems to be a Gaelicisation of the Pictish or British name *Elphin*. One important change associated with Cináed's acquisition of the Pictish overkingship is the disappearance of the Pictish language during the ninth, tenth and eleventh centuries and its replacement by Gaelic. This process of 'language death' could be explained by a scenario of war and conquest, but Gaelic influences – including Gaelic speech – had undoubtedly been permeating Pictavia since Constantine's overlordship of Dalriada in the late eighth century. The Pictish elite of Cináed's generation may have been fully bilingual, especially if Gaelic-speakers were already settling among them. It is likely, for instance, that large numbers of Dalriadan aristocrats had emigrated across Druim Alban to escape the Viking raids. These high-status Scots, displaced by Scandinavian colonists in the islands and coastlands of Argyll, may have arrived in Pictavia by invitation. It is not difficult to imagine their usefulness to a Pictish overking as extra manpower in his own struggles against the Vikings. If such a monarch was, in any case, an overlord to whom they and their kings owed allegiance, the refugees had a reasonable expectation of gifts of land in exchange for military service. Contrary to modern perceptions about the differences between the Celtic languages, the speech of a Dalriadan immigrant might not have been wholly unintelligible to Pictish ears.

In addition to the twelfth-century vision of Picto-Scottish warfare and Dalriadan conquest, another fictional scenario was created for Cináed. This envisaged him unifying Dalriada and Pictavia in a confederation, an act of statesmanship facilitated by his right to rule in each kingdom. The idea of some kind of negotiated merger between Picts and Scots became popular in the eighteenth and nineteenth centuries because it offered an ancient precedent for the union of the English and Scottish parliaments in 1707. Its proponents showed little understanding of the nature of early medieval kingship and sought instead to impose modern ideas about nationhood and statehood on an era when both notions were anachronistic.

Although Cináed is unlikely to have conquered Pictavia at the point of a sword, his accession as *rex Pictorum* surely involved some measure of conflict. In the wake of the disastrous defeat of 839, he is unlikely to have been the only claimant on the Pictish overkingship. Like the great Óengus 100 years earlier, Cináed would have had to dispose of his own rivals one by one, probably in a series of battles which echoed the dynastic strife of the 720s. Some or all of these rivals are identifiable in the Pictish king-list, the most prominent among them being Wrad or Ferat, whom a version of the St

Figure 10. Cross-slab from Meigle, Perthshire, showing horsemen and Biblical imagery on the reverse. Reproduced from J. Anderson, *Scotland in Early Christian Times* (1881).

Andrews foundation legend associates with a royal church at Meigle. Cináed's disposal of Wrad and the other claimants may have been a protracted process, drawn out over several years, but it appears to have been completed by 848 or 849. Only then could Cináed regard himself as *rex Pictorum*, the paramount sovereign of the Picts and overlord of the Scots. Regardless of his semi-legendary guise as the founder of medieval Scotland, this was a major achievement for Cináed and a clear testament to his capabilities. It placed him on a par with his illustrious predecessors Óengus and Constantine as a great king whose authority was acknowledged on both sides of Druim Alban.

The Treachery of Scone

Medieval chroniclers writing long after Cináed's reign were intrigued by the disappearance of a separate Pictish identity in the ensuing two centuries. In seeking to explain it they invented a suitable legend which became known as *Braflang Scoine* ('The Treachery of Scone'). According to this tale, Cináed and his Scots invited the Pictish nobility to a sumptuous feast at Scone in Perthshire. The supposedly amicable gathering turned into a bloody massacre when the treacherous Scots murdered their intoxicated guests. From this and similar traditions arose an erroneous belief that the entire Pictish nation had been exterminated. Although completely fictional, the story of the feast and the massacre of the nobles has some historical interest and is worth a closer look.

The legend is at least as old as the eleventh century and, ironically, was conceived by the Scots themselves. It portrays the Picts as honoured guests who were lulled into a false sense of safety before being brutally slaughtered in the feasting-hall. The *Prophecy of Berchan* casts the event in typically prosaic terms in its verses about Cináed: 'The fierce men in the East are deceived by him. [The Scots] dig the earth (mighty is the art!), a deadly pit, death by wounding, in the middle of Scone of the high shields.' Deception and betrayal are hallmarks of a twelfth-century Irish version of the story from which Gerald of Wales crafted his own report of the shameful incident. Gerald wrote that Cináed's henchmen

> noted their opportunity and drew out the bolts which held up the boards; and the Picts fell into the hollows of the benches on which they were sitting, in a strange trap up to the knees so that they could never get up; and the Scots immediately slaughtered them all, tumbled together everywhere and taken suddenly and unexpectedly, and fearing nothing of the sort from allies and confederates, men bound to them by benefits and companions in their wars.

The theme of a great banquet, during which a ruler deceives and slays his guests, is known elsewhere in medieval literature. As early as c.830 the Welsh author of the *Historia Brittonum* told how Hengist and Horsa, the legendary leaders of the Anglo-Saxon invasion, attended a banquet hosted by the Britons which turned into a massacre. Other versions of the same theme appear in Germany and Russia, but in all instances the motive behind the story is the total annihilation of one ruling elite by another. This, then, is the real historical value of *Braflang Scoine*, a legend created by Cináed's successors to show how his dynastic rivals in Pictavia were vanquished. It served a specific purpose as a powerful piece of propaganda in the tenth or eleventh centuries, at a time when Gaelic language and culture were supplanting their Pictish counterparts. In the late tenth century, many people of Pictish descent may have wondered why the customs of their ancestors were disappearing and why the customs of the Scots were gaining ground. They would have found a simple explanation in *Braflang Scoine*. The legendary or fictional aspects of the tale were unimportant to the Gaelic-speaking elite of what had once been Pictavia. What mattered to this group in the time of Cináed's descendants around c.1000 was the message conveyed by the tale's dramatic imagery: the Pictish period was over and a new 'Scottish' era had begun.

Dunkeld

The defeat of his rivals allowed Cináed to consolidate his position as an overking of Picts and Scots. He soon embarked on a process of political change that would eventually turn his kingdom into Alba, the precursor of medieval Scotland. One of his first and most significant actions was the transfer of relics from Columba's tomb on Iona to Dunkeld. This completed a process begun by the Pictish king Constantine three decades earlier. At the same time Indrechtach, abbot of Iona, conveyed the rest of the founder's remains and treasures to the Columban brethren's new home at Kells in Ireland. Significantly, one of the most sacred objects to reach Dunkeld at this time was the portable shrine known as *Scrín Choluim Chille* which – somewhat surprisingly – did not go to Kells. Its arrival in Perthshire showed Indrechtach's trust in Cináed's commitment to the Columban Church. For a while the church at Dunkeld, under the protection and patronage of the mac Ailpín dynasty, seems to have supplanted Kells as the true successor of Iona.

To some historians the division of relics is seen as breaking the long relationship between the respective successors of Columba and Áedán mac Gabráin. This relationship had been built upon pledges of mutual support whose benefits both parties had enjoyed for almost three centuries. With the leadership of the Columban *familia* migrating to Ireland, and with the elite of Cenél nGabráin perhaps moving eastward to serve Cináed and his heirs, it is easy to imagine the final curtain falling on the ancient link. However, the image of a symbolic parting of Ionan clergy and Kintyre royalty is not the only way to interpret the ninth-century division of Columba's bones. An alternative interpretation sees the enshrining of holy relics at Dunkeld as cementing rather than breaking the bond between abbots and kings.

Old traditions encountered in the previous chapter identified the Pictish king Constantine, son of Fergus, as founder of the first church at Dunkeld, but its status was elevated to new heights when Cináed made it a repository for Dalriada's patron saint. This was an act of great symbolism, for Columba was not only an icon for the Scots but also the leader of the Ionan monks whose missions had spread Christianity in Pictavia during the sixth and seventh centuries. The successors of these early missionaries were the bishops and abbots expelled in 717 by Nechtan, son of Derile, after his rejection of the Celtic Church in favour of the 'Roman' ecclesiastical customs of his English friends. By enshrining Columba's relics at Dunkeld, deep in the Pictish heartlands, Cináed reversed Nechtan's anti-Ionan policies and restored Gaelic primacy over religious affairs. More than this, he developed Constantine's earlier church as a pre-eminent religious foundation to rival the growing cult-centre of Saint Andrew on the coast of Fife. With Iona already evacuated and virtually abandoned, and with Dalriadan refugees probably arriving in Perthshire, Dunkeld became a new mother-church for Picts and Scots alike.

Under Cináed's patronage, Dunkeld enjoyed a special status as the main religious centre of his kingdom, inheriting the privileged position formerly enjoyed by Iona in a Dalriadan context. Dunkeld's abbot was acknowledged as chief bishop of the mac Ailpín realm, and therefore as spiritual head of Christianity east and west of Druim Alban. Within the next half century, however, this status was already being challenged by the clergy at St Andrews.

Residence and Ritual

One of Cináed's chief centres of power – perhaps his most favoured residence – was the palace of Forteviot in Strathearn. Here, on the valley floor beside the River Earn, he and his entourage made use of a site overlooked by the great cross of Dupplin which bore the name of his illustrious predecessor Constantine. Another place associated with Cináed is Scone, where later legend placed the treacherous slaughter of the Pictish aristocracy. Since Scone was a place of no significance in recorded history before Cináed's time, its important role in the rituals of kingship may have been first established by him. One Irish text calls him the first Scot to rule at Scone, a statement which implies that the place already had Pictish royal connections, but the information is late and almost certainly fictional. No reliable source mentions Scone before 906, when a royal proclamation of Scottish ecclesiastical law was made there by Constantine II, Cináed's grandson. This event took place at the oddly named *Collis Credulitatis*, 'The Hill of Credulity', a low mound which can still be seen adjacent to Scone Palace. Today the site is known as Moot Hill, a name derived from public meetings or 'moots' at which kings affirmed their authority by dispensing justice and performing rituals. A royal moot was a type of open-air meeting that became popular in Britain from the eighth century onwards. Such assemblies carried no implication of democracy or debate but instead marked a new development in the evolution of kingship. Their public aspect represented the increasing centralisation of power around a single individual to whom all the attendees owed loyalty. Moots allowed a king to summon all the chief men of his realm – lords, warriors and priests – to receive his commands and decrees *en masse* in a 'national' rather than in a local or provincial context. In this respect a moot replaced some functions of the royal circuit of earlier times when a king and his entourage toured the provinces of the kingdom to conduct formal ceremonies at high-status residences. Local issues were forgotten at a moot, where attendees were left in no doubt that they all belonged to one large kingdom and that their allegiance was owed to one powerful sovereign. The royal proclamation of Constantine II at Scone in 906 was conducted at such a gathering and probably followed similar ceremonies dating back to Cináed's reign. The mac Ailpín kings selected Scone because it nestled among sites of ancient significance: the Roman fort of *Bertha*, several prehistoric monuments and an important ford on the Tay all lay in close proximity. It was therefore an appropriate setting for the royal moot, although it is unlikely that the place had been used in this way by earlier Pictish kings.

Cináed's Foreign Policy

After his elevation as *rex Pictorum* and his adoption of Forteviot as a primary residence, Cináed gave thought to the security of his older domains in Argyll. The Viking presence in the western seaways posed a continuing menace to the homeland of the Scots and disrupted the ancient links between Dalriada and northern Ireland. To meet the threat, Cináed forged an alliance with his Irish counterparts by giving his daughter Mael Muire in marriage to the powerful Uí Néill king Áed Findliath. The political dimension of this union probably involved pledges of military co-operation against Scandinavian raiders. After Áed's death in 879, Mael Muire married his successor Flann Sinna, an equally powerful king, and helped to sustain her father's Irish policy until her death in 913. As well as being the wife of two Uí Néill kings she was mother to another and grandmother to a fourth. Her position in Irish dynastic affairs enabled Cináed and his sons to maintain mutually beneficial relationships with Ireland at a time when their primary concerns lay in the eastern part of their kingdom.

Dealing with the predatory Norsemen was trouble enough for the kings of the British Isles, but the situation worsened in the middle of the ninth century when a second wave of Scandinavian pirates appeared on the horizon. These were the Danes, whom the Irish annalists called 'Black Foreigners' to distinguish them from the 'White Foreigners' of Norway. There was little affection between the two groups. In 851 a Danish fleet plundered the Norse settlement at Dublin and, for the next couple of years, the eastern coast of Ireland became a battleground for rivalries between Norse and Danish warbands. These eventually fell under the sway of Norway in 853 when Olaf, the Norwegian king's son, came to Ireland to place the Scandinavian colonies under a yoke of tribute. The protection conferred upon Dalriada by Cináed's friendship with the Uí Néill seems, however, to have maintained an effective defence. The only major incursion into his territory at this time came in the East, when a Danish raid on Fortriu ravaged as far south as Dunkeld. The year of the attack is unknown, but its location shows the ease with which Danish forces were able to harass the interior of Pictavia.

Cináed had other enemies apart from predatory Vikings. During his reign the Clyde Britons attacked and burned Dunblane in southern Perthshire, where a Pictish church once stood near the site of the medieval cathedral. The place was an important religious centre in the south of Cináed's kingdom, but its frontier location made it vulnerable. Neither the date nor the cause of the raid are known but further hostilities with the Britons were avoided by a marriage between one of Cináed's daughters and a Clyde prince called Rhun. This union produced a son, Eochaid, a controversial figure who seemingly ruled as a mac Ailpín overking of Picts and Scots. Cináed's own military ambitions along his southern border drew him across the River Forth to launch a series of assaults on English territory. The sources credit him with six campaigns in Northumbria, during which he burned the coastal fortress of Dunbar and the monastery at Old Melrose on the River Tweed. Dunbar was an important stronghold in the defence of Northumbria's Pictish frontier and may have been the residence of Berht, the leader of Ecgfrith's raid on Ireland in 684. Cináed's assault on Dunbar may have had special significance for his Pictish subjects in the troubled border zone around the Firth of Forth. Not since the great victory at Dunnichen in 685 had an army from the Pictish heartlands inflicted such a damaging blow against the English. The raids into Northumbria show Cináed as an ambitious and confident ruler whose resources gave him the capability not only to defend his borders but also to launch aggressive strikes beyond them.

Beyond the Spey the northern lands lay exposed to Viking attacks, but it was here that the former Pictish sub-kingdom or province of Moray flourished under its own rulers. The Moravian elites chose not to acknowledge Cináed as their overlord. Like him they had links to Dalriada and were Gaelic-speakers, their forefathers having migrated from Argyll to escape the Scandinavian menace. They claimed descent from a family of Cenél Loairn princes who had evidently seized power in Moray during the late eighth or early ninth centuries. The Pictish rulers of this region had been supplanted by some process now invisible to modern historians. Whether the transfer of power was achieved amicably or violently is unknown, but it seems to have been accomplished before Cináed's own eastward migration from Argyll to Perthshire. Just as later Scottish writers traced Cináed's lineage back to the Cenél nGabráin king Domnall Brecc, so the ruling house of Moray claimed as their ancestor Ferchar Fota ('The Tall'), a seventh-century king of Cenél Loairn. Ferchar's grandson was the villainous Dungal whose incitement of the wrath of Óengus, son of Fergus, had brought the first period of Pictish domination over the Scots. The scenario of Ferchar's later descendants transferring Cenél Loairn interests to Moray and establishing there a new Gaelic kingdom need not be doubted, despite the absence of reliable information in the sources. Their likely route from Lorn is indicated by a chain of place-names suggesting a ninth-century movement from Argyll to Moray via the Great Glen. However, if the immigrants hoped to escape from the Vikings they were soon to be disappointed. After the middle of the century the northern Pictish provinces of Caithness and Sutherland came under severe pressure from Norse settlers moving south from colonies in Orkney. Cináed mac Ailpín felt no inclination to confront this new peril and was content to leave these territories to their fate. But the new rulers of Moray successfully defended their lands and maintained a fierce autonomy throughout those troubled times. In the following century, when they fell under the sway of Cináed's successors, they retained much of their former power but were no longer ruled by their own kings. Under the overlordship of the mac Ailpín dynasty, the ruler of Moray became instead a *mormaer* or 'great steward', the most famous bearer of the title being Macbethad mac Findlaich, Shakespeare's Macbeth, who attained the kingship of Scotland in the mid-eleventh century.

After Cináed

Cináed mac Ailpín died in his palace at Forteviot on 13 February 858, the cause of his demise being a tumour rather than the sword of an enemy. His sixteen-year rule over the Picts and Scots is often seen as a period of transition marking the birth of medieval Scotland, and this was perhaps true to some extent. He may have been the first Gaelic-speaking monarch to rule Pictavia and Dalriada as a single kingdom. During the reigns of his sons and grandsons this extensive realm was given a new name: *Alba*. This ancient name, formerly applied by Irish writers to Britain as a whole, seems to have been adapted as a label for the lands under mac Ailpín rule. Within two generations of Cináed's death, the chroniclers were calling his heirs 'kings of Alba' rather than 'kings of the Picts', thus heralding the notion of a single political entity spanning the highlands of northern Britain.

Cináed's final journey brought him back to the old Cenél nGabráin lands in the West. Like many of his alleged forefathers he was buried on Iona among the revered heroes of Dalriada, resting in peace in the graveyard of the deserted monastery. He was succeeded by his brother, Domnall mac Ailpín, who ruled for only four years. The main event of Domnall's reign seems to have been reported rather vaguely in the sources: 'The Gaels, with their king, in Forteviot made the rights and kingdom-laws of Áed, son of Eochaid.' These words refer back to Áed Find, king of Dalriada, whose victory in 768 probably freed the Scots from a Pictish overlordship first imposed by Óengus, son of Fergus. By c.800, this overlordship had been restored and was evidently still in place in Cináed's time. Perhaps it then lapsed after Cináed's death, before being restored by his brother? The king of the Gaels who 'made the rights and kingdom-laws of Áed' at Forteviot may have been a Dalriadan ruler compelled by Domnall mac Ailpín to renew the old oaths of allegiance. Later tradition remembered Domnall as 'a vigorous soldier' and noted that his life ended in violence with his assassination in 862. His death took place in the ruins of the Roman fort of *Bertha* at the junction of the Rivers Almond and Tay. This fort had been built by Agricola's troops during the first invasion of the Highlands, but its occupation by Rome was brief. However, to the Caledonians and their Pictish descendants it had long carried the footprint of imperial authority and remained an enduring symbol of power in the landscape. Its later name was *Rathinveramon*, a Gaelic name meaning 'earth-walled fort at the mouth of the River Almond'. Although its original function as a military site lay in the distant past, it may have hosted formal ceremonies for kings of the Pictish era. The mac Ailpín dynasty perhaps continued this tradition and, if so, it was a plausible venue for Domnall's murder in 862.

Domnall's successor was his nephew Constantine mac Cináeda, whom modern historians sometimes call Constantine I of Alba. Like his father and uncle he was described by the Irish annalists as *rex Pictorum*, 'king of the Picts'. This title was soon to disappear from the annals and was bestowed for the last time upon Áed mac Cináeda, Constantine's brother and successor. After Áed's death in 878 the notion of Pictish monarchy disappears entirely from the sources. The term *rex Pictorum* was replaced by *rí Alban*, 'king of Alba', probably to reinforce the point that the mac Ailpín dynasty now held the combined overkingships of East and West as an indivisible entity transcending ethnic affiliations. In battle the armies of Alba included warriors from Perthshire and Argyll marching under one banner on behalf of their sovereign, and it is this type of mixed Picto-Scottish force that the Vikings faced in a series of clashes during the reign of Constantine I. In his time the main Scandinavian menace was posed by Dublin, the greatest of the Norse realms in Ireland. From here in 866 came a large and powerful warband, led by King Olaf, to ravage Constantine's Pictish domains. Four years later, Olaf attacked Alt Clut, the great citadel of the Clyde Britons at Dumbarton, subduing it after a four-month siege. This was no random raid by pirates but a sustained, well-organised campaign whose objective was the destruction of one of the great northern powers. When the well between Dumbarton's two rocky summits dried up, the exhausted defenders were doomed and the mighty fortress fell. The jubilant Vikings stormed inside to ransack the ancient halls before capturing large numbers of Britons, including their king, Arthgal. These forlorn prisoners were herded to longships moored in the Clyde and taken back to Dublin to be sold as slaves. With them on the same ships went numerous folk of

English and Pictish stock whom the Vikings had captured during earlier raids.

The fall of Dumbarton was an important event in the history of those times. The Britons of the Clyde, many of whose kings had been stern adversaries of the Picts and Scots, were left bruised and temporarily leaderless. But the royal family survived the onslaught to recover its strength in the ensuing years. It transferred its main centre of power upstream to where the River Kelvin meets the Clyde in the vicinity of Partick and Govan. The sources acknowledged this move from the older stronghold at the head of the firth by referring to the post-870 kingdom as 'Strathclyde' and by ceasing to mention Alt Clut. From the late ninth to the early eleventh centuries the North Britons became once again a major power. Led by a vigorous native dynasty, they long resisted external threats before being absorbed into the kingdom of Alba. In the meantime, however, their king Arthgal, whom the Vikings had captured at Dumbarton, was murdered in 872. The slaying was carried out at the instigation of Constantine I who, in the fluid nature of political relationships, was now on friendly terms with Olaf of Dublin. By requesting Arthgal's execution, Constantine not only removed a potential foe from the northern arena but also demonstrated his prestige and influence.

Soon after the sack of Dumbarton a new Scandinavian army harassed Constantine's Pictish subjects before wintering among them. It was while attempting to gather tribute from the plundered territory that these Vikings were brought to battle by Constantine and defeated. The victory was followed by a battle at Dollar in 875 which marked a defeat for the men of Alba, this time at the hands of a Danish warband. In the aftermath the victorious Danes undertook a year-long campaign of slaughter and plunder, driving deep into Perthshire and ravaging as far as Atholl. Constantine's soldiers in the defeat at Dollar are called 'Scots' in one source but are elsewhere referred to as 'Picts', a confusion which shows that the old distinctions between the two peoples were becoming less relevant. Conflict with the Danes eventually led to Constantine's death in battle in 876 at *Inverdubroda*, probably Inverdovat on the Fife coast.

He had done his best to protect the heart of his realm from Viking raids but, against such relentless pressure, his chances of success were small. One tradition remembered him as a staunch protector of his people and called him 'the cow-herd of the byre of the cows of the Picts'. Another credited him with defeating the Clyde Britons, presumably before the siege of Alt Clut in 870. In the end, like the Dumbarton king Arthgal, Constantine was overwhelmed by Scandinavian enemies.

Constantine's successor was his brother Áed mac Cináeda, who held the kingship for barely a year before being slain in battle at Strathallan. Two royal deaths in so short a time brought a response from the leaders of the Columban Church, who now became anxious about the security of Dunkeld. The continuing Danish raids made Perthshire an unsafe location for Columba's relics, and their removal became a priority. In 878 the venerated shrine *Scrín Choluim Chille* was sent to Ireland, probably to Kells, 'to escape the foreigners'. With the shrine went other objects not named by the sources, but it is likely that Dunkeld was completely emptied of sacred relics at this time. It was not, however, the Danes who slew Áed mac Cináeda. The annals identified his killers as his own companions, but other sources name the slayer as Giric, a controversial figure whose origins are cloaked in mystery. Giric is credited by later tradition with liberating the Church of the Scots 'which was in servitude up to that time, after the custom and fashion of the Picts'. This may refer to high levels of taxation previously imposed on ecclesiastical estates by Pictish kings seeking to swell their own coffers. Perhaps Giric reduced this burden? Little is known about his reign, but it seemingly coincided with that of Eochaid, a grandson of Cináed mac Ailpín, whose father Rhun was king of the Clyde Britons and a son of the slain Arthgal. Eochaid and Giric may have jointly ruled Alba, at least for a time, with Giric serving as Eochaid's guardian and therefore as the real wielder of power. Giric died in 889 at the old Pictish hillfort of Dundurn, his death returning the kingship to the mac Ailpín dynasty. The new king was Domnall II, son of Constantine I. Domnall reigned for eleven years and is the first of his house to be called by the Irish annalists *rí*

Alban, 'king of Alba', rather than *rex Pictorum*, 'king of the Picts'. Domnall's successor in 900 was his cousin Constantine II, another of Cináed's grandsons. In the third year of this Constantine's reign the church at Dunkeld was attacked by Norse marauders, but the precious relics of Columba had already been moved to Ireland. Dunkeld's status as the principal church of Alba was in any case already waning and the primary focus of church-state affairs was shifting eastward to St Andrews. In 904, Constantine II vanquished the Norsemen at a battle in Strathearn. The victory was noted by the Irish annalists and contains their last mention of an identifiably 'Pictish' group, in this case the men of Fortriu. The lands formerly associated with the Picts are thereafter called Alba, eventually becoming part of *Scotia*, 'Scotland', during the eleventh century. With this brief notice of an obscure battle near the River Earn comes the end of Pictish history in the sources.

CHAPTER 12
Legends and Legacies

Contrary to the tales of mass destruction and genocide presented in some later chronicles, the Picts did not vanish in any literal or physical sense. Their disappearance was entirely political: they merged with the Scots to eventually become the 'Scottish' nation. Their separate identity was forgotten and their lands were subsumed into the Gaelic-speaking kingdom of Alba. The process of change, which may have begun as early as *c.*800, continued during the ninth, tenth and eleventh centuries. Nowhere was it seen more profoundly than in the upper levels of Pictish society, where an ability to speak Gaelic became a requirement for social advancement, especially after the elevation of Cináed mac Ailpín as *rex Pictorum*. With familial roots in Kintyre where he had previously ruled as a king, Cináed came to Pictavia with a strong Gaelic background and with ambitious Scots in his entourage.

Positions of status under the mac Ailpín kings were no longer open to aristocratic Picts unless they were willing to move with the times. The Pictish language, although no doubt lingering among the peasantry, gradually lost its role in elite communication and eventually vanished altogether. The fact that it has left scant traces in Scottish Gaelic indicates the rapid pace of its extinction. Some aspects of Pictish society, mostly those relating to how agricultural land was apportioned and managed, survived the transition to be adopted by the new Picto-Scottish elite of Alba.

To some modern eyes Cináed mac Ailpín was the exterminator of all things Pictish, but this view is not borne out by the sources.

Cináed was an overking of the Picts in an era when their culture was subject to Gaelic influences, but there is no evidence that he or his heirs consciously sought to eradicate the old Pictish identity. On the contrary, a chronicle written at Dunkeld in the second half of the ninth century continued to call the folk of Cináed's kingdom 'Picts' rather than 'Scots'. It was not until the reigns of his grandsons that the term *fir Alban*, 'Men of Alba', became the new name for the people under mac Ailpín rule.

In demographic terms the population of Alba was predominantly Pictish. People who identified themselves as Picts formed a majority group in the new kingdom, and most of them remained *in situ*. Under the rule of an elite whose cultural affinities were increasingly Gaelic, the descendants of these Picts became 'Scots'. Eventually, after several generations, the people of what had once been Pictavia forgot that their ancestors had ever been anything but Scots. The process happened quickly and was helped by a growing belief, spread by deliberate propaganda from the ruling elite, that the entire Pictish nation had been wiped out. This belief became so firmly embedded that it was openly stated at the highest levels of political discourse. It appeared in the Declaration of Arbroath, the great affirmation of Scottish independence drawn up in 1320 in defiance of English aggression. The Declaration was sent to the Pope, urging him to recognise the Scots as rightful masters of Scotland because – among other achievements – they had conquered the country and *Pictis omnino deletis*, 'utterly destroyed the Picts'.

Legends: The Picts of Galloway

By the Norman period the Picts no longer existed as a distinct group. Their descendants had long since been absorbed into the Gaelic-speaking population of medieval Scotland. The people whose ancestors had tilled the fertile lands of what had once been the Pictish heartlands were now the Scots of the East. However, in the minds of some twelfth-century chroniclers, a people called *Picti* could still be found in one remote corner of Britain. These 'Picts' were in fact the Gallovidians, the inhabitants of Galloway, whose geographical isolation and toughness gave them a barbarous image and a terrifying reputation. In Anglo-Norman eyes the men of Galloway were the most savage warriors in the armies of the Scottish kings and were reputed to drink human blood. At the Battle of the Standard, fought near Northallerton in Yorkshire in 1138, the army of the Scottish king David I included large numbers of these 'Galloway Picts' when it suffered defeat at the hands of superior Anglo-Norman forces. Contemporary English writers such as Richard of Hexham gave lurid accounts of the brutality of David's soldiers and singled out the Galloway contingent as the worst culprits.

When Richard of Hexham called these men 'Picts' he distinguished them from the 'Scots' in David's army and regarded them as a different ethnic group. In making this distinction he was at least partly correct, for the Gallovidians of the twelfth century were a hybrid folk descended from indigenous Britons, Northumbrian settlers and an influx of Gaelic-speaking Norsemen. Their Viking ancestors were the fearsome Gall-Gáidhil, 'Foreign Gaels', of Argyll and the Isles. These appeared in the ninth century as marauders in the northern waters of the Irish Sea, but some groups colonised south-west Scotland to eventually give Galloway its name. They were not 'Picts' in any real sense and it is not known why this label was applied to them by Richard of Hexham and his contemporaries. The situation is complicated by Bede's claim that Saint Ninian of Whithorn converted the 'Southern Picts'. Until quite recently this was interpreted by some historians as evidence for Pictish settlement in Galloway in the fifth and sixth centuries. The idea is no longer taken seriously, but it provides an interesting example of how the real history of the Picts has become entangled with myth and ambiguity. Another confusing anomaly as far as Galloway is concerned is the presence of a Pictish symbol stone not far from the Whithorn peninsula. This stone stands outside an ancient fort on Trusty's Hill and was apparently carved in Early Historic times. Its uniqueness in south-west Scotland has prompted historians to wonder if it shows the existence of a Pictish colony in the area. Since there is no other evidence for a settlement of Picts in the vicinity, the idea has little substance. The most that can be said of the symbols on Trusty's Hill is that they were carved either by a visiting Pictish craftsman or by a Briton who was familiar with the symbols. No Pictish colonies are likely to have been founded in Galloway during the Early Historic period, nor did any exist when the Gall-Gáidhil, the 'Foreign Gaels' or 'Viking Scots', gave the region its name in the ninth and tenth centuries. By the twelfth century, when Richard of Hexham wrote about the Battle of the Standard, the real Picts of the far northern Highlands were already a forgotten people.

Legends: Brochs and Pigmies

A number of place-names in the Scottish landscape suggest that the term 'Pictish' was used in medieval times to imply the unknown purpose or uncertain origin of ancient structures and features. North-east of Dunkeld an earthwork was erected in the twelfth century as an obstacle for deer but, in the later folklore of the locality, it was said to be a Pictish construction. On modern maps of the area it is still marked as the Picts' Dyke. Further south on the Anglo-Scottish border near Carlisle and far beyond the Pictish heartland, another mysterious earthwork, the Catrail, appears on old maps as 'The Picts' Work'. Neither of these features has any connection with the historical Picts, but the folklore shows how some communities came to regard well-known local landmarks as Pictish in origin.

The custom of attaching the names of ancient peoples or legendary figures to old landmarks is a widespread phenomenon and is not confined to Scotland. In England there are numerous places traditionally associated with King Arthur and Robin Hood, or erroneously linked to Danes and Romans. It is hardly surprising, then, that Scottish folklore should mistakenly describe as 'Pictish' so many features and monuments whose origins lie well outside the period of the historical Picts. The custom was sometimes applied in reverse, with genuine Pictish monuments being given non-Pictish connections. At Meigle, formerly the site of a Pictish monastery, a famous sculptured stone showing the Biblical figure of Daniel became in local folklore a commemoration of 'Vanora' or Guenevere, King Arthur's queen. The process would hardly be noteworthy at all were it not for the parallel development of a rather bizarre belief that the Picts were a race of dwarfs or pigmies. The impressive stone structures known as brochs, which were built by the ancestors of the Picts, were often referred to as 'Pictish towers' in popular folklore, despite their abandonment before the true Pictish era. Similarly, the chambered underground dwellings now called souterrains, which ceased to be used after the third century AD, were once considered to be 'Pictish houses'. Some souterrains continued in use, or were re-occupied during the sixth to eighth centuries after a period of abandonment, but many were simply filled in with earth. In so far as the brochs and souterrains had any Pictish connection, it is fair to say that these structures were built by the ancestors of the Picts but not by the historical Picts of the centuries after AD 300. In the Middle Ages, however, the connection was firmly rooted in old lore. An explicit link was made between the Picts and the builders of brochs and souterrains by the writer of the *Historia Norwegiae*, a Scandinavian text of the thirteenth century. The relevant passage concerns Orkney and is worth quoting here:

> These islands were at first inhabited by the Picts and
> Papae. Of these, the one race, the Picts, little exceeded
> pigmies in stature. They did marvels in the morning and
> in the evening, in building walled towns, but at mid-day
> they entirely lost all their strength and lurked, through fear,
> in little underground houses.

The 'Papae' were Celtic priests, specifically the monks and hermits who made their dwellings on remote isles around the coasts of Scotland. The 'walled towns' are brochs while the underground houses are souterrains. The particular design of the latter made them look like the homes of tiny occupants and this led to an idea that the Picts were pigmies, a tradition persisting into modern times in the folklore of the Northern Isles. In Fife there long persisted a similar image of the Picts as 'short, wee men with red hair and long arms and broad feet' whose repertoire of arcane knowledge included a secret recipe for the brewing of heather ale.

The Invisible Picts

Not all medieval traditions chose to diminish or denigrate the Picts. In England, for example, a fourteenth-century chronicler whose objective was 'to declare the right of the king of England to the said dominion of Scotland' used the story of the Treachery of Scone to cast the Scots in a poor light. The old tale of deceit and slaughter at Cináed's banquet had already been given an anti-Scottish flavour in the version presented by Gerald of Wales in c.1190, and this was eagerly borrowed by later English chroniclers. Part of Gerald's narrative on the banquet story has been quoted in the previous chapter, but his comparison of the Picts and Scots is equally interesting, for he regarded the former as 'far superior in arms and valour' and goes on to lament their murder at the feast:

> And thus the more warlike and powerful nation of the two peoples wholly disappeared and the other, by far inferior in every way, as a reward obtained in the time of great treachery, have held to this day the whole land from sea to sea and called it Scotland after their name.

By the end of the Middle Ages, the true story of Scotland's origins was barely visible through a haze of myth and legend. Out of the mists arose a belief that the Picts had no place in real history and were a mythical race whose deeds belonged in the realm of folklore. To a twenty-first century tourist admiring the Dupplin Cross or the St Andrews Sarcophagus, or to anyone familiar with the writings of Bede and Adomnán, the very existence of such beliefs might seem astonishing. More surprising, perhaps, is the persistence of these views into the modern era. To some historians of the nineteenth and twentieth centuries the Picts had no place in Scottish history because they bequeathed no written records of their own. To others the mysterious *Picti* were nothing more than an invention by Roman writers. The idea of 'Pictish Studies' as a serious topic for research would have been greeted with derision in academic circles less than a century ago. As recently as the 1950s an early pioneer of the subject bemoaned the fact that 'archaeologists who value their reputation are reluctant to introduce the Picts into archaeological discussion'.

The situation has changed since then, and Pictish Studies is now a respected academic discipline. Knowledge of people, places and events in Early Historic Scotland has advanced greatly in the past fifty years. Meticulous excavation by archaeologists has yielded a far clearer picture of the settlements and material culture of the Picts and their neighbours. Linguistic experts have confirmed that the Pictish language was not an outlandish non-Indo-European gibberish but a variant of the P-Celtic or Brittonic group of languages represented today by Welsh, Cornish and Breton. Historians have probed the various chronicles, annals and other texts to identify not only when and why they were created but also to assess their usefulness as sources of information. Cumulatively, the work of numerous scholars in several disciplines means that the public can now come to 'know' the Picts in the way that they know the Scots, Romans, Anglo-Saxons and Vikings.

Aliens

One part of the enduring mystery of the Picts is the fundamental question of their ethnic origin: who were they and where did they come from? With the benefit of recent advances in knowledge this question can now be answered: the Picts were one of three Celtic-speaking groups who inhabited parts of North Britain during the first millennium AD. Such a response might not be to everyone's taste, for in making the Picts less mysterious than the Scots and Britons it makes them less unique and less special. It instantly brings them into the mainstream of Scottish history by reeling them in from their solitary position on the fringe. However, it is unlikely to completely dissipate the air of mystery surrounding all things Pictish. This pervasive aura will continue to thrive for a long time, or at least as long as people continue to read the Venerable Bede. It was this studious English monk who asserted that the Picts were not true natives of Britain but came originally from Asia, from the faraway Scythian steppes. Such an exotic origin-tale was always likely to set the Picts apart from other nations of the British Isles. As for themselves, they undoubtedly knew that they differed from their neighbours in several important aspects, but these differences were less of an issue than they might appear today. In any case, being different from everyone else does not necessarily make a group of people outlandish or enigmatic in their own time. If the Picts were a strange folk, then so too were the Scots of Dalriada who, alone of the peoples of mainland Britain, spoke a Gaelic language. More alien still were the Northumbrian English, whose frontier settlements lay within sight of Pictavia. To the threatened Britons of Lothian in the fifth and sixth centuries, it was surely these land-hungry newcomers rather than the familiar Picts who deserved the label of a strange people who did not quite fit in. There was no need to create for the English an exotic origin-legend about a journey from an ancestral homeland far away: it was a well-known fact that their forefathers had sailed over from Germany after the Romans left Britain. Despite Bede's tale about the mysterious Picts and their alleged Scythian heritage, the real outsiders from an eastern land across the North Sea were his own people.

The Picts were strange and alien only in so far as their northerly location sundered them from other folk or hindered their ability to keep abreast of developments elsewhere. They themselves were hardly likely to have been ignorant of this obvious geographical fact. When their king Nechtan, son of Derile, requested Northumbrian help in ecclesiastical matters he acknowledged his kingdom's isolation and, according to Bede, 'he also said that he and his people would always follow the customs of the holy Roman and apostolic Church, so far as they could learn them, remote though they were from the Roman people and from their language'. This echoes the words placed by Tacitus in the mouth of Calgacus, chief of the Caledonians, on the eve of the Battle of Mons Graupius: 'There are no more nations beyond us, nothing is there but waves and rocks ... even our remoteness and isolation, while they give us protection, are bound to make the Romans wonder what mischief we are up to.'

The Pictish Legacy

Scotland is Scotland because the Picts became Scots and adopted the Gaelic language. This was not a historical inevitability but rather an unforeseen by-product of a lengthy Pictish overlordship of the Scots which eventually led to the Gaelicisation of Pictavia. The reverse scenario – a gradual Pictification of the Scots – may have been a more expected result and might indeed have occurred if the Vikings had not been added to the mix. Scandinavian raids seem to have had a corrosive effect on both peoples, resulting in major losses of territory and a westward migration of fearful Dalriadan elites. Accommodation of the latter by their Pictish overkings placed high-status Scots in positions of power east of Druim Alban, thereby injecting a Gaelic element into the upper strata of Pictish society. The accession of Cináed mac Ailpín, a Gaelic-speaking monarch, as the paramount *rex Pictorum* undoubtedly accelerated the process of change. Things might have gone the other way, with northern Britain becoming Greater Pictavia rather than Scotland, but external forces intervened to turn the situation on its head. It is surely ironic that, by forging a single nation as a bulwark against the Vikings, the last kings of the Picts unwittingly condemned their own culture to oblivion.

Nowhere is the irony more evident than in how the two main population groups of medieval Alba are remembered today. Visitors who come to Scotland seeking traces of the 'Dark Ages' generally

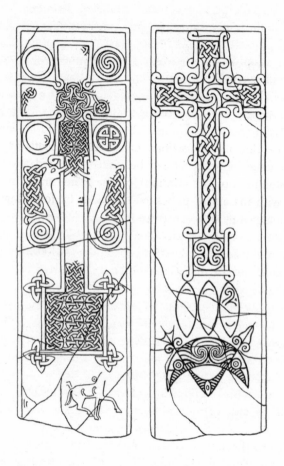

Figure 11. Pictish cross-slab from Skinnet, Caithness, now in Thurso Museum. Reproduced from J.R. Allen and J. Anderson, *The Early Christian Monuments of Scotland* (1903).

want to see Pictish symbol stones. This is largely because, in the eyes of many people, it is the Picts rather than the Scots who most vividly represent the period. The impressive sculpture of the Picts, together with their esoteric symbols, has ensured that they are far more famous than their Dalriadan contemporaries. The Scots of Cináed mac Ailpín's time left no equivalent artistic legacy and seem to lurk in the background, their role in history largely hidden from the eyes of passing travellers.

The sculptured stones, especially those bearing symbols, are vivid and potent reminders of the Pictish past. They are chiefly responsible for the current upsurge of interest in the Picts. Most of the surviving stones are accessible in museum collections or at ancient church sites, or in their original settings in the landscape. Under the care of organisations such as Historic Scotland, many of these unique monuments can be visited, admired and studied. Some stand in obscure locations 'off the beaten track' but can be found with the aid of published guides or by following 'Pictish Trails' mapped by local tourism authorities. The symbols continue to provoke lively debate and many ingenious theories, published and unpublished alike. Some of the more well-known theories appear in the publications listed at the end of this book. As well as being inspected and discussed by experts and laymen, the symbols provide inspiration for artists working in various media. Examples of artistic projects include full-size carved replicas of famous stones, modern sculptures in wood and bronze, and engravings of Pictish symbols on jewellery.

The group of stones categorised as Class II – upright slabs displaying symbols on one side and a cross on the other – are rightly regarded as among the finest examples of Early Christian art. Among this category are two of the most famous Pictish monuments of all: the cross-slab outside Aberlemno Kirk with its vibrant scenes of battle, and the Hilton of Cadboll stone depicting a noblewoman riding to the hunt. The standard of workmanship in both cases is breathtaking and provides an enduring testimony to the skill of Pictish craftsmen. The same can be said, too, of sculptured stones bearing no symbols, such as the Dupplin Cross. All of these monuments are outstanding pieces of visual art and, collectively, represent the greatest gift of the Picts to the people of modern Scotland.

The stones do more than bear witness to an outstanding artistic culture. They proclaim their creators and patrons as members of a sophisticated elite who wielded enormous wealth and power. Throughout this book such elites have sometimes been identified as 'barbarians', but the term does not mean barbaric or savage in an anthropological sense. It is simply a convenient label for the various European nations who lived outside the Roman Empire and whose leaders seized the initiative when imperial power collapsed in the fifth century. The kings and aristocrats who commissioned the Pictish monuments were no more and no less deserving of the label 'barbarian' than their peers in France, Germany and other developing regions of Western Europe. The lady riding side-saddle on the Hilton of Cadboll stone, with her ornate brooch and mounted servants, would not have seemed out of place on one of Charlemagne's royal hunts. Despite having bequeathed no literature of their own, the Picts were not backward or primitive in any aspect of their society or culture. On the contrary, they were a vigorous and powerful people who played an important role in the shaping of medieval Britain. Far from peering out of a mystical twilight on the fringe of the Celtic world they were major players in the social, political and cultural developments of their time. They did not simply vanish into the Highland mists: they merged with another Celtic nation and eventually relinquished their identity. Their modern descendants provide a reminder of the significant Pictish component in the population of Scotland, even if this genetic heritage is invisible and rarely acknowledged. In their continuing blood-lines, and in a majestic Highland landscape adorned with sculptured stones, the Picts have indeed bequeathed a lasting legacy.

Kings of the Picts

This is based on the Pictish king-list but excludes the twenty earliest (and possibly legendary) kings before Wradech Uetla. The dates show approximate reign-lengths.

Wradech Uetla (late fourth century)
Gartnait Diuperr (early fifth century)
Talorc son of Achivir (early fifth century)
Drust son of Erp (early fifth century)
Talorc son of Aniel (454–8)
Nechtan Morbet son of Erp (458–82)
Drust Gurthinmoch (482–512)
Galam Erilich (512–24)
Drust son of Girom and Drust son of Wdrost (524–9)
Drust son of Girom (529–34)
Gartnait son of Girom (534–41)
Cailtran son of Girom (541–2)
Talorc son of Muircholaich (542–53)
Drust son of Munait (553)
Galam Cennaleph (553–4)
Brude son of Maelchon (554–84)
Gartnait son of Domech (584–99)
Nechtan grandson of Uerb (599–620)
Ciniod son of Lutren (620–31)
Gartnait son of Gwid (631–5)
Brude son of Gwid (635–41)
Talorc son of Gwid (641–53)
Talorcan son of Eanfrith (653–7)
Gartnait son of Donuel (657–63)
Drust son of Donuel (663–72)

Brude son of Beli (672–93)
Taran son of Entifidich (694–7)
Brude son of Derile (697–706)
Nechtan son of Derile (706–24)
Drust (724–6)
Alpín (726–8)
Nechtan son of Derile (728–9)
Óengus son of Fergus (729–61)
Brude son of Fergus (761–3)
Cioiod son of Feradach (763–75)
Alpín son of Ferat (775–80)
Talorcan son of Drostan (780)
Talorcan son of Óengus (780–2)
Drust son of Talorcan (782–9)
Constantine son of Fergus (789–820)
Óengus son of Fergus (820–34)
Drust son of Constantine and Talorcan son of Wthoil (834–7)
Eoganán son of Óengus (837–9)
Ferat son of Bargoit (839–42)
Brude son of Ferat (842–5)
Ciniod son of Ferat (845)
Brude son of Fotel (845–6)
Drust son of Ferat (846–8)
Cináed mac Ailpín (842–58)

APPENDIX B

Pictish Timeline

AD

43 Roman invasion of Britain

82 Agricola's first assault on Caledonia

83 Agricola's second assault on Caledonia

84 Battle of Mons Graupius

122 Construction of Hadrian's Wall begins

143 Antonine Wall constructed

208 Severus arrives in Britain to fight a campaign in the North

297 Roman sources mention Picts for the first time

367 Picts join other groups to form the Barbarian Conspiracy

410 End of Roman rule in Britain

520 Approximate date of Saint Ninian's mission to the Picts

559 First record of war between Picts and Scots

563 Saint Columba arrives in Britain

565 Columba visits the Pictish king Brude son of Maelchon

580 Scots under Áedán mac Gabráin attack Orkney

584 Death of Brude son of Maelchon

597 Death of Columba

598 Scots defeated by Picts in Circinn

603 English victory over the Scots at *Degsastan*

640 English conquest of Edinburgh

643 Clyde Britons defeat Scots at Strathcarron

654 Picts defeat Scots at Strathyre

655 Oswiu of Northumbria defeats Penda of Mercia

664 Synod of Whitby

670 Ecgfrith, son of Oswiu, becomes king of Northumbria

672 Brude son of Beli becomes overking of the Picts

681 Abercorn is established as an English bishopric for the Picts

682 Brude son of Beli devastates Orkney

684 Ecgfrith's army attacks Ireland

685 Picts defeat Ecgfrith at Dunnichen

687 Death of Cano of Skye, leader of Cenél nGartnait

693 Death of Brude son of Beli

697 Adomnán organises a synod at Birr in Ireland

698 Picts defeat Northumbrians in battle

704 Death of Adomnán

711 Northumbrians defeat Picts in Manau

717 Nechtan son of Derile expels the Columban clergy from Pictavia

724 Nechtan retires to a monastery as dynastic warfare begins

728 Battle of Moncrieffe Hill between Óengus and Alpín

729 Óengus son of Fergus becomes overking of the Picts after victory at *Druim-Derg-Blathuug*

731 Bede publishes the *Ecclesiastical History*

733 Dungal of Cenél Loairn captures Brude son of Óengus

734 Óengus invades Dalriada

736 Battle of Ederline where Picts defeat Cenél Loairn

740 Óengus and the Mercians launch joint attack on Northumbria

741 'Smiting of Dalriada' by Óengus

750 Clyde Britons defeat Picts at Mugdock

756 Óengus and the Northumbrians launch joint attack on Dumbarton

761 Death of Óengus

768 Áed Find, king of Cenél nGabráin, attacks Fortriu

789 Constantine son of Fergus becomes paramount king of the Picts

793 Vikings attack the Northumbrian monastery on Lindisfarne

820 Death of Constantine

834 Death of Óengus II

839 Danes defeat Picts and Scots at a great battle in Fortriu

842 Cináed mac Ailpín claims the Pictish overkingship

848 Cináed secures his postion as *rex Pictorum*

849 Relics of Columba arrive at Dunkeld

858 Death of Cináed at Forteviot

870 Sack of Dumbarton by Vikings

904 Last reference to the land of the Picts in the Irish annals

APPENDIX C
Some Pictish Puzzles

At many points in Pictish history the sparse or ambiguous information given by the sources can be interpreted in more than one way. In this book one or more alternative interpretations are often presented even if one is eventually preferred. The following list gives a selection of 'puzzles' or areas of uncertainty for which more than one plausible theory can be offered. Most of these theories appear in publications listed in the bibliography at the end of this book.

1. The site of the Battle of Mons Graupius.
   In this book: The battle took place near Bennachie in Aberdeenshire.
   An alternative: The battle took place at Duncrub, near Dunning in Perthshire.

2. The reign of Brude son of Maelchon.
   In this book: Brude was the overking of all the Picts.
   An alternative: Brude's rule was confined to the northern Picts and did not extend south of the Mounth.

3. The Maeatae and Manau.
   In this book: The Maeatae or Miathi were Britons who inhabited the district of Manau around Stirling.
   An alternative: The Maeatae were Picts from southern Perthshire.

4. The Scots of Dalriada.
   In this book: The Scots were a Gaelic-speaking people who were indigenous to Argyll.
   An alternative: The Scots migrated from northern Ireland to colonise Argyll in c.500.

5. Pictavia, Alt Clut and the two Nechtans.
   In this book: The Picts and the Clyde Britons were ruled separately by kings called Nechtan in the early seventh century.
   An alternative: The two Nechtans were in fact one king who ruled both kingdoms at the same time.

6. Matrilineal succession.
   In this book: In matters of royal inheritance the Picts generally used a system of matrilineal succession in which kings were rarely succeeded by their own sons.
   An alternative: Pictish royal inheritance was mainly patrilineal, frequently passing from father to son or from brother to brother.

7. The cross-slab in Aberlemno kirkyard.
   In this book: The battle scene on the stone cannot be identified with certainty and might represent an eighth-century event.
   An alternative: The stone commemorates the Battle of Dunnichen in 685.

8. Bishop Curetán and Saint Boniface.
   In this book: Curetán and Boniface were names borne by a Pictish bishop of c.700.
   An alternative: Curetán and Boniface were separate figures and both may have been mythical.

9. Óengus son of Fergus and his relationship with Nechtan son of Derile.
   In this book: Óengus and Nechtan were rivals who briefly joined forces during the Pictish dynastic wars of the 720s.
   An alternative: Óengus was Nechtan's designated heir in the Pictish overkingship.

10. Óengus son of Fergus and his relationship with Aethelbald, king of Mercia.
    In this book: Óengus and Aethelbald were allies against Northumbria.
    An alternative: The alliance between Óengus and Aethelbald is fictional. In reality they had no direct contact with one another.

11. The reign of Constantine son of Fergus.
    In this book: Constantine was a Pictish king who subjected the Scots of Dalriada to his rule, imposing overlordship by force.
    An alternative: Constantine was a legitimate king of the Scots as well as of the Picts and ruled both peoples simultaneously.

12. Kings of the Picts and Scots in the late eighth and early ninth centuries.
    In this book: The later kings of Dalriada ruled as vassals of Pictish overlords.
    An alternative: Both kingdoms remained independent until the time of Cináed mac Ailpín.

13. The cultures of Picts and Scots in the early ninth century.
    In this book: They were already beginning to merge as one people.
    An alternative: They shared some cultural traits but remained distinct and separate.

14. Cináed mac Ailpín.
    In this book: Cináed had a legitimate claim to kingship over the Picts as well as over the Scots.
    An alternative: Cináed was a Scot from Kintyre who conquered the Picts by invasion and war.

15. The foundation of Dunkeld.
    In this book: The first church at Dunkeld was established by Constantine son of Fergus.
    An alternative: There was no church at Dunkeld before the time of Cináed mac Ailpín.

16. The Pictish symbols.
    In this book: The symbols represent personal names.
    Some alternatives: The symbols represent families or territories or marriage alliances.

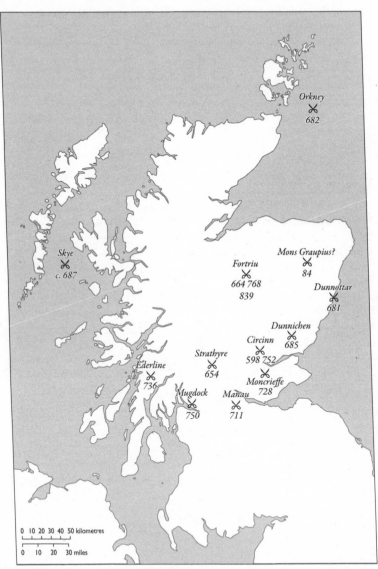

The Picts at war: a selection of battle-sites.

Postscript to the 2016 edition
Pictish Archaeology

Centres of Power

Before the ninth century, Pictish ruling elites tended to establish their main residences and strongholds in elevated locations. Hilltops and coastal promontories were favoured for the residences and strongholds of kings and powerful nobles. Such sites offered natural defensive and strategic capabilities, as well as commanding wide views across landscapes or seascapes. The natural defences were usually supplemented by artificial ditches and ramparts, some of which were refurbishments of pre-existing works while others were new creations of the Early Historic period. Ancient hillforts re-used in Pictish times include three already mentioned in this book – Craig Phadraig, Bennachie and Moncrieffe Hill – as well as others such as Turin Hill in Strathmore and Clatchard Craig in Fife. In some cases the older prehistoric defences were quite extensive, with the Pictish settlement being placed within what had once been a substantial enclosed space. At both Moncrieffe Hill and Turin Hill, the Pictish phase was represented by strong-walled circular citadels or 'ringforts' surrounded by earlier Iron Age ramparts. Nevertheless, many Pictish forts seem to be located on sites with no previous defensive features. At the large promontory fort of Burghead in Moray, which may have been built as early as the fourth century, an older settlement seems to have existed but might not have been fortified. Here, the Pictish fortress lay on the tip of the headland and comprised two enclosed areas, one of which was probably the main stronghold or citadel. Three ramparts across the neck of the headland provided an additional defence. Visitors in the sixth and seventh centuries were most likely presented with a particularly impressive sight when they reached the fort itself: thirty or more stone plaques, each inscribed with the image of a bull. Their original purpose is unknown, but they may have adorned the mighty wall of the citadel as emblems of strength and power, or to symbolise a pagan bull-cult.

Although Burghead is one of the oldest Pictish forts, the current candidate for the title of most ancient lies on the summit of Dunnicaer, an isolated rock-stack off the Aberdeenshire coast, 1 mile south of Stonehaven. Perched above towering cliffs, this site had long been regarded as almost inaccessible. In 2015, however, it was reached by a team of archaeologists and subjected to a modern excavation. The project revealed that the summit had been enclosed by a drystone wall reinforced with beams of oak. Traces of a hearth and floor were also found, suggesting the presence of a wooden house or lordly hall. Carbon dating indicated that the fort may have been occupied as early as the third century AD. At some point, the summit wall had been decorated with stone plaques inscribed with abstract designs, some of which are recognisable as Pictish symbols. Unfortunately, many of these were lost in the early nineteenth century when a group of local youths climbed up and threw them into the sea below. The few that were saved are now regarded as the oldest surviving Pictish symbol stones. Dunnicaer appears to have been abandoned by its occupants, no doubt because of the sea-stack's vulnerability to erosion and collapse. It is likely that they moved a short distance further south, to the distinctive promontory where Dunnottar Castle stands today. In the late seventh century, Dunnottar was known as *Dun Foither* but this name might originally have been borne by Dunnicaer.

Fortress ramparts of the Early Historic period were frequently made from unmortared stone reinforced with a wooden framework. Archaeologists refer to this method as 'timber lacing' and have identified it as a construction technique at a number of sites around the British Isles. The framework sometimes supported massive ramparts. At Burghead, the timber-laced inner wall of the fortress was 8 metres thick. Interestingly, some ramparts are known to have been timber-laced, not because the wood itself has survived but because it has fused with the stone to produce a glassy or 'vitrified' mass. Vitrification can only be produced by intense heat, which means that the walls must have been deliberately set alight, no doubt by enemies during an assault or siege.

The scale and complexity of fort defences varied considerably, from a single wall encircling a small summit to a series of enclosed terraces descending from a hilltop. At complex sites, each fortified zone may have been part of a hierarchical design in which the highest tier emphasised the importance of whoever dwelt there. Indeed, it is possible that defensive concerns were less of a factor in the layout of some forts than the desire to display the wealth and status of elite occupants. Military activity was nevertheless a fact of life for kings and lords, and it is no surprise that the forts became embroiled in conflict. Contemporary references in annals and other sources show Pictish strongholds playing important roles in warfare from the mid-sixth century to the ninth, whether as targets for attack or as landmarks for battlefields. Instances previously noted in this book include sieges at Dunnottar (681) and Dundurn (683) together with battles near iconic hillforts at Dunnichen (685) and Moncrieffe (728). One notable absentee from the documentary record is Burghead, undoubtedly a major centre of power with a significant military and maritime role. The evidence of topography and archaeology suggests that Burghead may have been an important naval base within the northern Pictish kingdom of Fortriu.

Not all early Pictish power centres were on hilltops or coastal headlands. Some were in less elevated positions such as low ridges or valley floors. One such complex has been discovered in recent years at Rhynie, a village nestling above the west bank of the River Bogie in Aberdeenshire. Rhynie's Pictish connections have long been known: at least eight 'Class I' monuments once stood in the vicinity, among them the symbol-incised Craw Stane and the enigmatic Rhynie Man. The place is not mentioned in contemporary sources but, as noted below, it was certainly a centre of power in Pictish times despite being neither particularly elevated nor strongly fortified. In similar mould and likewise absent from the documentary record is the Brough of Birsay in Orkney. Here, a natural defence may have been provided at high tide, when the site becomes an island, but otherwise there is no trace of fortification. The inhabitants in the seventh and eighth centuries were Picts of very high, probably royal, status who oversaw craft activities such as metalworking and stonecarving.

Fortresses on hillforts or coastal headlands were the settlements of choice for Pictish kings, at least until c.800. References in contemporary texts, supported by archaeological data, suggest that they were eventually replaced by weakly defended sites on valley floors. This transfer of royal power from elevated strongholds to low-lying 'palace' complexes may reflect changes in the way territory was ruled and administered, with easy access to farmlands and roads perhaps becoming more important than residences that were harder to attack. External influences might also have played a part, bringing ideas on the design of royal settlements from other parts of Britain and from Continental Europe. The shift from hilltop to valley can be seen most clearly in Strathearn, where the ninth-century royal palace at Forteviot may have supplanted an ancient fort on Moncrieffe Hill as the main focus of authority in the valley. Forteviot has already been mentioned in Chapter 10, where we saw that the palace of the mac Ailpín dynasty was deliberately placed within a 'ritual landscape' of prehistoric monuments. Although the precise location of the palace has yet to be identified, it almost certainly lay on the edge of the present-day village, in an area of farmland where Pictish graves have been found. A simple wooden palisade, rather than a stronger rampart of stone, may have been the only defensive feature. Forteviot's importance as a centre of power for Pictish royalty is confirmed not only by contemporary texts but also by the inscription on the Dupplin Cross, which commemorates King Constantine (died 820). The cross originally stood on the north side of the valley, directly opposite the similarly impressive Invermay Cross. These two ninth-century monuments were simply late additions to the ritual landscape, their presence reinforcing a longstanding aura of power associated with the prehistoric remains. The relationship between old and new landmarks of authority is a fascinating topic in itself. Continuing archaeological investigations by the Strathearn Environs and Royal Forteviot project (SERF) may enable us to understand it more clearly.

Some Pictish fortresses were abandoned after c.800 only for their sites to be re-used in later periods. At Urquhart, on the shore of Loch Ness, the rocky mound that had supported a lordly stronghold in Pictish times was incorporated within a large stone castle erected in the thirteenth century. Likewise, the site of the Pictish promontory fort of Dun Foither is now occupied by Dunnottar Castle. No such continuity is seen at Dundurn, an important place in the Pictish era that was seemingly abandoned in later times. Further along Strathearn, the kings of Alba long maintained a presence at Forteviot after the main focus of their authority shifted to Scone in the early tenth century. Scone itself appears to have functioned more as a ceremonial venue rather than as a royal residence.

Other Settlements

Archaeological investigation of individual centres of power can tell us a great deal about them: how and when they were built, how long they were occupied and what types of activity took place. The wider context – how they fitted into the surrounding landscape – requires a broader kind of study in which all types of settlement are considered, not only those of the kings and nobles but also those of the majority population. This is not always easy, for it relies on being able to identify low-status sites that may have left few visible traces. Moreover, some Pictish farmsteads undoubtedly lie beneath modern ones at sites where there has been no break in habitation for a thousand years or more. Unlike hillforts, ringforts and other high-status structures, the settlements of ordinary Pictish folk are likely to have disappeared altogether. Houses and barns made from wood will have rotted away, while the ruins of small stone buildings may have vanished beneath ploughland. Fortunately, a number of these non-elite sites have been rediscovered through aerial photography, usually as cropmarks which cannot be seen at ground level. It is a characteristic of cropmarks that they show best in areas of good quality soil. They thus emerge quite clearly in the arable farmlands of present-day Fife, Angus and Perthshire, but are less evident in hilly districts further north, where soils are poorer. In southern Pictland, then, the ancient pattern of settlement can sometimes be revealed by aerial photography. Dating the individual features is not always easy, for the cropmark outlines include settlements from all periods. Nevertheless, archaeologists are often able to identify those of Early Historic date – including the farms and houses of the agricultural peasantry. This kind of overview, in which low-status as well as high-status settlements are studied as elements in a landscape, can help us to understand how different groups within Pictish society interacted with one another and with their environment. It broadens our perspective in a way that studying individual sites in isolation cannot. The landscape approach has been adopted in Strathearn, where the SERF project has studied the multi-period settlement pattern. Ground-based surveys and excavations have been undertaken at selected sites but the guiding principle is to study the valley as a whole.

The homes of ordinary Picts could be round or rectangular, the former being generally assumed to be the earlier style. Local preferences must have played a part in design and construction, with availability of building materials a key factor. At Buckquoy in Orkney, a farmstead of round buildings was constructed in stone, this being easily obtained in the vicinity. Much further south, at Easter Kinnear in Fife, the buildings of a Pictish farm were wooden and square. There was also much variety in size and in how the interior was partitioned. A type known today as the 'longhouse', first recognised as Pictish on a settlement at Pitcarmick in Perthshire, includes examples more than 20 metres in length. Whether round, rectangular or long, the home of a Pictish farming family was typically a group of buildings surrounded by cropfields and grazing land. Archaeological evidence from Buckquoy shows how one such farm was worked: barley and oats were cultivated; cattle were bred for meat and milk. Several farmsteads would have constituted the estate of a local lord who received regular tithes of agricultural produce. In return, the farmers could expect protection from marauders. They would also have had certain legal rights, such as access to justice and arbitration when grievances or disputes arose.

Symbols on Stone

The Picts used a unique 'alphabet' of symbols as a form of visual communication, inscribing them on a range of objects and surfaces. Today, these strange designs can still be seen in the Scottish landscape on standing-stones, Christian monuments and living rock. They also appear on smaller stones as well as on objects of silver and bone. More than 30 distinct symbols are known, ranging from realistic animal-shapes to abstract designs. While there is some variation in detail, the symbol alphabet is remarkably consistent across a wide geographical area encompassing all of the known Pictish territories.

Experts in the fields of archaeology and art history have long debated the purpose of the symbols, wondering what meaning or message they conveyed to Pictish eyes. The question was discussed briefly in the fourth chapter of this book. There we noted the lack of any broad agreement on what the symbols mean, although a theory that they might represent personal names was given tentative support. At present, this view does seem to be favoured by many in the academic community, even if a definitive answer is likely to remain elusive. There is no doubt that each symbol repre-sented something that could be easily understood in the Pictish period. What cannot be assumed is that the meaning remained unchanged over time, or that a particular symbol served the same purpose on Orkney or Skye as in Perthshire or Fife. On one important point there does seem to be broad agreement: the date when the symbols first appeared as carvings on stone. The earliest symbol-stones can be assigned with confidence to the sixth century AD and are commonly designated as 'Class I' to distinguish them from later monuments of the Christian period. Most are unshaped, upright stones with two or three incised symbols. Roughly one third occur as solitary monoliths, the rest being associated with others in a locality. A photograph in this book shows an example of a solitary Class I stone, or rather its modern replica, at Dunnichen in Angus. It has three carved symbols: flower; double-disc and Z-rod; mirror and comb. Another photograph shows the stone at Abdie in Fife, bearing a double-disc and Z-rod beneath a cauldron. Both stones are typical of Class I. Rather more unusual, though carved in the same style, are the plaques from Dunnicaer and the symbol-carvings on cave walls and natural outcrops.

One well-known group of cave carvings is found at East Wemyss in Fife and has recently been the subject of a detailed archaeological study. The caves look out across the Firth of Forth and have been used for various purposes from ancient times to the present day. They carry the scars of human activity and remain at risk of further damage through vandalism, neglect and natural erosion. Some eighty Pictish carvings have been identified, most of them symbols incised in the sixth to eighth centuries. Since 2013, an archaeological project has been using photography and laser-scanning to create 3D images of the cave interiors. The results have been put together to provide a virtual tour that allows the carvings to be appreciated in digital form. Another instance of Pictish symbols carved into 'living rock' rather than on standing-stones occurs at the ancient fort on Trusty's Hill in Galloway. The location seems so far from the traditional Pictish heartlands that many experts doubted whether the symbols were genuine and not merely fakes. In Chapter 12, we noted that Trusty's Hill is part of the enduring mystery of the 'Galloway Picts'. Since that chapter was written, an archaeological excavation has established not only that the hillfort was occupied by people of high or royal status in the sixth century AD but also that the two symbols – carved on a rock near the fort entrance – belong to the same period. This is a significant discovery, not least because it casts aside any suspicion that the carvings are later forgeries. However, part of the puzzle still remains unsolved, for we still have no idea why Pictish symbols should be found so far south. Were they put there by a Pictish stonecarver? If so, who commissioned them to be carved, and what message did they convey to a population that was presumably non-Pictish?

Case Study: Rhynie

At Rhynie in Aberdeenshire, no less than eight Class I stones are known to have stood in or around the present-day village. All but one of this group have been moved from their Early Historic settings, the lone exception being the Craw Stane which stands on a low hill in what may be its original position. Two other stones – including one carved with an enigmatic figure known as 'Rhynie Man' – were discovered further down the same hill but might originally have stood higher up. Another two were found near the bottom of the hill among the ruins of St Luag's church. The remaining three – one of which is now lost – came from the village itself.

An interesting aspect of the Rhynie stones is that some, perhaps all, may have been used as monuments long before the Pictish period. One even has cup-shaped marks usually associated with prehistoric art. Likewise, the Craw Stone and two others look like prehistoric standing stones that have been re-used by Pictish carvers. Similar recycling could account for a number of Class I stones elsewhere in Pictland, with symbols being incised on ancient monoliths that were already significant features in a landscape. An aura of ancestral power would have surrounded re-used monuments and this was no doubt intended to be transferred to local Pictish elites. Archaeologists now know that the Craw Stane stands beside what was once the entrance of a circular enclosure consisting of an earthen bank, ditch and wooden palisade. Within the enclosed space stood a timber hall, clearly a high-status building, together with pits containing the burned bones of oxen. Aside from the Craw Stane itself, none of these features are now visible above ground but some were revealed by aerial photography and the rest have been discovered by excavation. Archaeologists found evidence of metalworking inside the enclosure, the most interesting object being a tiny axe-hammer cast in bronze. This miniature weapon is reminiscent of a larger one borne by the carved image of Rhynie Man whose stone may originally have stood close by. Drawing all the evidence together, the most obvious interpretation is that the hilltop enclosure was a pagan cult centre in Pictish times, a place where animals were sacrificed in the presence of people of high status. Attendees at these rites may have been given small bronze gifts, like the miniature axe-hammer, as souvenirs of their visits. The chronological context is the sixth to seventh centuries, when paganism still held sway among the Picts. However, it is likely that the enclosure had been used as a ritual venue in the ancestral past, perhaps as far back as the middle of the first millennium BC. The Craw Stane may have played a ceremonial role throughout this very long period, first as a bare monolith and later as a canvas for Pictish symbols.

Places like Rhynie, where Class I stones occur in a group, offer an alternative way to search for 'meaning' in the symbols. Instead of concentrating on individual designs and trying to work out what each one represents, we can approach the puzzle from a wider perspective, by considering the landscape context. It is surely significant, for instance, that some symbol-bearing stones were placed next to important routes, almost like signposts or waymarkers.

Others were erected on low ridges or knolls overlooking streams and rivers that today define old parish boundaries. There is little doubt that many of these watercourses similarly separated units of land in Pictish times, with a symbol stone marking either the boundary itself or a specific (and special) location beside it. An example of a special location would be a single grave or small cemetery, these having been found at the original sites of some stones. A common feature is the placement of a symbol stone within view of an ancient hillfort, a relationship that must be more than coincidence. One question that remains unanswered is why two or more stones might stand in close proximity to one another while others stood in isolation. What was the significance of grouping some stones together while leaving others on their own? At Rhynie, we might wonder if there was a specific connection between the symbols on the Craw Stane and the nearby figure of Rhynie Man. Perhaps by stepping back from the purely artistic or representational aspect of symbol stones to study their broader landscape context we might begin to understand the role they played in Pictish society, even if we come no closer to solving the mystery of what the symbols themselves actually mean.

Church and Cross

By c.700, Christianity had established itself as the main religion of the Picts, having displaced the pagan cults of their ancestors. During the seventh century, churches and monasteries were founded all over Pictish territory, predominantly by clerics from the Gaelic west. Some, perhaps many, of these missionaries came from Iona as followers of the teachings of St Columba. Others were sent from non-Columban foundations, such as St Maelrubha's monastery at Applecross which, despite its western location, remained independent of Iona. Important monasteries in the Pictish lands included Meigle and St Vigeans (both in Angus), Rosemarkie and Portmahomack (both in Easter Ross), and St Andrews in Fife. Whether St Andrews existed as a Christian settlement before 700 is open to question but its importance in the ninth and later centuries is undeniable. Of the others, we can probably assume that Meigle and St Vigeans were in existence before the eighth century. Rosemarkie, as we saw in Chapter 8, was certainly the seat of a bishop in 697. The fullest picture comes from Portmahomack, a place that is now emerging as a primary ecclesiastical centre for the northern Pictish kingdom of Fortriu.

Case Study: Portmahomack

Portmahomack stands on the Tarbat Peninsula in Easter Ross, on the shore of the Dornoch Firth. Its role as an important Christian settlement in the Pictish era has long been acknowledged. The old parish church, St Colman's, carries the name of an early Irish saint, possibly Colman of Lindisfarne (died 675). From the eighteenth century onwards its graveyard has yielded sculptured stones from the time of the Picts. There has never been any doubt that this was a religious site of considerable antiquity. Confirmation eventually came through an archaeological programme that began in the mid-1990s. Among the key discoveries was a *vallum* or boundary-ditch, a feature typical of early monasteries, enclosing not only the church and graveyard but a much larger area.

We now know that Portmahomack was indeed an important Pictish site, with roots extending back to the sixth century. It seems to have begun in an area to the south of St Colman's, where a settlement of roundhouses was inhabited by folk who were involved in crop-growing and metalworking. These people buried their dead on high ground near the site of the present-day church, in a cemetery of stone-lined 'cist' graves. Whether they were already Christians, or simply pagans who shared the Christian fashion for stone-lined burial, remains an open question.

More certain is that their settlement was a high-status one, the residence or estate of a prosperous landowning family. By the end of the seventh century, the estate had been supplanted by the dwellings and workshops of a vigorous monastic community. The transition might have come about through a formal gift of land, of the kind seen in the foundation-tale of St Columba's monastery on Iona. Whatever process was involved in the founding of Portmahomack, its inhabitants were engaging in a range of craft activities from c.700 onwards. To this phase we can assign the construction of the vallum and, in all likelihood, the first stone church where St Colman's stands today. Within the enclosed area a variety of goods were produced. Silver and bronze were worked into chalices, plates and other religious vessels; cattle were butchered so that their hides could be turned into vellum for manuscripts; stone was carved into richly decorated monuments such as cross-slabs. Glassmaking and woodworking were also undertaken. This community was, to some extent, self-sufficient, except for specialised items that had to be acquired from outside, such as raw materials for metalworking. Imports would have been exchanged for surplus produce from the monastery, most likely beef and leather, via local trading networks. In fact, the monastic coffers are likely to have been full, not only from trade but also from gifts donated by rich patrons in the secular world beyond the vallum. Eventually, the monastery may have grown so powerful that it controlled the entire Tarbat Peninsula as an ecclesiastical estate. This might be the context for three large, ornate cross-slabs erected around the peninsular coastline at Nigg, Shandwick and Hilton of Cadboll. These impressive, expensive monuments may have marked the zenith of the monastery as an economic and spiritual powerhouse in the late eighth century. The situation then changed around the year 800, at the dawn of the Viking

Age. One or more violent raids on Portmahomack led to the destruction of the craft workshops by fire. Evidence from the burial-ground shows that the monks themselves were targeted, some being slain by sword-wielding attackers. We can probably assume that the culprits were Vikings. Nevertheless, in spite of the violence and destruction, the site was not abandoned. Formal religious activity certainly ceased, as did the specialised crafts associated with it – stonecarving and vellum production – but metalworking continued, albeit in a different way. Instead of chalices and other religious objects, the ninth-century metalsmiths produced personal items such as brooches and buckles. These were intended for new trading networks based on secular goods. Whether the artisan community included former members of the monastery is unknown, but it cannot be ruled out.

Pre-Viking Portmahomack was one of a number of Pictish monasteries that, by the end of the eighth century, were producing sculpture of the highest quality. Today, the surviving monuments from these places provide striking evidence of the power and vigour of Pictish Christianity. An exquisite showcase of the stonecarver's art is presented to the modern visitor. Much has undoubtedly been lost or destroyed, making the surviving monuments all the more precious. There are, however, enough survivors to show how a sophisticated sculptural style developed from the simpler techniques displayed on Class I symbol stones. Art historians have recognised a distinctly Pictish blend that flowered in the eighth century, a style in which native stonecarving traditions met influences from other parts of the British Isles and from Continental Europe. The monuments in question occupy two of the three categories or 'classes' of Pictish sculpture: Class II and Class III. The classes were devised more than a hundred years ago as a means of dating and distinguishing key phases in the development of Pictish sculpture. Class I stones are usually unshaped monoliths incised with Pictish symbols. As noted above, they seem to be pre-Christian, having probably been carved in the sixth to early seventh centuries when pagan beliefs still held sway among the Picts. By contrast, Christian influences are strongly emphasised on Class II stones – upright slabs with a richly decorated cross on the front and Pictish symbols on the back. These are usually dated to the eighth and early ninth centuries and are rightly regarded as the high points of Pictish sculpture. They overlap with the Class III stones which have crosses and other Christian motifs but none of the esoteric symbols. The date-range of Class III brings the sculptural tradition to the end of the Pictish period c.900. None of the boundaries between the classes should be regarded as solid, for the dating of early medieval sculpture is not an exact science. There was plainly much overlap and many regional variations. Some parts of Pictland will have been quicker than others to adopt new sculptural trends. There is, in fact, a case for abandoning the entire classification system, not least because of its rigid focus on the presence or absence of symbols. However, it is so well-established that it is likely to be around for the foreseeable future.

Places to Visit

It is advisable to check on access and opening times before visiting any of these places.

Museums with Significant Collections of Pictish Sculpture

National Museum of Scotland, Edinburgh
Meigle Museum, Angus
St Vigeans Museum, Arbroath, Angus
Groam House Museum, Rosemarkie, Easter Ross
Perth Art Gallery and Museum
Dundee Museum and Art Gallery
Montrose Museum and Art Gallery
Meffan Institute, Forfar, Angus
Aberdeen University Anthropological Museum
The Moray Society Museum, Elgin
Inverness Museum and Art Gallery
Dunrobin Castle Museum, Sutherland
Caithness Horizons Museum, Thurso
Tankerness House Museum, Kirkwall, Orkney
Lerwick Museum, Shetland

Individual Sites and Monuments

Aberlemno, Angus. Three sculptured stones, including the cross-slab depicting the famous 'battle scene'.
Dupplin Cross. This is now in St Serf's Church at Dunning in Perthshire.
Abernethy. The eleventh-century round tower, although later than the Pictish period, is an impressive structure well worth visiting. At its base stands a fine symbol stone.

St Andrews Sarcophagus. Housed in the museum of St Andrews Cathedral, which has a large collection of sculpture from the late Pictish period.

Dunkeld Cathedral and King's Seat (the Fort of the Caledonians).

Dundurn hillfort, Strathearn.

Schiehallion, the Fairy Hill of the Caledonians. This spectacular mountain can be viewed from various locations, including Loch Rannoch, or it can be climbed on foot.

Restenneth Priory. A medieval foundation on the site of a Pictish church, close to the battlefield of Dunnichen. The earliest surviving stonework is eleventh-century.

Dunnichen Hill. Suggested locations for the great battle of 685 lie below the northern and southern slopes of the hill.

Sueno's Stone. This very tall cross-slab stands in Forres, Moray, and is protected by glass. On one side it shows spectacular battle scenes involving ninety-eight human figures.

Tarbat Discovery Centre, Portmahomack, Easter Ross. An impressive display of Pictish material relating to the nearby archaeological excavation.

Dunadd hillfort, Argyll. An important royal stronghold of the Scots. The nearby visitor centre at Kilmartin gives useful information on Dunadd and Dalriada.

Dumbarton Castle. Chief citadel of the Clyde Britons. The castle on the summit of the rock can be visited, but nothing remains of earlier structures. A striking view can be gained from the southern shore of the Clyde at West Ferry.

Further Reading

Early Scotland

Alcock, L., *Kings and Warriors, Craftsmen and Priests in Northern Britain, AD 550–850* (Edinburgh, 2003)

Anderson, A.O., *Early Sources of Scottish History, AD 500–1286*. Vol. 1 (Edinburgh, 1922)

Armit, I., *Celtic Scotland* (London, 1997)

Clarkson, T., *The Makers of Scotland: Picts, Romans, Gaels and Vikings* (Edinburgh, 2012)

Duncan, A.A.M., *Scotland: The Making of the Kingdom* (Edinburgh, 1975)

Foster, S.M., *Picts, Gaels and Scots: Early Historic Scotland*. 3rd edition. (Edinburgh, 2014)

Ritchie, A. and Breeze, D.J., *Invaders of Scotland* (Edinburgh, 1991)

Smyth, A.P., *Warlords and Holy Men: Scotland, AD 80–1000* (London, 1984)

The Picts: General and Collected Studies

Carver, M., *Surviving in Symbols: A Visit to the Pictish Nation* (Edinburgh, 1999)

Cummins, W.A., *The Age of the Picts* (Sutton, 1995)

Driscoll, S.T., Geddes, J. and Hall, M.A. (eds), *Pictish Progress: New Studies on Northern Britain in the Early Middle Ages* (Leiden, 2011)

Friell, J. and Watson, W.G. (eds), *Pictish Studies: Settlement, Burial and Art in Dark Age Northern Britain* (Oxford, 1984)

Henderson, I., *The Picts* (London, 1967)

Henry, D. (ed.), *The Worm, the Germ and the Thorn: Pictish and Related Studies Presented to Isabel Henderson* (Balgavies, 1997)

Nicholl, E. (ed.), *A Pictish Panorama: The Story of the Picts and a Pictish Bibliography* (Balgavies, 1995)

Ritchie, A., *Picts* (Edinburgh, 1989)

Small, A. (ed.), *Picts: A New Look at Old Problems* (Dundee, 1987)

Wainwright, F.T. (ed.), *The Problem of the Picts* (Edinburgh, 1955)

Kingship and Society

Aitchison, N., *The Picts and the Scots at War* (Sutton, 2003)

Alcock, L., *Kings and Warriors, Craftsmen and Priests in Northern Britain, AD 550–850* (Edinburgh, 2003)

Anderson, M.O., *Kings and Kingship in Early Scotland* (Edinburgh, 1973)

Driscoll, S.T. and Nieke, M.R. (eds), *Power and Politics in Early Medieval Britain and Ireland* (Edinburgh, 1988)

Ralston, I., *The Hill-Forts of Pictland since 'The Problem of the Picts'* (Rosemarkie, 2004)

Wagner, P., *Pictish Warrior, AD 297–841* (Oxford, 2002)

Roman Period

Breeze, D.J., *The Northern Frontiers of Roman Britain* (London, 1982)

Breeze, D.J., *Roman Scotland* (London, 1996)

Breeze, D.J., *The Antonine Wall* (Edinburgh, 2006)

Fraser, J.E., *The Roman Conquest of Scotland: The Battle of Mons Graupius, AD 84* (Stroud, 2005)

Hanson, W.S., *Agricola and the Conquest of the North* (London, 1987)

Hanson, W.S. and Maxwell, G.S., *Rome's North West Frontier: The Antonine Wall.* 2nd edition. (Edinburgh, 1986)

Hunter, F., *Beyond the Edge of the Empire: Caledonians, Picts and Romans* (Rosemarkie, 2007)

Woolliscroft, D.J. and Hoffmann, B., *Rome's First Frontier: The Flavian Occupation of Northern Scotland* (Stroud, 2006)

Sixth to Ninth Centuries

Aitchison, N., *Forteviot: A Pictish and Scottish Royal Centre* (Stroud, 2006)

Clancy, T.O., 'Philosopher-King: Nechtan mac Der-Ilei', *Scottish Historical Review* 83 (2004), 125–49

Cruickshank, G., *The Battle of Dunnichen* (Balgavies, 1991)

Driscoll, S.T., *Alba: The Gaelic Kingdom of Scotland, AD 800–1124* (Edinburgh, 2002)
Foster, S.M., 'The State of Pictland in the Age of Sutton Hoo', pp.217–34 in M. Carver (ed.), *The Age of Sutton Hoo* (Woodbridge, 1992)
Fraser, J.E., *The Battle of Dunnichen, 685* (Stroud, 2002)
Fraser, J.E., *From Caledonia to Pictland: Scotland to 795* (Edinburgh, 2009)
Hudson, B.T., *Kings of Celtic Scotland* (Westport, 1994)
Woolf, A., *From Pictland to Alba, 789–1070* (Edinburgh, 2007)

Christianity

Broun, D., 'Dunkeld and the Origin of Scottish Identity', pp.95–111 in D. Broun and T.O. Clancy (eds), *Spes Scotorum, Hope of Scots: Saint Columba, Iona and Scotland* (Edinburgh, 1999)
Carver, M., *Portmahomack: Monastery of the Picts* (Edinburgh, 2008)
Clancy, T.O., 'The Real St Ninian', *Innes Review* 52 (2001), 1–28
Clarkson, T., *Columba* (Edinburgh, 2012)
Crawford, B.E. (ed.), *Conversion and Christianity in the North Sea World* (St Andrews, 1998)
Hughes, K., *Early Christianity in Pictland* (Jarrow, 1970)
MacDonald, A., *Curadán, Boniface and the Early Church of Rosemarkie* (Rosemarkie, 1992)
Macquarrie, A., *The Saints of Scotland: Essays in Scottish Church History, AD 450–1093* (Edinburgh, 1997)
Sharpe, R. (ed.), *Adomnán of Iona: Life of St Columba* (London, 1995)
Woolf, A., *The Churches of Pictavia* (Cambridge, 2013)

Neighbours of the Picts

Bannerman, J., *Studies in the History of Dalriada* (Edinburgh, 1974)
Campbell, E., *Saints and Sea-Kings: The First Kingdom of the Scots* (Edinburgh, 1999)
Campbell, E., 'Were the Scots Irish?' *Antiquity* 75 (2001), 285–92
Charles-Edwards, T., *Early Christian Ireland* (Cambridge, 2000)
Clarkson, T., *The Men of the North: The Britons of Southern Scotland* (Edinburgh, 2010)
Crawford, B.E., *Scandinavian Scotland* (Leicester, 1987)
Higham, N.J., *The Kingdom of Northumbria, AD 350–1100* (Stroud, 1993)
Koch, J.T., *The Gododdin of Aneirin: Text and Context from Dark-Age North Britain* (Cardiff, 1997)

Lowe, C., *Angels, Fools and Tyrants: Britons and Anglo-Saxons in Southern Scotland, AD 450–750* (Edinburgh, 1999)

Ritchie, A., *Viking Scotland* (London, 1993)

Rollason, D., *Northumbria, 500–1100: Creation and Destruction of a Kingdom* (Cambridge, 2003)

Pictish Art, Sculpture and Symbols

Clarke, D.V., 'Reading the Multiple Lives of Pictish Symbol Stones', *Medieval Archaeology* 51 (2007), 19–39

Cummins, W.A., *The Picts and their Symbols* (Stroud, 1999)

Foster, S.M. (ed.), *The St Andrews Sarcophagus: A Pictish Masterpiece and its International Connections* (Dublin, 1998)

Foster, S.M. and Cross, M. (eds), *Able Minds and Practised Hands: Scotland's Early Medieval Sculpture in the 21st Century* (Leeds, 2005)

Fraser, I., *The Pictish Symbol Stones of Scotland* (Edinburgh, 2008)

Henderson, G. and Henderson, I., *The Art of the Picts: Sculpture and Metalwork in Early Medieval Scotland* (London, 2004)

Jackson, A., *The Symbol Stones of Scotland: A Social Anthropological Resolution of the Problem of the Picts* (Stromness, 1984)

Jackson, A., *The Pictish Trail: A Guide to the Old Pictish Kingdoms* (Kirkwall, 1989)

James, H., Henderson, I. Foster, S.M. and Jones, S., *A Fragmented Masterpiece: Recovering the Biography of the Hilton of Cadboll Pictish Cross-Slab* (Edinburgh, 2008)

Jones, D., *A Wee Guide to the Picts* (Edinburgh, 1998)

Mack, A., *Pictures and Symbols: the Pictish Legacy in Stone* (Brechin, 2007)

Sutherland, E., *A Guide to the Pictish Stones* (Edinburgh, 1997)

Language, Literacy and Place-Names

Forsyth, K., *Language in Pictland: The Case Against 'Non-Indo-European Pictish'* (Utrecht, 1997)

Forsyth, K., 'Literacy in Pictland', pp.39–61 in H. Pryce (ed.), *Literacy in Medieval Celtic Societies* (Cambridge, 1998)

Nicolaisen, W.F.H., *The Picts and Their Place Names* (Rosemarkie, 1996)

Rivet, A.L.F. and Smith, C., *The Place-Names of Roman Britain* (London, 1981)

Watson, W.J., *The History of the Celtic Place-Names of Scotland* (Edinburgh, 1926)

Matrilineal Succession

Evans, N., 'Royal Succession and Kingship among the Picts', *Innes Review* 59 (2008), 1–48

Jackson, A., 'Pictish Social Structure and Symbol Stones: An Anthropological Assessment', *Scottish Studies* 15 (1971), 121–40

Miller, M., 'Eanfrith's Pictish Son', *Northern History* 14 (1978), 47–66

Ross, A., 'Pictish Matriliny?' *Northern Studies* 34 (1999), 11–22

Sellar, D., 'Warlords, Holy Men and Matrilineal Succession', *Innes Review* 36 (1985), 29–43

Woolf, A., 'Pictish Matriliny Reconsidered', *Innes Review* 49 (1998), 147–67

Origin-Legends and Other Pictish 'Problems'

Broun, D., 'Pictish Kings, 761–839: Integration with Dál Riata or Separate Development?' pp.71–83 in S.M. Foster (ed.), *The St Andrews Sarcophagus: A Pictish Masterpiece and its International Connections* (Dublin, 1998)

Broun, D., 'The Seven Kingdoms in *De Situ Albanie*: A Record of Pictish Political Geography or Imaginary Map of Ancient Alba?' pp.24–42 in E.J. Cowan and R.A. McDonald (eds), *Alba* (East Linton, 2000)

Broun, D., 'Alba: Pictish Homeland or Irish Offshoot?' pp.234–75 in P. O'Neill (ed.), *Exile and Homecoming: Papers from the Fifth Australian Conference of Celtic Studies* (Sydney, 2005)

Fraser, J.E., 'From Ancient Scythia to *The Problem of the Picts*: Thoughts on the Quest for Pictish Origins', 15–43 in S.T. Driscoll, J. Geddes and M.A. Hall (eds), *Pictish Progress: New Studies on Northern Britain in the Early Middle Ages* (Leiden, 2011)

Mac Eoin, G.S., 'On the Irish Legend of the Origin of the Picts', *Studia Hibernica* 4 (1962), 138–54

Miller, M., 'Matriliny by Treaty: the Pictish Foundation-Legend', pp.133–64 in D. Whitelock, R. McKitterick and D. Dumville (eds), *Ireland in Medieval Europe: Studies in Memory of Kathleen Hughes* (Cambridge, 1982)

Ritchie, A., *Perceptions of the Picts: From Eumenius to John Buchan* (Rosemarkie, 1994)

Smith, B., 'The Picts and the Martyrs or did the Vikings Kill the Native Population of Orkney and Shetland?' *Northern Studies* 36 (2001), 7–32

Woolf, A., '*Dun Nechtáin*, Fortriu and the Geography of the Picts', *Scottish Historical Review* 85 (2006), 182–201

Index